DATE DUE			

Joseph Conrad and Warrington Dawson

Joseph Conrad and Warrington Dawson:
The Record of a Friendship

Dale B. J. Randall

Your eager boat, with eagle's wings,
Will make a rapid passage,
And, steered by reason, governed with strength,
Will reach the shores of fame!

 But, resting from your journey,
 In the golden lands of fortune,
 Remember, o remember with a sigh
 Those who perished in the tempest!

APOLLO KORZENIOWSKI

Durham, N. C.
Duke University Press
1 9 6 8

*Printed in the United States of America
by Heritage Printers, Inc.*

To Phyllis

Preface

This work brings to light a minor but fresh aspect of Joseph Conrad's life. When Conrad died nearly half a century ago, his fifteen-year friendship with Francis Warrington Dawson somehow sank from view. Dawson's name surfaced briefly—without annotation—in the Conrad letters edited by Jean-Aubry, and it was mentioned kindly but fleetingly in a sentence by Joseph Retinger.[1] In their helpful Conrad bibliography, Lohf and Sheehy gave some further clues that would lead a devoted navigator to some evidential flotsam in Dawson's own books. And Jessie Conrad, in her biography of her husband, devoted most of a page to a few direct facts about the American friend whom she and her husband had entertained repeatedly and warmly in their home near Ashford. But such scattered, brief allusions are all that has been available thus far on the Conrad-Dawson relationship.

The present book is made possible by the fact that Dawson, shortly before his death in 1962, gave many of his papers and books to the Duke University Library (now the William R. Perkins Library). Included in the gift were numerous documents relating not only to himself, but also to his distinguished father, Francis Warrington Dawson I. This material, supplemented with a gift presented by Mrs. Ethel Dawson Barry, constitutes what has been called "The Francis Warrington Dawson, I and II, Collection." Most of the letters from Conrad to Dawson are here. Since beginning to work on the Conrad-Dawson friendship in October, 1963, however, I have been in touch with a number of Dawson's friends and relatives, and thanks to their generosity, particularly that of Dr. Herbert Barry and his daughter Miss Lucy Barry, and of Lady Phyllis Benton, the Dawson Collection has continued to grow. In addition, a separate collection has been set up in the name of Dawson's lifelong friend Dr. Bernard Lytton-Bernard, who has been most generous in contributing papers which throw light on Dawson.

The study at hand consists of two parts. The first presents the back-

1. Reference is made in this paragraph to the following books: G. Jean-Aubry, *Joseph Conrad: Life and Letters*, 2 vols. (Garden City, N.Y., 1927) and *Lettres Françaises* (Paris, 1930); Joseph H. Retinger, *Conrad and His Contemporaries* (New York, 1943); Kenneth A. Lohf and Eugene P. Sheehy, *Joseph Conrad at Mid-century: Editions and Studies, 1895–1955* (Minneapolis, 1957); and Jessie Conrad, *Joseph Conrad and His Circle* (New York, 1935, and Port Washington, N.Y., 1964).

ground of the friendship, traces its course, and then briefly outlines Dawson's career until his death. Analysis here has sometimes been difficult because Conrad's feelings, like everyone's, were masked as much as revealed by his words, and because Dawson in later years tended to reminisce in rather roseate generalities. For this latter problem, of course, the letters of Part Two have been of great help, cryptic though some of them are. In Part Two there are a total of one hundred and nineteen communications. Sixty of these—some of them mere notes—are by Conrad. Only two, so far as I know (Nos. 4 and 9), have been printed in previous volumes of Conrad letters. Fifty-one are from Conrad to Dawson and are of special interest for being the first bona fide Conrad letters to Dawson ever printed, as well as for being all, or nearly all, of Conrad's extant correspondence with this particular American friend. Of the fifty-nine non-Conrad documents thirty-six have been selected from among the unpublished letters of Mrs. Conrad, and thirteen from those of Dawson himself. Other correspondents include Borys Conrad, Theodore Roosevelt, Walter Hines Page, Lord Plymouth, and Ellen Glasgow. In other words, because the book as a whole is focused on a relationship rather than an individual, I have collected letters not only from the two central figures, but also from a few of the people who played relevant roles in their lives.

A few comments on procedure may be in order. All letters and works by Dawson, all letters to him, and all letters from the Conrads may be understood to come from the Dawson Collection at Duke unless otherwise specified. Although eleven of the undated documents have thus far proved impossible to date (Nos. 9, 18, 28, 30, 33, 42, 43, 45, 50, 51, and 72), I have tried to guess sensibly at the position of each in the correspondence. Only two letters are presented in fragmentary form, the first from Roosevelt to Mrs. Roosevelt (No. 1) and the second from Dawson to a cousin (No. 118). For the most part documents are reproduced very much as they were written, though I have regularized some of the spacing and capitalization. For instance, I have placed at the end certain postscripts which are scribbled at the tops or sides of the original letters, and the indentation of complimentary closes I have regularized without comment. As for capitalization, both Conrad and his wife created a minor snag for editors by their tendency to make initial letters of words somewhat larger than other letters. Since it is difficult to decide which words they meant to capitalize, I have in all but a few instances followed standard practices. Furthermore, even when a quoted source has blazed forth in large capitals a large-and-small-capital system is maintained here, and in Part Two printed stationery headings are always indicated by means of large and small capitals, whatever their original form. One sort of change, however, I have tried to resist: I have tried to preserve each writer's spelling (or misspelling) and resort only sparingly to *sic*.

Now that the time has come to write this preface, the job of putting final touches to the manuscript seems somehow more real than the earlier and much bigger job of wading through masses of manuscript material, or even the job of reading Dawson's own numerous works. Now I am down to such problems as keeping the *see* references to a minimum, when the two parts of the book are intended, after all, to throw light on each other. One particular problem which has plagued me both early and late is that of compressing a relatively large body of information on a subject of modest importance so as to produce a book of modest proportions. If the reader finds himself forming the opinion that my solution is imperfect or that I come trailing too much scholarly foam for the size of my ship, I urge him at least to skip any remaining footnotes. He will surely survive without them.

Fortunately it is no problem to offer sincerest thanks to the many who have helped make this book a pleasure to write. Besides those persons named in Section 1 of the Bibliography, and the many librarians at institutions listed in Section 2, I should like to thank the Duke University Council on Research, which has generously helped to defray my costs, and the Cooperative Program in the Humanities (sponsored by the Ford Foundation at Duke and the University of North Carolina, Chapel Hill), which granted me the fellowship that has enabled me to bring my work to a close. I should like also to thank J. M. Dent & Sons Ltd. and the trustees of the Conrad Estate for permission to use the Conrad materials herein. More personal thanks are due to Dr. Mattie Russell and Dr. Virginia Gray of the Manuscript Department at Duke, who have been kindness itself in making available their experience and resources; to Miss Florence Blakely, Miss Mary Canada, and Miss Mary Frances Morris of the Reference Department, who have attacked a large variety of puzzles with unfailing sympathy; to Mr. John Menapace of the Duke Press, who has processed most of the photographs used here as illustrations, to say nothing of designing the finished book; to Dr. Theodor Schmidt and Mrs. Noma Flint, who have been generous with their linguistic first aid; and to Professors Elgin W. Mellown, John M. Rhoads, and Grover C. Smith, and, again, Dr. Virginia Gray, each of whom has read and commented helpfully on all or parts of the manuscript. Nor am I unmindful of the special value of that friend who found me an elusive Conrad quotation while reading in the bathtub one blazing summer day when it seemed as though the Carolina breeze was itself short of breath.

Having reached this point, I understand why so many writers save their final thanks for those closest to them, those who have endured if not prevailed. My last and greatest thanks are for her to whom I dedicate this book.

D. R.

21 July 1967

Contents

Contents

Contents

Contents

Illustrations

Part One

An Account of the Friendship

1

Introduction

Joseph Conrad met Warrington Dawson in May, 1910. An eager, earnest-eyed young American, Dawson never really was to be one of Conrad's secret sharers—if, indeed, there could be any—and yet he became one of those privileged few to partake of Conrad's late-night talks before the fire in the low-beamed, book-crammed study at Capel House. "Pray believe in my most genuine regard for your opinions," Conrad assured him after one visit, "for your feelings for your judgement and your sincerity."[1] In fact, Conrad's entire family came to look on Dawson as a friend. Conrad told him that young Borys "could not fail to respond to the warmth of your heart and the absolute sincerity of your whole personality. It is irresistible."[2] And of Mrs. Conrad he wrote, "Jessie as you know is always your very particular friend. . . . It's extraordinary how that woman understands you."[3] When the right reservations have all been made about Conrad's verbal extravagance in personal relations, the fact remains that in passages like these he is writing to a man who means something to him.

A clue to Conrad's view of Dawson may be found, paradoxically, in Joseph Retinger's comment that Conrad, "a gentleman of manners belonging to the old school," generally disliked Americans for lacking "the subtleties of civilization."[4] Dawson was every inch

1. From a letter of 17 August 1911, included in Part Two of the present volume (No. 12).
2. Undated letter, perhaps of 1 November 1912 (No. 30).
3. Undated letter, written perhaps in 1913 (No. 50).
4. *Conrad and His Contemporaries* (New York, 1943), pp. 10, 97. Retinger is sometimes unreliable, but these phrases ring true. A more extreme statement is made by Eloise Knapp Hay, who finds in Conrad an "insuppressible antipathy to American politics, institutions, and character" (*The Political Novels of Joseph Conrad* [Chicago, 1963], p. 167). Hugh Walpole reported him as saying it was "easier to have an intellectual friendship with a Chinaman than with an American," and that on 19 July 1920 Conrad "Got very angry as usual at the mere mention of Americans or

a gentleman. He was a cultivated, sensitive, responsive young Southern patrician who had gravitated to Paris some years before, lived at
first in the Faubourg St. Germain, then settled in the quiet elegance
of a flat in Versailles. Furthermore, he had a special taste and talent
for conversing with the great and near-great. Conrad could write in
a novel and maybe feel in his bones that "Difference of nationality
is a terrible obstacle for our complex Western natures,"[5] but as a
genteel *déraciné* himself, he was in many ways prepared to be sympathetic to the polished young American from Versailles.

Much will be said here of Dawson. It is necessary to have a
sketch of him to hold up among the several portraits by Conrad's
biographers. Yet there should be no mistaking the fact that Conrad's
stature as a major writer is the main justification for the present
work. Dawson himself was a fascinating figure. He was an intensely
proud, romantic, ambitious young man who succeeded in making
himself into a novelist and newsman. He wrote over twenty books
of various kinds, edited and translated still more, and for an incredible span of over sixty years he turned out a seemingly endless barrage of newspaper articles; but the sad truth is that he was armed
with little in the way of literary talent, and he never beat down the
public's terrible, great shield of unconcern. Dawson knew more
people and did more things than any ten average men. His variety of
lives surpassed Conrad's own. He cannot be called a failure as a man
if for no other reason than that his life was so full. Still it must be
admitted that he was not a success as a creative writer, and that is
what mattered most to him.

Since any discussion of the Dawson-Conrad friendship must
lean on such of their letters as survive, it should also be admitted at
the outset that Conrad's letters to Dawson, moving though a few
may be, are not really fine pieces of prose. Conrad's letters were sel-

Russians, both of whom he detests" (quoted by Rupert Hart-Davis, *Hugh Walpole:*
A Biography [London, 1952], pp. 179, 195).
Probably the truth is that Conrad's ideas about Americans were always mixed, from
the time when, as a young man, he considered settling in the New World, to the close
of his life when he was warmly welcomed in the United States as one of the greatest
living writers. Material on the subject is both plentiful and conflicting, but Borys
Conrad, looking back over his father's life, has come to think that the anti-American
vehemence of "J. C." was more habitually displayed than profoundly felt. It became
one of his set reactions (interview of 21 November 1964).
5. *Under Western Eyes* (London, 1911), pp. 114–115.

dom that, and those he wrote to Dawson are particularly offhanded and scrappy. A reconstruction of their friendship therefore runs the risk of becoming "wrapped . . . in the futilities of historical anec-dotes," to use one of Conrad's own phrases.[6]

Nevertheless, an attempt at reconstruction is justified. Though the shadow-line between significance and triviality varies always with the angle of one's vision, the letters gathered here constitute a valu-able memento of not merely one but two men, both of whom are worth remembering. Moreover, there is an attractive spontaneity in these letters, a casual freshness which enlivens not only the jottings of Conrad, but also those of the other correspondents—Jessie Con-rad, for instance, and Dawson himself. The letters may even have a certain usefulness. At any rate they cast new light on Conrad's life, and in a number of important ways Conrad's life may be shown to illuminate his books. As he himself knew, "every novel contains an element of autobiography . . . , since the creator can only express himself in his creation. . . ."[7]

If Conrad was likewise correct in thinking that a man's real life is the one allowed him in the minds of other men, then Dawson's random reminiscences have value, too. One may cavil about them, naturally. Like Eliot's April they mix memory and desire. But that is part of the story.

6. *Nostromo* (London, 1904), p. 339.
7. *A Personal Record* (New York, 1912), p. 8.

2

Dawson's Background and Early Years (1878-1909)

Conrad thought of the Suffolk seaport of Lowestoft as his English birthplace.[1] Disembarking from the steamer *Mavis*, on which he held an ordinary seaman's berth, he arrived here first in mid-June, 1878. A month or so later he signed on a coal carrier called the *Skimmer of the Sea*, and for ten weeks during that summer and fall he sailed back and forth between Lowestoft and Newcastle, practicing his English and earning a shilling a month. On 23 September he signed off, and several days later, at the age of twenty, wrote his first English. It was a modest enough beginning. He wrote a letter in answer to the following advertisement, which had appeared in the London *Times* of 25 September: "SEA.—WANTED, respectable YOUTHS. . . ."[2] That same week, on 27 September, Francis Warrington Dawson, the younger, was born.

Dawson's birthplace was Charleston, South Carolina, which he himself would eventually call "the most conservative of Southern towns."[3] More specifically, he was born in the Lightwood House, at the southeast corner of Meeting Street and Lightwood Alley, a fact which enabled him to speak in later years of his "proud heritage of having been 'born south of Broad Street.' "[4] The room in which the event took place was mahogany-panelled, huge, and haunted. Reputedly it was still frequented by the unhappy sister of the Revolutionary War "martyr" Colonel Isaac Hayne, who had been hanged by the British in 1781. Whatever the true whereabouts of the Colonel's sister, however, the Lightwood House may be viewed in retrospect as a suitably romantic setting for the start of Warrington Dawson's colorful life.

1. J. G. Sutherland, *At Sea with Joseph Conrad* (Boston, 1922), p. 48.
2. Quotation and preceding facts from Jerry Allen, *The Sea Years of Joseph Conrad* (New York, 1965), pp. 100, 317.
3. *The Pyramid* (London, 1922), p. 31.
4. From Dawson's carbon of a memorandum to James I. Robertson, Jr., written 26 December 1958 (p. 7).

6

His next home had its appropriateness, too. Built from plans imported from abroad, the house where he grew up at 43 Bull Street[5] was both beautiful and strangely untypical of its environment, "an imposing structure," according to one contemporary account, "with a broad piazza, the roof of which is supported by massive pillars. The drawing-rooms extend the whole length of the house and are the handsomest in Charleston."[6]

The head of this imposing house was a newspaperman known to his enemies as "the Czar of South Carolina," the "Autocrat of Bourbonism."[7] To his many staunch friends, on the other hand, Francis Warrington Dawson, Sr., was rather more a St. George. The Honorable James Simons, for one, declared that he "combined extraordinary brilliancy with extraordinary energy. Fearless, undaunted, prompt, and abounding in resources, he was at his best in the most trying emergencies."[8] Viewed from any angle, the elder Dawson was clearly a major figure of his time and place. Probably his friend J. C. Hemphill was correct to call him "the controlling spirit in the political life of South Carolina."[9]

To begin with, however, he was not a Southerner and his name was not Dawson.[10] Born in London on 17 May 1840, he had been baptized in the Roman Catholic Church as Austin John Reeks. The Reeks family (pronounced "Ricks") was at that time old and quite respectable, but suffering from fading fortunes as a result of some unwise investments. The son of Joseph Austin Reeks and Mary Perkins Reeks, young Austin retained his original three names throughout boyhood. Then, growing to maturity at the time of the American Civil War, he became fired by the idea of running the Yankee blockade. In fact he grew so determined to fight for the Confederacy that he set aside his whole previous life—including some playwriting, a languishing love affair, and a clerkship in a real estate office—

5. The house is now No. 99.
6. From a newspaper article (5 February 1887?) by Josiah Carter, preserved in F. W. Dawson, Sr.'s, Scrapbook No. II, p. 65.
7. From an article in the *Commercial Gazette*, Columbia, S.C., 2 December 1883, in Dawson's Scrapbook No. I, p. 126.
8. Quoted by J. C. Hemphill in *Library of Southern Literature*, ed. Edwin Anderson Alderman and Joel Chandler Harris, III (Atlanta, 1909), 1374.
9. Hemphill, III, 1372.
10. The following biographical sketch is based on numerous printed and manuscript sources. The most complete of these is the excellent M.A. thesis of S. Frank Logan, "Francis W. Dawson, 1840–1889: South Carolina Editor," Duke University (1947). See also Jonathan Daniels, *They Will Be Heard: America's Crusading Newspaper Editors* (New York, 1965), pp. 187–207.

and took the *nom de guerre* Francis Warrington Dawson. The name emerged from a family quarrel. His father had declared that no son of his would violate the Queen's neutrality and dishonor the name of Reeks by getting himself hanged, and the young man had replied in a self-righteous outburst that he would get himself hanged, then, under a name of his own. The surname which he chose had its special relevance. It was that of an uncle by marriage who had fallen in the final British charge of the Sepoy Rebellion (1858). In December, 1861, therefore, a young man named Dawson shipped out of Southampton as a common sailor on the C.S.S. *Nashville*. He was "common" only in the technical sense. When he boarded the *Nashville*, he brought a suit of dress clothes, a black Inverness cape, and a bowie knife. Like his son many years later, he obviously had a strong romantic streak. In the elder Dawson, however, this was tempered by an equally strong strain of hardheaded masculine practicality. Of his voyage to the Confederacy he wrote later: "I expected no reward and wanted none, and had no intention whatever of remaining permanently in the Southern States."[11]

Dawson sought more action than he was able to find in the Confederate Navy. Being attached to a vessel in the James River Squadron at the time when McClellan was advancing toward Richmond, he volunteered to the officers of the Richmond "Purcell" Battery, C. W. Field's Brigade of A. P. Hill's Division, and in June, 1862, was enlisted as a private in the Army of Northern Virginia. From August of that year (when he became a First Lieutenant) until October, 1864, he served under Longstreet as Assistant Ordnance Officer, and after that as Ordnance Officer under Fitzhugh Lee. For over three years he fought well. In April, 1865, however, there was no longer a Confederacy to fight for, and Dawson emerged from the chaos a Captain.[12] He had a single postage stamp and the change from a five-dollar greenback.

For a while Captain Dawson worked as a farmhand, and for another while he was a bookkeeper in a dry goods store. The turning point came soon, however, in the winter of 1865, when he took a job as assistant editor and reporter on the *Daily Richmond Examiner*. At this time he met his future partner, Bartholomew Roche-

11. *Reminiscences of Confederate Service, 1861–1865* (Charleston, 1882), p. 3.
12. He had been wounded at Mechanicsville (1862), Harrisonburg (1864), and Five Forks (1865), and was captured once near Williamsport (1862). See Ella Lonn, *Foreigners in the Confederacy* (Gloucester, Mass., 1965), esp. pp. 178–180.

fort Riordan. In November, 1866, he arrived in Charleston, and on 6 October 1867 a new firm called Riordan, Dawson & Co. purchased the Charleston *Daily News*. For Dawson the purchase marked the beginning of a remarkable career. In early April, 1873, when the same company bought the Charleston *Courier* and merged it with the *News*, Dawson became editor of what was to become the most powerful paper in South Carolina, one which laid claim to the "LARGEST CIRCULATION IN THE COTTON STATES." Dawson's climb had been fast and sure. A naturalized citizen as of 1 April 1868, he proceeded to take a place among the distinguished Americans of his day.[13]

Throughout his career Captain Dawson showed strength, courage, and conviction. In 1883, Pope Leo XIII made him a Knight of the Order of St. Gregory the Great because of the stand he dared take against duelling. In 1886, when a severe earthquake struck Charleston, he hurried to the *News and Courier* building while the walls were still crumbling, and almost before the dust had settled he organized reconstruction efforts, and thereafter maintained the morale of the citizens in such a way that they made him a bronze plaque "For Unequalled Services in Unparalleled Calamity." But on 12 March 1889, protesting to his neighbor at 95 Rutledge Street, Dr. Thomas B. McDow, a married man who secretly had been seeing the Dawsons' Swiss governess, the editor met a violent end. During the course of a quarrel the doctor shot Dawson, and beneath "a sky weeping rain and craped with clouds, Charleston, like a great family bereft," struggled to grasp the "heart-chilling truth" that the great man was gone.[14] His son, Francis Warrington Dawson, Jr., was ten years old.

13. Dawson's success has been attributed to the fact that "He applied the lesson of England's progress to the stricken Southern States—he preached industrialism, crop diversification, immigration of agricultural workers from Europe and artisans from the North" (Broadus Mitchell and George Sinclair Mitchell, *The Industrial Revolution in the South* [Baltimore, 1930], pp. 74–75). Constantly he drove home the slogan, "The Mills Must Come to the Cotton," and, with the help of his editorials, drew fresh capital from within and beyond the South. "In a day when newspapers were regarded as the voice of their editors, the editors of city dailies—Francis W. Dawson of the Charleston *News and Courier*, Henry Watterson of the Louisville *Courier-Journal*, Henry W. Grady of the Atlanta *Constitution*—were public figures of supreme importance" (C. Vann Woodward, *Origins of the New South 1877–1913*, Vol. IX of *A History of the South*, ed. W. H. Stephenson and E. M. Coulter [Baton Rouge, La., 1951], 145).

14. Newspaper clipping, Sarah Dawson's Scrapbook No. II, p. 4. See Thomas K. Peck, "The Killing of Captain Dawson," in *Charleston Murders*, ed. Beatrice St. J. Ravenel (New York, 1947), pp. 71–107.

Over twenty years earlier, on 1 May 1867, at a nuptial mass, Captain Dawson had married a Charleston girl named Virginia M. Fourgeaud. This first Mrs. Dawson died on 6 December 1872, after only five years of marriage. A few months before her death, however, James Morris Morgan, a friend from Dawson's navy days, had introduced the editor to his sister Sarah. This introduction proved fortunate because it was Sarah Morgan, more than anyone else, who helped Dawson to regain his equilibrium. The whole situation was delicate, of course, and the well-bred young lady was suitably reluctant about returning the widower's growing affection, but on 27 January 1874 they were married. In the Gadsden House on Meeting Street, where Miss Sarah lived with her mother, Bishop Patrick N. Lynch of Charleston married the Catholic editor to an Episcopalian bride.

Sarah Ida Fowler Morgan Dawson was the youngest daughter of a wealthy Louisiana family. She had been born in New Orleans on 28 February 1842, the child of Thomas Gibbes Morgan and his second wife, Sarah. Morgan was Collector of the Port of New Orleans at the time, but soon afterward he was made Judge of the District Court in Baton Rouge. Hence most of Miss Sarah's childhood was spent in the up-river city. Ante bellum Baton Rouge was a place of culture and grace, and the girl flowered prettily. Blue-eyed and golden-haired, with a magnolia-petal complexion, she had wit, intelligence, and charm. Not only could she write well, sing a bit, and play the guitar, but as the seventh child of a seventh child (her mother) she was thought by some to have special psychic talents. Yet even Eden sank to grief. Judge Morgan died in November, 1861, and in May, 1862, the Federal ships came up the Mississippi from New Orleans. Although the first Yankees in Baton Rouge were gentlemen, the Morgan mansion was looted and sacked in August of that same year, and an era came to an end.[15] Two of

15. A woman coming into town "on errands of mercy" later described what happened:

> Seeing the front door of the late Judge Morgan's house thrown wide open, and knowing that his widow and daughters, after asking protection for their property of the commanding general, had left before the battle, I entered. No words can tell the scene that those deserted rooms presented. The grand portraits, heirlooms . . . , stabbed and mutilated in every brutal way! The contents of store-closets had been poured over the floors; molasses and vinegar, and everything that defaces and stains, had been smeared over walls and furniture. Up-stairs, *armoires* with mirror-doors had been smashed in with heavy axes or

Sarah's brothers were killed during the war, the rest of her family was scattered, and Sarah herself was threatened with poverty. Making matters worse, her back was permanently injured when she fell from a buggy in the spring of 1863. At last, after the war, she and her mother did find temporary refuge with her brother Jimmie—Colonel James Morris Morgan. In fact, Jimmie had purchased Wade Hampton's plantation on the Congaree River, some four miles below Columbia, South Carolina, and it was here that Sarah met Captain Dawson. But when Jimmie was married a short time later, Sarah and her mother moved on once again. Finally, and perhaps naturally, the two ladies settled in Charleston, and here, at Dawson's urging, the young woman began to write articles and editorials for the *News and Courier*. Presumably it was not quite proper for a lady to engage in journalism, so all her efforts appeared either anonymously or signed discreetly with a nom de plume. Perhaps more surprising, she continued to write for the paper even after her marriage to the editor in 1874, though above all she devoted herself now to being a wife and, before long, a mother. The Dawsons' first child was Ethel, born in 1874. Francis Warrington, Jr., was born in 1878. Another son, Philip, was born in 1881, but died before the year was out. Then eight years later came Captain Dawson's death.

The New Orleans writer Grace King never forgot her first meeting with Mrs. Dawson and young Warrington. It took place at Blowing Rock, a mountain resort in western North Carolina, not long after Captain Dawson was killed. Mrs. Dawson, she remembered, "was clad in deep mourning, and was frail of body almost to the limit of vitality. She would have been beautiful but for the extreme pallor of her face, and her haughty rigid expression of reserve." Warrington was "coming down the path through the woods . . . , walking by the side of his mother, whose hand he held to guide her over the rough way. He was a sturdy boy, about twelve, with fine, dark-blue eyes and an engaging smile."[16] It was a symbolic scene. As the years passed, Mrs. Dawson leaned more and more on the comfort of Warrington's hand. At the same time she was urg-

---

hammers . . . (Eliza McHatton Ripley, *From Flag to Flag* [New York, 1889], pp. 49–50).

Sarah herself recorded many details of her story in *A Confederate Girl's Diary*.

16. "American Writers in Paris: Warrington Dawson," *Ex Libris*, American Library in Paris, II (1924), 35. A slightly different version is given in her *Memories of a Southern Woman of Letters* (New York, 1932), pp. 206–208.

ing her boy to remarkable attainments, she was also holding on to him in a way she might have feared if she could have understood. Between them, of course, there were many kinds of ties. Not least was the precious memory of the man who had dominated their home and given meaning to their lives. There were also certain business deals which Mrs. Dawson felt had victimized both her children and herself. After the acquittal of Dr. McDow there even came to be a shared feeling that Charleston, whatever good things it had given them, was no longer really home.[17] Then on 16 February 1898 Warrington's sister Ethel was married to a lawyer, Herbert Barry, who had been born in Wilmington, North Carolina, but now had an office on Wall Street. Sarah Dawson's immediate family was down to two. When her mainstay, Warrington himself, sailed for France in October, 1889, her loneliness must have been profound. In February of the following year, however, before that winter was over, she followed after him, and, reunited in Paris, the dignified, quietly embittered mother and her ambitious young son took an apartment on the superb old Boulevard St. Germain. Although the captain's widow never again wore colors and her stationery stayed rimmed in black, at least the closing years of her life were brightened by the company and accomplishments of her "wonderful boy." Warrington in his twenties was fair, tall, and handsome, rather mild-eyed and not always well, but physically well built and nearly indefatigable when his zeal was aroused. Take him for all in all, he was a promising young man. Assured of his devotion as well as his ultimate success, Mme. Dawson sold her Charleston home, settled permanently in France, cultivated a small group of friends, and once more took up her pen.[18] It was a comfortable, genteel life. At its end, though, she was again deprived of her mainstay. When she died in Paris in May, 1909, Warrington was away on one of his

17. "The verdict was generally regarded throughout South Carolina and the nation as an outrage on justice" (Logan, p. 320).

18. *The National Cyclopaedia of American Biography*, XXIII (New York, 1933), 301, lists some of her publications: *Round about Marriage* (1892–1893), trans. of *Autour du Mariage* (1883) by Gyp (pseud. for Countess Sibylle Gabrielle Marie Antoinette de Martel de Janville); *Les Aventures de Jeannot Lapin* (1903), a version of the Brer Rabbit stories which was well received; *Les Prisonniers* (1907), trans. from Mary Cholmondeley, *Prisoners*, published serially in *La Revue Hebdomadaire*; *A Confederate Girl's Diary*, one of the finest works of its kind, published posthumously by her son (1913); and—perhaps the best of her magazine work—a story called "A Tragedy of South Carolina," *Cosmopolitan* (1895). See Elizabeth Vignier, "Sarah Morgan Dawson," *The Southern Club Woman*, IV (1929), 1–2.

journalistic trips, this time in British East Africa. He was engaged, in fact, in the adventure which was to lead eventually to Joseph Conrad's door.

In 1933, looking back on his childhood, Dawson recalled his parents as "highly cultured and . . . brilliant conversationalists." He told of growing up "in an atmosphere of artistic, literary, and scientific thought, which at the same time always remained intensely vital."[19] The statement is characteristically spacious. The scientific thought at Bull Street cannot have been deep. On the other hand, there is no doubt of the Dawsons' artistic and literary interests.

One literary work of special importance to Warrington, which he first read as a boy, was Sir Thomas Malory's *Morte Darthur.* For some reason Malory's story of King Arthur and his knights had a special impact on him. Of course his own father had been knighted, and that fact would not have been lost on anyone of his romantic and rank-conscious disposition. Moreover, he had read *Idylls of the King* with great care, and pondered over parallels between Malory and Tennyson. Nevertheless it is impossible to state what specific attractions the Arthurian matter may have had for him. All one can say for sure is that he repeatedly came back to it, and particularly to the character of Gareth. A young man called Gareth was to be the most frequently recurring of several autobiographical figures in Dawson's fiction, most notably in his novel called *The True Dimension,* but also in *The Guardian Demons* and in such short stories as "The News That Wasn't," "The Cross-Channel Tunnel," and "Gareth's Beat," as well as, more perfunctorily, *The Green Moustache* (in which the main Dawson-character is called something else). Dawson even wrote a five-act play which he entitled with Gareth's nickname, *Beaumains.*[20]

19. From Dawson's copy of his reply of 28 January 1933 to a questionnaire from Miss Alberta Lawrence, editor of the Golden Syndicate Publishing Co., New York.

20. The proper use to be made of such facts is problematical. Of course Dawson's Gareths have their individual roles to play in his stories, and of course one may learn by viewing them in the light of Dawson's life. I am also tempted, though, to use the evidence of Dawson's Gareths as a more or less unconscious invitation to look at his life in the light of Malory's work. What parallels between himself and his fictional prototype would have occurred to Dawson? Despite the fact that Malory's Gareth pretends, in the beginning, to so poor and weakened a condition that he needs support on both sides from lesser men, the handsome young prince is endowed with such sterling qualities that men of insight recognize his fineness at once. The sources on Dawson all agree that there was something noble in his character and bearing, and his life story, as we shall see, was to become an increasingly complex

Dawson's earliest education, literary and otherwise, was conducted at home. In 1886, however, his father escorted the family to France, established Mrs. Dawson in Paris, and registered the children in school, Ethel in the exclusive convent of the Sacré Cœur (in the former Hôtel Biron) and Warrington in the École Saint-Guillaume, directed by the Frères des Écoles Chrétiennes.[21] Warrington contracted pneumonia—his whole subsequent life was to be shaped by matters of health—and virtually the entire stay abroad turned into a prolonged convalescence as far as he was concerned, first in the Forest of Fontainebleau and later in Lausanne. Then in August, 1887, he was back in Charleston, enrolled with his sister in Mrs. Isabel Smith's School. A model child, Warrington proceeded to win prizes in recitation, conduct, and French.

Young though he was, Warrington had at this time already begun to write. Much later he remembered the "scent of printer's ink blending with copy paper," and he deemed it "as welcome to my nostrils as the tang of salt air in the Southern sea-breeze. . . . My initiation with proof-correcting came under my father's supervision when I was nine, on the 'copy' of my own reviews of children's books."[22] Captain Dawson had acted on his belief that an articulate child like Warrington could best express what children like.

Between the ages of eleven and fourteen, after his father's death, the boy attended Mr. W. D. McKenney's University School in Charleston, where he did very well once again. Reaching fifteen in the fall of 1893, he enrolled as a freshman in the municipal College of Charleston. Meanwhile he was continually writing on the side. He turned out feature articles for the *News and Courier* and even tried his hand at a novel. Sometimes the kindly poet-newsman Carlyle McKinley, an old friend of his father, would go over his "scribblings" and offer encouragement.[23] Then in 1895, in order to "brush up" some of his college subjects (he had failed geometry and

---

pattern of contrasting power and helplessness, strength and weakness. The fact that Gareth's weakness is merely a helpful illusion of his own devising is almost too easy, too devastating a key to carry as one approaches Dawson's life. Dawson's last, long years of paralysis were surely not built on conscious pretense, and yet they were very probably built on illusion.

21. The school is described in Dawson's *Gift of Paul Clermont* (London, 1921).

22. "Newspaper Luck in the Paris of the Old Days" (MS in the Ralph Foster Museum, The School of the Ozarks), p. 77.

23. "Newspaper Luck. . . ," p. 77. McKinley should have been a good mentor. Despite his slim output, the *DAB* refers to him as "one of the chief Southern poets of the period" (Robert Duncan Bass, XII [New York, 1933], 104). Herbert R. Sass

done badly in German), Dawson enrolled in McCabe's University School, an excellent private academy in Richmond.[24] But here "his health broke down," and for many months "he was incapable of connected work."[25] In later years Dawson chose to forget the importance of this episode. More and more he became one who saw things as he wanted to see them. Yet the basic situation, at least to begin with, was simply that he contracted scarlet fever from a friend.[26] Mrs. Dawson wrote to J. C. Hemphill, who was editor now of the *News and Courier*, that Warrington had been taken to St. Luke's Hospital in New York and had been "found to be a rare and 'singularly interesting case' of partial paralysis from Diphtheria or Scarlet Fever—probably both."[27] The fact is that Warrington's paralysis probably was caused by neither of these diseases.[28] Whatever the cause, though, his general recovery was slow and perhaps, in a sense, never complete. As for immediate results, the most important was that the young man's formal education was ended.

When he felt sufficiently strong for what he called "a convalescent trip," Dawson, back in Charleston, signed as purser on the

---

(*Outspoken: 150 Years of the News and Courier* [Columbia, S.C., 1953], p. 46) writes of him as an "almost legendary figure . . . who made a name as a reporter when in 1878 he met the famous moonshiner outlaw Lewis Redfield at a rendezvous in the Blue Ridge mountains and wrote for the *News and Courier* the story of his exploits." However, "McKinley's more enduring work was that of editorial writer and poet. . . ." See also William Ashmead Courtenay, ed., *In Loving Memory of Carlyle McKinley, 1847–1904* (Walhalla, S.C., 1904); Mildred Lewis Rutherford, *The South in History and Literature* (Athens, Ga., 1907); and George Armstrong Wauchope, *The Writers of South Carolina* (Columbia, S.C., 1910).

24. Not only had Dawson's father known William Gordon McCabe during the war, but McCabe, like McKinley, was a friend with literary leanings. Dawson later maintained that he went to the school to meet his father's friends. (See Louise Manly, *Southern Literature from 1579–1895* [Richmond, Va., 1895]; Mildred Lewis Rutherford, cited above; and Edd W. Parks, ed., *Southern Poets* [New York, 1936].)

25. Frank C. Lockwood, "Mr. Warrington Dawson and His Books," *Allegheny Literary Monthly*, XVI (1910), 55.

26. Dawson letter of 30 March 1897 to Mrs. Lucy Parke Bagby. Original in Virginia Historical Society, Richmond.

27. 22 January 1897 (Hemphill Family Papers, Perkins Library, Duke).

28. Post-diphtheritic paralysis rarely lasts as long as Dawson's paralysis (somewhat over a year). Furthermore, there is no record of diphtheria in Dawson's official hospital history. Scarlet fever—which he did have—would seldom lead to paralysis. Altogether, considering evidence from Dawson's later life, it seems that the entire episode, involving an incapacitation of some fourteen and a half months, had a strong psychological aspect. (This note is based on discussions with Dr. John M. Rhoads of Duke University Hospital. A case transcript was kindly furnished by Miss A. Rose Toddonio and Mr. F. Dennis Harrington, St. Luke's Hospital, Morningside Heights, New York City.)

British merchant steamer *Sam Handford,* outward bound for Spain on 1 March 1898. Though this was the time of the Spanish-American War, Dawson's move was a rather dim shadow of the action which his father had taken many years earlier.[29] For Dawson, in any case, the move was crucial. During the trip he seemed to realize for the first time who he was and how he might fulfil himself. In 1899 he returned home but stayed only briefly (Warrington "could not endure the scene of his father's martyrdom," his mother confided to her journal). Then on 16 October he sailed from New York on what she called "his European Destiny."[30] The complexity of his aspiration is suggested best by his own words:

> My adventures in connection with the Spanish-American War having fixed my destinies, I had returned home in 1899 to pull up my roots and come back to Paris for the 1900 Exhibition, planning to do free lance journalism as an immediate means of live[li]hood, wishing to make something out of my voice and having inclinations towards grand opera, but nursing in the depths of my brain and heart and soul the passion for novel-writing which has been the dominant aspiration of my existence. . . .
>
> I did not intend, however, to write hack novels ground out per pattern and sold "like chunks of cheese dealt over the counter by a cheese-monger," to quote the explosive simile once used by Joseph Conrad in telling me why he had never been able to satisfy the demands of certain publishers for something really popular and conventional. . . . So I started off, arming myself with some social and professional introductions. . . .[31]

For Dawson the opening years of the new century were studded with a dazzling series of successes. In 1900 there was a silver medal for his reporting of the Paris Exposition. There were interviews with President Émile Loubet, General William Booth, Augustus Saint-Gaudens, Edmond Rostand, Mary Garden, and Sarah Bern-

29. In some ways the move was closer to that of the young Joseph Conrad, who had been allowed to go to sea before finishing his secondary education partly because "the doctors seem to have been convinced that the sea air and plenty of physical exercise were going to restore the boy's nervous balance and put an end to the recurring attacks of migraine" (Zdzislaw Najder, ed., *Conrad's Polish Background,* trans. Halina Carroll [London, 1964], p. 14).

30. From Sarah Dawson's notebook labelled "As It Was Told," p. 132.

31. "Newspaper Luck . . . ," pp. 70–71.

hardt (whom his father before him had interviewed). There were notable friendships with Rodin and the popular astronomer Camille Flammarion. Partly on the basis of a "scoop" concerning Queen Wilhelmina's trousseau (it was being created in Paris, not, as given out, in Holland), he was appointed to organize and manage the Paris bureau of what was to become the United Press.[32] Here was an important job and he did it well. "He is going on from success to success," his mother wrote home;[33] "the spirit of his father seems upon him."[34] Still, indefatigably, he attempted more. He went to Brussels for the Socialist strike riots of 1901; to St. Petersburg in 1904 to organize a cable service and observe the first of the Russo-Japanese War; and to The Hague for the Second Peace Conference in 1907. In Paris in 1905 he attended the hearings of the North Sea Tribunal, and in 1908 he not only witnessed the shooting of Alfred Dreyfus, but beat his brother reporters in telegraphing the news because he slipped out a back door of the Pantheon, while they were blocked by police at other exits. Acclaimed Secretary General of the Foreign Press in Paris, he became the intermediary between the French government and all resident foreign correspondents. He was the first American journalist ever granted a permanent annual seat in both French houses of Parliament. He was even offered the position of General European Manager of the United Press Associations. Grand though this last post must have seemed, however, he refused because it would have ended his fondest dream of all—a literary career. Throughout his life, whatever else befell him, Dawson kept working on his books.

> My first novels, *The Scar* and *The Scourge*, were written between 5 and 7 A.M. . . . Which did not prevent me from taking my singing courses with Manoury of the Paris Opera, and on other days my fencing lessons . . . , before the arduous part of my daily programme began.[35]

Despite incredible stress, which told on him physically, the years 1900 to 1908 were probably the best in Dawson's life. The world lay before him, and his mother stood by his side. "Keep an eye on

32. It was then called the Publishers' Press and Scripps-McRae Press. It merged with Scripps News Association and became the United Press Associations in 1907.
33. Sarah Dawson to Mrs. Eunice (William Huger) Dunkin, 21 May 1901 (Dawson Collection, Duke).
34. Sarah Dawson to Eunice Dunkin, 22 April 1901.
35. "Newspaper Luck . . . ," p. 94.

that boy!" she wrote back to the States. "He is destined to great things."[36]

Objectivity and the passage of time make it clear that Sarah Dawson loved more intensely than wisely, and that she wanted too much from her son. Probably this was true from the time when Warrington was a child, but the situation grew more acute in the years following her husband's death. "I am bewildered by his resemblance to his father," she wrote in 1900. "There is the movement of the hands, the volubility, the backward motion of the head that I have seen no where else."[37] What is more, he was all hers. "Poor boy!" she wrote; "his one idea is to lavish things on me as though I were a girl."[38] She even reported that once when they had gone out together in Versailles they

> suddenly saw one of his [journalistic] brethren, a man of forty-odd, seated on the boulevard with a gross scullion whom he was kissing and odiously caressing—and I thanked God for the beautiful boy who believes his mother to be the supreme object of love and adoration, and who keeps himself free of all taint, waiting for a higher calling.[39]

After Warrington had achieved one particular triumph she felt "incapable of telling . . . the full extent of the honor and fame and responsibilities and—Thank God—Income, that are about to befal[l] my boy. Forgive me if I seem hardly lucid. . . . Warrington, not only independent of the world and its cruelties, but commanding, as he was born to command?"[40] She could scarcely believe her good fortune.

It was also during this opening decade of the new century that Dawson first realized the literary stature of Joseph Conrad. Though he had come across Conrad's work earlier, it was Edward Abram Uffington Valentine, himself a novelist and poet, who impressed upon Dawson the importance of Conrad's achievement.[41] Like Daw-

36. Sarah Dawson to Eunice Dunkin, 1 January 1904.
37. Sarah Dawson to Eunice Dunkin, 26 April.
38. Sarah Dawson to Eunice Dunkin, 28 March 1902.
39. Sarah Dawson to Eunice Dunkin, 23 July 1901.
40. Sarah Dawson to Eunice Dunkin, 25 January 1901.
41. Among Valentine's works are *The Ship of Silence* (1902), with poems which reviewers found Keatsian; *Hecla Sandwith* (1905), his best-known novel; *The Red Sphinx* (1907), with S. E. Harper; *Camilla of the Ridges* (1910); *The Road to Thebes* (1910); and *The Labyrinth of Life* (1912), a novel about the American colony in Paris.

son, Valentine was a man of many talents. He had trained for careers in music and law, and during the Cuban War he had even tried soldiering. For a while he settled down to serve as literary editor of the Baltimore *Evening News*.[42] Then in 1907 he set off still again, this time to pursue a literary career in the American colony in Paris. Perhaps realizing, as Dawson had, that he was embarking on a hazardous venture, he arranged to keep in touch with journalism, serving now as a special foreign correspondent for the New York *World*. Because Dawson at this time was Secretary General of the Foreign Press in Paris, and because the two men had known each other since about 1894, it must have seemed only natural that they should meet again, and, once met, that their talk should turn to literary matters.[43]

Dawson's own first novels appeared first in England, *The Scar* in 1906 and *The Scourge* in 1908. Both were Southern novels with a Virginia setting, and both were attempts at realism. Dawson explained that his purpose in *The Scar* was "to chronicle truthfully what I have seen and lived of the South's development within my own experience."[44] He wanted to show "the hardships and fortitude in a remote corner of Southern country a quarter of a century after the war had ended and wounds were supposed to be healed. . . ." He cushioned himself from criticism, however, with the characteristic statement that, "judged superficially, it must needs alarm the South's pride and excite the North's prejudice." Whatever his private thoughts, Dawson's face-saving stand on the matter of recognition was from this time forward much the same. It was essentially that of Frank Norris, who wrote (with more force than Dawson would have deemed proper), "By God, I told them the truth. They liked it or they didn't like it. What had that to do with me?"[45] As a matter of fact, while the critics found fault with Dawson's first two books, they also found much to praise. The New York *Times* greeted

42. He built his Baltimore column into "one of the most carefully-read and closely-watched features of the paper. Publishers and writers generally recognized him after a time as among the leading reviewers of the country" (Paul Winchester and Frank D. Webb, eds., *Newspapers and Newspaper Men of Maryland Past and Present* [Baltimore, 1905], p. 95).

43. I have had to conjecture here, but the dating fits. According to Dawson, Valentine first spoke to him of Conrad about 1907.

44. From Dawson's carbon of a letter to "the Editor of the [Richmond] TIMES-DISPATCH" (i.e., James Calvin Hemphill), 16 August 1910.

45. *The Responsibilities of the Novelist and Other Literary Essays* (New York, 1903), p. 22.

the American publication of *The Scar* (1910) with words as harsh as any, perhaps, when it reported that

> The book is so good, so strong, and apparently so true in many of its phases that the reader marvels all the more that the author did not himself realize how bungling, illogical, and unconvincing it is in certain other phases. . . .
>
> But Mr. Dawson's theme is big and vital and he handles it, in many ways, so capably and invests his gray, forbidding picture with so much human interest that one is inclined to praise rather than to be captious.[46]

Dawson's first two books had a certain freshness, a rather petulant irony which contrasted favorably with the rosy glow of the conventional Southern romance of the day. Ellen Glasgow, who later recalled that a maiden aunt had given her a Confederate novel every Christmas of her girlhood,[47] preceded Dawson in this field of Southern realism, and yet both authors, known to each other, began to write at about the time "when the idealistic treatment of the romantic material of Southern life had reached its climax of popular approval." Like Ellen Glasgow, Dawson "did not break sharply with the traditions of that school," but hoped to take "the best lessons it had to teach," and to turn "them into a new achievement."[48] The main difference between them, of course, was one of talent. Ellen Glasgow went on to become a major writer, while Dawson, with less literary ability, spent his energies in a number of different fields, and sometimes, it turned out, on barren ground. Long before his death in 1962 Dawson had had to resign himself to literary oblivion. For some perverse reason not only the public and the scholars but even the list-compilers had overlooked his fiction, even when their concern was not quality, even when all they tried to catch in their nets were novels with satirical elements or historical novels or novels of the South. It was a fate more grim than he deserved.

Though Theodore Roosevelt did not pretend to be a literary critic, he did take a special joy in reading, and just prior to the American

46. *Times*, 2 April 1910, p. 183.
47. Cited by Jay B. Hubbell, *The South in American Literature: 1607–1900* (Durham, N.C., 1954), p. 842.
48. This diagnosis, made in terms of Ellen Glasgow, is given by Arthur Hobson Quinn, *American Fiction: An Historical and Critical Survey* (New York, 1936), p. 681. Like all other students of the subject, Quinn overlooks Dawson.

debut of Dawson's works he allowed himself to wonder publicly how the United States could ignore Dawson. "It seems rather queer," he wrote,

> to go abroad and discover an American author. Two books have appeared in England during the last year or two, named 'The Scar' and 'The Scourge.' They have been a success, not only in England, but on the Continent; for translations have appeared or are appearing in German, French, and Russian. Yet they are by an American, Mr. Warrington Dawson, of South Carolina; and they deal with localities, questions, and types exclusively and typically American. It is not very creditable to us that this American, writing with unusual power of American scenes and problems, should have an exclusively European audience.[49]

From an article in *The Bookman* it appears that Gertrude Atherton must have seen the case more clearly. Though she wrote in general terms, her words come so close to describing Dawson's situation that she may well have had him, among others, in mind:

> A very few American writers have obtained a certain circulation in England and remained practically unknown in their own country. I have noticed this from time to time, but do not recall their names, and it is not worth while to make the attempt. It is all very well to obtain your first recognition in a foreign country if hostile critics and a puzzled public prevent your advancement at home, but if the native does not follow that foreign success as a matter of course, it means that you lack the power to interest a vast public. . . . If your own people keep on rejecting you, after the *réclame* of English acceptance, you can call yourself a failure. . . .[50]

Such *réclame* as Dawson received was short-lived, and yet it helped arouse the interest and sympathy of Joseph Conrad. Never a good critic, Conrad wrote on 27 September 1910 to tell Dawson that *The Scar* had "*power* . . . and a great charm of style, a soberness of presentation which appeals to me extremely, l'œil artiste as to details, with a large conception of the whole. In short, mon cher,

49. "A Southerner's View of the South," *Outlook*, XCII (1909), 310.
50. "The American Novel in England," *Bookman* (New York), XXX (1910), 639.

beaucoup de talent. Talent, I mean, of the sort that is on the way of becoming *exceptional*." For a time, at least, it was possible to believe that Dawson was to reverse the process of his English father, who had come west across the Atlantic and found success in America.

3

Conrad's Introduction to Dawson (1910)

The meeting of Conrad and Dawson on Saturday, 28 May 1910, was not only the beginning of a friendship but also, in a sense, the culmination of Dawson's adventures in Africa.[1]

Immediately following the inauguration of President Taft on 4 March 1909, former President Theodore Roosevelt left Washington to go on a hunting expedition. Though lame in one leg and nearly blind in one eye, Roosevelt had made himself a symbol of "strenuous Americanism," and now he was to throw his tremendous enthusiasm into an exploration of the game trails of the Dark Continent. When his safari finally set out, it broke all records "for immensity and organisation."[2] His encounter with the bongo, the kudu, the dikdik, and the wildebeest were reported only sketchily in the world's newspapers, however, because he insisted on his new right to be a private citizen. He refused to be stalked by reporters.

Dawson, undaunted, left Paris for Naples, where Roosevelt was to pause on his way. With typical flair, Dawson went out in a launch to meet Roosevelt's ship, and that same afternoon he presented himself to the great man at his hotel, a place called appropriately the *Excelsior*. Roosevelt was cordial, but insistent on privacy. He had sailed from Naples to Messina and, in fact, was about to depart from Messina before Dawson managed to have a real talk with him. Once this second contact was made, Dawson's path was clear. Here was no mere reporter, obviously. Here was the youthful, enterpris-

1. I deduce the date with the aid of a Conrad letter to Galsworthy collected by Jean-Aubry (*Joseph Conrad: Life and Letters*, II [Garden City, N.Y., 1927], 107) and reprinted here (No. 4). Undated by Jean-Aubry, the letter was written 31 May 1910.

2. Elspeth Huxley, *White Man's Country: Lord Delamere and the Making of Kenya*, I (London, 1935), 250. "There were 500 porters, each carrying his 60-lb. load." A map of Roosevelt's route precedes the foreword to Vol. I of his *African Game Trails* (New York, 1910).

23

ing, ingratiating incarnation of Roosevelt's own belief that "The joy of living is his who has the heart to demand it."[3] Here, by Godfrey, was a journalist with style enough to think of providing himself with a letter of introduction from the Ambassador to France, Henry White. Moreover, Dawson was the son of a famous father. The young man wrote home to his mother—in the usual French of their private correspondence: "Il a parlé avec beaucoup d'admiration de papa. Il a dit 'I never knew your father, but I know of his splendid work. . . . Your father was not only a great and able man, but also a man of remarkable breadth. . . .' "[4] A few days later he was even able to quote Roosevelt on the subject of himself: "There *are* some newspaper men I object to—but you see, *you* happen to be a gentleman!"[5]

Mrs. Dawson, as always, was very proud of her boy. On the eve of his departure from Paris she had read him, as she usually did when they parted, the scene from Thackeray's *Henry Esmond* in which Henry returns from the wars and meets Lady Castlewood in the cathedral, bringing home his sheaves. When Dawson returned with his sheaves this time, however, there was no one to receive them. On the last day of April, 1909, the news was cabled from Paris that Mrs. Dawson had fallen ill, and on the fifth day of May she died.

Four days later and half a world away, in British East Africa, Dawson registered his "Revolver 6ch."[6] By this time he had become more or less affiliated with the Roosevelt party. He was certainly still a correspondent of the United Press, but his rather anomalous position seems to have been less that of a journalist than that of a particularly pleasant and helpful companion. Roosevelt had been intent all along on avoiding a mob of reporters. On the other hand, the discreet release of a few brief, authentic news items was an altogether different matter. As it turned out, Roosevelt even asked Dawson to come along on some side trips, "more to have someone to talk with," Dawson said later, "than for any other reason. He didn't talk politics, . . . but rather literature, arts and sciences."[7]

3. *A Book-Lover's Holidays in the Open* (New York, 1916), p. x.
4. Dawson to Sarah Dawson, 7 April 1909.
5. Dawson to Sarah Dawson, 11 April 1909.
6. *The Official Gazette of the East African Protectorate*, XI (Nairobi, 1909), 317.
7. Quoted by the Boston *Globe*, 26 March 1910, from a lecture delivered that afternoon to the Twentieth Century Club (clipping, p. 79 of Dawson's Scrapbook No. 67898).

Making everything easier was the fact that Dawson hit it off especially well with Roosevelt's son Kermit. On one occasion the two young men set out on their own private expedition around Lake Naivasha, with two gunbearers, two tent boys, and seventeen porters, all in search of bushbuck. Dawson even acquired an African name. The American people were to learn eventually that Africa had transformed Theodore Roosevelt to *Bwana Makuba* (Great Master), but only *Bwana Makuba's* immediate companions knew also that *Bwana Mazarowe* (Trumpet Voice) was Warrington Dawson.[8]

Dawson, of course, never relied on charm alone to carry the day. Like Gareth before him, he had learned to polish kettles. When Roosevelt discovered that the young man could type fast and write longhand as quickly as most secretaries write shorthand,[9] he was happy to accept Dawson's offer of clerical help. Though the world never knew, it was partly thanks to Dawson that Roosevelt's articles for *Scribner's* kept emerging from the interior. Later on, when Dawson lectured about his African experiences, he recalled that one day he had sat "at the typewriter taking dictation . . . from 9 in the morning until 2:20 at night, our only pause being for meals."[10]

It was while they were together in Nairobi that Dawson and Roosevelt met one of Joseph Conrad's best friends. Three hundred and twenty-seven miles up the Uganda Railway from Mombasa, Captain Edward Lancelot Sanderson was a well-established public official. A few years earlier Conrad had been a frequent guest at Sanderson's home in Hertfordshire, where Sanderson's father was headmaster of Elstree School. At Elstree, young Ted Sanderson and his mother, "Mrs. Kitty," are even said to have joined forces to help with the polishing of *Almayer's Folly*.[11] Some years earlier still, in

8. The name was a memorial to "one catastrophic day when the carrying quality of my voice inadvertently cleared the entire plains of game thereby spoiling the hunt" (from a Dawson MS filed under "Miscellaneous Fragments on Africa").

9. This detail is recalled by Archibald B. Roosevelt (interview of 9 September 1964).

10. From the *Globe* article cited earlier. Furthermore, leaving Africa before the rest of the party, Dawson was able to offer aid to Roosevelt from Paris. On 17 July 1909 Roosevelt wrote Robert Bridges, assistant editor of *Scribner's*, "I suppose you have arranged about the foreign publishing rights. If you have not done so in France, my personal friend Warrington Dawson will not as a matter of business but as a matter of friendship make arrangements for you . . ." (*The Letters of Theodore Roosevelt*, ed. Elting E. Morison *et al.*, VII [Cambridge, Mass., 1954], 20).

11. M. E. Reynolds, *Memories of John Galsworthy* (London, 1936), p. 26. *The Mirror of the Sea* (London, 1906) was dedicated to Katherine Sanderson.

1892, as a new B.A. of King's College, Cambridge, Ted Sanderson had undertaken a tour to the South Seas with his friend John Galsworthy. One aim of the young men was to find Robert Louis Stevenson. Another aim for Sanderson was to regain some of the strength he had lost from overstraining at rowing and running. What happened is now a familiar story. Stevenson was not to be found, but at the beginning of the trip home in March, 1893, on board the passenger-and-wool clipper *Torrens,* "one of the fastest sailing ships of her day,"[12] out of Adelaide, Australia, Sanderson and Galsworthy met Conrad. Sanderson never forgot the Polish First Mate. Though the docking of the *Torrens* in London four months later brought Conrad virtually to the close of his career as a sailor, Sanderson always thought of him afterwards as "a bold and hardy seaman first and foremost. . . ."[13] Back in England, Sanderson received the M.A. degree in 1894, then settled down to serve for a while as Assistant Master at Elstree. In 1898 he married Helen Mary Watson, daughter of the sheriff of Wigtownshire, Scotland. (Conrad thought of the young Mrs. Sanderson as "a Scotch girl of great intelligence.")[14] Then in 1899 he sailed with the Third Battalion, Yorkshire Regiment, for duty in the South African War. At first things went badly. The British had underestimated the Boers, and even after the largest British army in history began to make major gains—Orange Free State and the Transvaal were declared annexed—the Boers managed to wage a guerrilla war. Lord Kitchener, Commander-in-Chief, proceeded to occupy the country bit by bit, however, and peace was finally achieved in 1902. By this time Captain Sanderson's health was damaged again, and he decided not to return to England just yet. Instead, he took employment in Johannesburg in the Transvaal Education Department, and both he and Mrs. Sanderson settled in South Africa until late in 1904. On 1 October of that year the *Official Gazette* announced that he had been appointed Town Clerk of Nairobi.[15]

The Roosevelt visit to Nairobi proved memorable. To begin

12. Jerry Allen, *The Sea Years of Joseph Conrad* (New York, 1965), p. 285.

13. Cmdr. Ian Sanderson to Randall, 11 January 1966. Miss Allen, in *The Sea Years,* explains that although Conrad was subsequently attached briefly to the *Adowa,* the *Torrens* was his last ship of importance (p. 325).

14. Letter to Edward Garnett, 9 November 1899, now in The Philip H. & A. S. W. Rosenbach Foundation, Philadelphia.

15. *Official Gazette of the East Africa and Uganda Protectorates,* VI (Mombasa, 1904), 375. Captain Sanderson remained Town Clerk until November, 1910, when he returned to succeed his brother-in-law as Headmaster of Elstree. He served as

with, both Roosevelt and Dawson were delighted to find that the heart of darkness had a civilized corner. Roosevelt reported how, a short time before, "a lady on a bicycle, wheeling down to a rehearsal of [Gilbert and Sullivan's] 'Trial by Jury,' had been run into and upset by a herd of frightened zebras."[16] And though a lion had taken to prowling in the outlying residential neighborhood, Dawson told of finding "at the house of Captain and Mrs. E. L. Sanderson an entire shelf of books by Joseph Conrad with his autograph in each. . . ."[17] Most of the time in Nairobi, Roosevelt was the guest of William Northrup McMillan, the rancher and big-game hunter, but one night he was invited to dine "with the Provincial Commissioner, Mr. Hobley, and the next with the town clerk, Captain Sanderson. In each case the hostess, the host, and the house were all delightful, and the evening just like a very pleasant evening spent anywhere in civilization. . . ."[18] Over half a century later Mrs. Sanderson was still to recall how Roosevelt's confidential advisers recommended that he visit her and her husband rather than some higher official, and how Roosevelt sat on the floor to read in the Sandersons' library.[19] Captain Sanderson himself long remembered the story of how Roosevelt found in Thackeray's *Book of Snobs* a passage which he vowed he would send to the Kaiser. In all respects, then, the new relationships were a success. It appears, however, that Roosevelt was impressed most of all by Mrs. Sanderson. In the privacy of a letter to his sister, Anna Roosevelt Cowles, the former President confided on 17 December 1909 that "There are a certain number of the people I have met here of whom I am really fond; two of the women, Lady Delamere and Mrs. Sanderson, are delightful."[20] On the same day he wrote to Bridges at *Scribner's*:

> I . . . enclose some little sketches by a Scotchwoman here, which seem to me to have real value. They give with vividness the sense, the feel, of this life, as it strikes a cultivated, rather

Headmaster from 1911 until 1935 and died on 23 March 1939. See London *Times*, 25 March 1939, p. 1; J. A. Venn, comp., *Alumni Cantabrigienses*, Pt. II (1752–1900), Vol. V (Cambridge, Eng., 1953), p. 414; and scattered references in official Gazettes of the East Africa and Uganda Protectorates.

16. *African Game Trails*, II, 325–326.
17. *Opportunity and Theodore Roosevelt* (Chicago, 1924), p. 162.
18. *African Game Trails*, II, 325.
19. Interview of 8 December 1964.
20. *Letters*, ed. Morison, VII, 43. Lady Delamere was the wife of Hugh Cholmondeley, Baron Delamere, an important settler in B.E.A.

lonely woman who knows herself to be an exile. Will you read them yourself? If you publish them, I think they should be signed only with the initials, H. S.[21]

Mrs. Sanderson's sketches—delicate, poignant, formless little things —were eventually published by *Scribner's* under the pen name "Janet Allardyce." In passing they paid the Sandersons' friend Conrad the compliment of subtle allusion: "Johannesburg has long been for us an experience of the past, and our home is now in an 'Outpost of progress,' in the land of the lion and the Masai."[22]

By the autumn of 1909 Dawson had returned to the States. He resigned from the United Press on 7 October and wrote to Roosevelt that he was "at least momentarily out of journalism."[23] For the time being he was quite smitten by the idea of mounting the lecture platform. Still in his mind, however, was that day in East Africa when Roosevelt had said, "What you plan to do, do now. You have at thirty an adaptability which you won't have in ten years. You believe in yourself, and because of the novels you have already written I believe in you. . . . Be a novelist."[24] Roosevelt later became still more explicit: "Cling to South Carolina" was his advice.[25] Take a man like Joel Chandler Harris as a model insofar as identifying yourself with a region, and take Bret Harte as a model of what to avoid. (Harte had settled in England and continued to write mechanically of the American West even after he had forgotten that California poppies are yellow.) Dawson proceeded to arrange a number of lecture engagements during the winter of 1909–1910. He delivered "With Roosevelt in Africa" at least ten times between 29 November 1909 and 29 March 1910. But back in Paris he admitted in a letter to his sister's husband, Herbert Barry, that while he had "made good in several different directions," he had "not yet made good financially." After nine and a half furiously busy years he was "not much

21. *Letters*, ed. Morison, VII, 44.
22. "African Sketches and Impressions," *Scribner's Magazine*, XLVIII (1910), 627–632, esp. 629. "More African Sketches" appeared in LI (1912), 103–110. Jean-Aubry included Conrad letters which refer both to the sketches and to the news of the Sandersons which Dawson brought from Africa, but he failed to identify Dawson and apparently knew nothing of "Janet Allardyce" or the part that Roosevelt played in publishing her work.
23. From Dawson's carbon copy of a letter to Roosevelt, 14 October 1909.
24. Quoted by Dawson in the introductory matter to his *Crimson Pall* (Chicago, 1927), p. 18.
25. Dawson reported this to Herbert Barry in a letter of 27 April 1910. Quoted from Dawson's copy.

better off than I was when I started, save for my experience, my ripening, and the friends I have made. . . ." He could live and work in Paris for relatively little, he wrote,

> and be considered a person of consequence in Charleston; but to attempt living on the same income in Charleston would mean that I would be considered a failure. My effort must therefore be to make enough money by books and articles to be able to go back to Charleston to settle several years from now, and become an editorial contributor to the News & Courier to have influence on the spot, living part of the year there dealing with local questions, and part of the year in the North or abroad so as to avoid getting provincial. But this will take money, and I am now out for earning it if I possibly can through real literature.

This was written 27 April 1910, just a month before he met Conrad. In other words, when Dawson went to England in May to "cover" the funeral of Edward VII (though "out of journalism," he was an inveterate reporter), he regarded his status as "largely of a literary and artistic nature. . . ."[26] All things considered, it is not surprising that he wrote to Conrad and introduced himself as one who bore greetings from Roosevelt and the Sandersons, nor that the contact, once made, proved to focus on writing.

It was Dawson's good luck to come to Conrad's home in Aldington, Kent—"four tiny rooms in half a cottage"[27]—just as Conrad was emerging from one of the blackest times of his life. Jean-Aubry goes so far as to characterize the whole period between 1910 and 1914, the time of all Dawson's visits, as one of "great loneliness" for Conrad: "For months he did not even go up to London, saw almost no one. His only link with the world was his letters, few in number and limited to a handful of loyal friends. . . ."[28] Though known to some readers both at home and in the States, Conrad at this time was by no means the famous author he was to become. Moreover, his small private circle, which was very important to him, had recently shrunk significantly.

First had come his alienation from Ford Madox Hueffer. Hueffer

26. Dawson's "Think It Not Strange," a MS memoir, p. 24.
27. Conrad to William Rothenstein, 17 December 1909, in Jean-Aubry, *LL*, II, 104.
28. *The Sea Dreamer* (London, 1957), p. 257.

had entered Conrad's life toward the end of 1898, another crucial period because Conrad had then recently and rather reluctantly acquired an infant son. Despite differences in age, background, and temperament, Conrad and Hueffer had become good friends, entered into an intimate creative collaboration, and eventually fathered jointly three books, all less important as novels than as literary experiments, concrete evidence of long literary discussions. Whatever problems Hueffer may have caused Jessie Conrad, who disliked him intensely, he provided Conrad himself with some of the admiration and encouragement, some of the opportunity for self-definition, that he needed. After eleven years, however, the break came. There were a number of causes, none simple and perhaps all related. Some grew out of the men's joint effort to make a go of the ill-fated *English Review*.[29] Some were probably related to Hueffer's extramarital liaison with the writer Violet Hunt (whose *Tales of the Uneasy* appeared in 1910). Such a relationship as that between Hueffer and his lady assistant at the *Review* was almost sure to strain Conrad's rigid morality, and it may have wounded him also in a private way which he himself could not have articulated.[30]

Next came Conrad's break with James Brand Pinker, his friend, agent, and creditor. With the greatest of effort Conrad had managed to finish *Under Western Eyes* on 22 January 1910. Then he had gone up to London to see, first, his publisher, and then Pinker—"the Imperatively Necessary Pinker," Conrad had called him in 1907.[31] Pinker was a hard-boiled little man with a mind of his own, and yet, according to Jessie, he could usually succeed in soothing Conrad.[32]

29. See also pp. 35–36.
30. Bernard C. Meyer relates Conrad's "emotional climate" at the time to *Under Western Eyes*, the book he was finishing, a "story of the lonely Russian youth Razumov, who betrays a fellow student" ("Psychoanalytic Studies on Joseph Conrad," Pt. 4, "The Flow and Ebb of Artistry," *Journal of the American Psychoanalytic Association*, XII [1964], 815). However valid this may be, the total situation in which Conrad found himself should not be oversimplified. Both wives, for example, became involved. Shortly before *Under Western Eyes* was completed, the estranged Mrs. Hueffer summoned Conrad to her home and infuriated him by letting loose a bitter barrage at writers in general and Conrad's friend Galsworthy in particular. Jessie later connected this incident with Conrad's trip up to London, where he wrecked a chair and, at Galsworthy's that night, apparently still seething inside, kicked out the foot of the bed in his sleep (see Jessie Conrad, *Joseph Conrad and His Circle*, 2nd ed. [Port Washington, N.Y., 1964], pp. 140–141).
31. Conrad to Henry James, 20 September, in Jean-Aubry, LL, II, 55.
32. *Joseph Conrad and His Circle*, p. 228.

But not this time. An explosive quarrel between the two led not only to another long estrangement, but also, as Conrad said later, to "a severe illness which seemed to wait like a tiger . . . on the turn of a path to jump on me. . . ."[33]

Conrad's physical symptoms, those of a severe case of gout, were dreadful enough. Still worse, though, the gout was merely part of a breakdown of major dimensions.[34] On 6 February 1910 Jessie confided to Alice Rothenstein,

> The book is finished and now Conrad has had a complete nervous breakdown and gout. Gout everywhere, throat tongue head. There are two swellings on the back of his head as big as my fist. Poor boy, he lives the novel, rambles all the time and insists the Dr and I are trying to put him into an asylum. He is not to be allowed the least mental exertion or to see anyone at present.[35]

By 20 May Conrad was at least sufficiently improved to inform William Rothenstein that

> I can just, just hobble over 50 yards or so of smooth ground but am too tottery and generally shaky to venture on the pavements of Babylon. Also one wrist is dead lame.
>
> The mind is not much better. Can't concentrate for more than ½ hour at a time.[36]

Yet the next day Conrad wrote his first letter to Dawson. Considering the circumstances, it was cordial and surprisingly cheery, an

---

33. *Notes on My Books* (Garden City, N.Y., 1921), p. 117.

34. Conrad was well aware of the neurasthenic qualities of his affliction. On 7 May 1936 Jean-Aubry wrote to Herr Paul Wohlfarth:

> Conrad . . . considerait la goutte comme une maladie d'ordre nerveux. Il est indubitable qu' à plusieurs époques de sa vie, il eut de très violentes crises de goutte après des moments où il avait eu de grandes préoccupations, de grandes fatigues nerveuses. . . . Cela ne veut pas dire que toutes ses attaques de goutte ont été déterminées ainsi. J'ai connu Conrad intimement pendant près de dix ans, et l'ai vu très souvent, trop souvent, hélas! en proie à la goutte; mais ses plus fortes crises ont toujours coincidé avec des crises d'ordre moral, et par conséquent [*sic*] nerveuses. Il y en a même eu des cas troublants, telle la crise de goutte très violente qui semble bien avoir attendu juste le moment où il venait de terminer 'Under Western Eyes' comme si l'écrivain avait eu la faculté de retenir cette crise jusqu'au moment où il aurait achevé son travail.

(From a MS in the Wellcome Historical Medical Library, London.)

35. From a MS in the Houghton Library, Harvard.

36. Quoted from *Men and Memories: Recollections of William Rothenstein 1900–1922* (New York, 1932), p. 159.

invitation couched facetiously in such safari terms as seemed appropriate to a reader who brought news from Africa.

Dawson's Saturday afternoon visit was eventually described by Jessie in *Joseph Conrad and His Circle* (1935). A few years earlier, however, at Dawson's request, she had written a longer and somewhat less formal account. On 20 February 1929 Dawson had made explicit his hope of capitalizing on his old connection with Conrad:

> I wonder if some time you could find the leisure to write a short sketch of Conrad's friendship with me. . . . It would be a help to me in getting before the public some day my own view of "my dear Conrad". . . . But this consideration is not the main one I am holding in view. I am thinking that such a sketch by you would help now to get a new public in America for Conrad. . . .[37]

Jessie's warmhearted, voluble, hastily written response was a thoroughly characteristic piece called "Friendship's Friend." Though her memory was shaky and she leaned toward overstatement, her essay gives a close and rare glimpse of the Conrad-Dawson relationship. Because of its inaccessibility and its relevance, and despite its rambling, the strange little document is perhaps best preserved here:

> To my mind there is no dearer word than "friend". I do not mean by this a mere acquaintance, made one moment and forgotten the next, so to speak, but a bond between two individuals. That bond based upon the keen appreciation each one feels for his fellow.
>
> Friendship is more lasting than love, first because it has usually a more substantial foundation, is less personal, less swayed by jealousy, perhaps. True friendship should endure through long years of silence, should be capable of recalling at will those happy hours of close companionship that mark some epoch in all our lives.
>
> There are some people who seem to possess a genius for friendship, whose personality makes a lasting impression, and in most cases claims a feeling of equal intensity from the object of its regard. In those cases no length of time, or absence can sever or even weaken. I have heard it said that some friendships

37. The entire letter is included in Part Two (No. 111).

last longer if the friends are parted. It may be so in some cases. But I think there must be something wanting, some little thing that does not ring true.

So many friendships made by Joseph Conrad began with a letter, a letter in which he detected the real sentiment of friendliness. Sometimes even when the letter contained a fair measure of criticism. If he considered that unfair, or uncalled-for, he might perhaps indulge in a sharp retort, but even so the letter usually served as an introduction, and more often than not the foundation of a new friendship was laid.

Joseph Conrad's friendship with Warrington Dawson had such a beginning, if I remember rightly.[38] The outcome of this was a visit paid to our tiny cottage in Aldington for lunch.

Warrington Dawson arrived late for that meal, not due to any fault of his own, however. My husband's minute directions for finding our modest abode, tucked away under the hill, would have been perfect had our postal address given Smeeth as our railway station. Instead the note paper bore the heading "Aldington Nr Hythe." Small wonder then that our guest insisted upon being driven to Hythe.

The preparations for that meal had perforce to be made under difficulties, owing to the very limited space, and my husband's instructions were that everything was to be the very best I could provide. Picture my consternation when the hours passed by and the lunch was in due course cleared away.

Joseph Conrad retired in high dudgeon to the fastness of the little study drawing-room, and I was left with the small boy.[39] Slowly the hours slipped by, till suddenly my husband called out joyously, "Here he is, Jess. Lets have lunch in again at once."

Somehow I achieved this, and the guest ate and the two talked like old friends.

Warrington had brought a flattering message from Theodore Roosevelt. I recall Conrad's pleasure at this kindly message. Also that when he was in America in 1923 he made a point of

---

38. It is hard to imagine that Dawson's introductory letter contained criticism, unless on some innocuous topic such as Conrad's failure to write very regularly to the Sandersons. On the other hand, perhaps Jessie means only that the "foundation" of the Conrad-Dawson friendship was laid by a letter.
39. Apparently John, not yet four. Borys was twelve at the time.

calling upon Mrs Roosevelt, and expressed delight at her friendly and cordial reception. I have here by my side a tiny envelope containing her card. This card accompanied her subscription to the Joseph Conrad Memorial Fund and was given to me by Canon Ashton-Gwatkin, of Bishopsbourne.

These few facts seem easier to record here, having mentioned the name of President Roosevelt. I have wished very much that it had been my privilege to have accompanied my husband upon that call, more I think than upon any he made while in America.

More than fifteen years of close friendship between Warrington Dawson and my husband resulted from that delayed lunch, a friendship that it was my joy to share. The complete understanding between the two artists never waned, never grew cold or indifferent.

All through the great world war letters passed between them, recording their hopes and fears, laying bare their most intimate impressions. Impressions of youth on one side and of a father on the other.

Often Conrad has said to me how great was the understanding displayed by this man who was young enough to have been a son to him, how well he understood that dread and pride he felt in the fact that his own flesh and blood was out there, facing the odds with his full measure of pluck and courage.[40]

There is something fearful in the mere fact of recalling one's impressions of that terrible conflict. Everyone's memories must perforce bear a close resemblance. And yet there is sufficient agony for each to feel personally that their ordeal was almost too great to bear. Those months of war made their deep impression on all of us, but I have yet to see or hear of anyone who is better for that suffering. I cannot see how such gigantic and intimate torture could have that effect. I know I felt almost apologetic when my own boy escaped death, when all around were lamenting their loss. Some few have said to me how much they wished they had a son to give to the war! These people, it is almost needless to say, were in every case childless.

Nearly five years ago, the friendship between Joseph Conrad and Warrington Dawson was cut short by my husband's death.

40. For a brief comment on Borys's war experience, see p. 96.

Yet I do not feel that it is at an end. There are some few friends of his, of ours, that still seem to be friends of us both.

It is with those that I feel most at ease. At ease in mind and at rest, free from the feeling that I am being criticised, secure in the belief that they will understand and not misjudge or attribute motives to me of which I am innocent. To these friends I can talk of Conrad, can recall mentally his personality and charm, and can be certain of being in accord with those with whom I may be.

Warrington Dawson has made me feel that I had a real place in his affections, that I did indeed share in his friendship with Conrad. . . .[41]

In trying to give her overall impression of the friendship Jessie neglected to say that Conrad's other guest that first afternoon was Arthur Pearson Marwood. (With some domestic sleight-of-hand, which was her forte, Jessie transmuted lunch into tea.) Marwood was a very good friend. A Yorkshire squire with mathematical inclinations, he had been introduced to Conrad by Hueffer in August, 1908, and in November of that same year Marwood and Hueffer had laid out the money to found the *English Review*, with Hueffer as editor and Conrad very much in the thick of things. Not only was the first issue of the *Review* put together under Conrad's Aldington roof, but the whole undertaking may have been intended "to start a Movement and to found, in the French sense, a 'school,' " with Conrad and Hueffer as headmasters.[42] When the breach occurred between the two novelists, in any event, Arthur Marwood was left in a difficult position. As Violet Hunt saw it, "Marwood, in his noble simplicity, was caught between two deeply sophisticated personalities, and went about looking ill and unhappy."[43]

41. This transcription is based on a typescript corrected in ink by Jessie (Dawson Collection, Duke). I have made a few additional corrections of mechanical errors and omitted the following words, which are bracketed out of the final sentence of the original: "and that when we meet, as assuredly we must very soon, that our pleasure in that meeting will be mutual."
There is reason to think the essay appeared in a magazine called *Health and Life* during the early 1930's, but I have been unable to find it.
42. So says Douglas Goldring, *South Lodge: Reminiscences of Violet Hunt, Ford Madox Ford and the* English Review *Circle* (London, 1943), p. 25. Actually there were multiple motives. Hueffer himself gave contradictory explanations for the founding.
43. *I Have This to Say: The Story of My Flurried Years* (New York, 1926), p. 62. As Hueffer saw the situation, he and Marwood had financed the *Review* but been forced to sell when they could not keep it going. Unfortunately, according to Hueffer,

Nevertheless, Marwood was a good man for Conrad to know. Archibald Marshall described him as one who

> read voluminously, and seemed to have forgotten nothing of what he ever had read. He was the most remarkable instance of the encyclopaedic mind that I have ever come across. There seemed to be no subject upon which he did not possess a store of detailed information. He wrote with difficulty and wrote very little, but he had a clear and convinced appreciation of literary values.[44]

In Conrad's own words, Marwood was "a great reader with a profound knowledge of literature, in whose judgment I have an absolute confidence; a man whose critical instinct is of marvellous justness."[45] It was this man, then, whom a convalescent Conrad shared with Dawson that May afternoon in 1910. Later on, Marwood was to read and be impressed by Dawson's fiction.

Conrad marked the event by presenting his young American visitor with a copy of *The Mirror of the Sea*, which he inscribed "To Warrington Dawson on the auspicious occasion of our first meeting."

---

the men who took over happened to be liberals and the managing director a Russian. The result was that, "Marwood being a strong Tory and Conrad a Pole with a violent hatred for all Russians, they decided between them that Conrad's contributions should cease, Marwood having by that time taken my place as general cook and bottle-washer in Conrad's literary establishment" ("Working with Conrad," *Yale Review*, XVIII, n.s. [1928–1929], 706–707). The Russian was David Soskice, Hueffer's own brother-in-law. Soskice was unsuccessful in forming a syndicate to purchase the magazine, however, and it passed into the hands of Sir Alfred Mond. Hueffer's testimony is generally suspect because of the creative cast of his memory, but his comment here touches enough personal, political, and literary factors to suggest the intricacy of the situation. See also p. 30.

44. *Out and About: Random Reminiscences* (London, 1933), p. 275.

45. Quoted by E. L. Grant Watson, *But to What Purpose: The Autobiography of a Contemporary* (London, 1946), p. 149.

4

The Friendship Well Launched (1910-1912)

Two days after Dawson met Conrad he wrote an article for the Charleston *Sunday News* on Kipling, whom he had met at a recent reception in London.[1] It was the big year of "If": "*If you can dream —and not make dreams your master. . . .*"

For the most part, however, in keeping with the plan he had outlined to Herbert Barry, Dawson in 1910 buckled down to literary work. He settled in a well-appointed "little flat" at 1 bis rue Hardy in Versailles and worked hard on an autobiographical "Paris novel" which was published eventually as *The Pyramid* (1922). He launched into an autobiographical children's book about a Charleston boy and his dog, *Buz and Fury*, published thirteen years later (1923). And he laid out the plot of "Sibylla," a rather wild foray into the occult which was set in magnolia country and professedly based on actual characters, but withheld from public view for some eighteen years, appearing finally as *The Guardian Demons* (1928).

The Conrads, meanwhile, in June, 1910, moved from their Aldington cottage to the delightful old farmhouse called Capel House, near Hamstreet. After Conrad's horrendous winter things began to look better. In August life was eased a bit by a civil list pension. Then, too, Conrad was able to finish "The Partner" and "A Smile of Fortune." Nevertheless, writing was still unusually hard for him, and a visit from the Sandersons late in the year must have proved a welcome diversion.[2]

The first significant development in the friendship of the two expatriate novelists came about through Dawson's enthusiastic *bonhomie*. Looking back at the Dawson of this period, Archibald Roosevelt, the president's youngest son, supposes "that the reason we all liked him was that he was so genuinely interested in every-

1. The article appeared in the issue of 12 June 1910, p. 25.
2. On 11 November 1910 Captain Sanderson was granted official permission to resign his post as Town Clerk of Nairobi.

body else's affairs in the right way. Not in an interfering way."[3] Apparently it was only a matter of time before Dawson was bound to try to help Conrad, and Conrad, with his refined sensibilities, was bound to respond warmly.

In a letter of 15 February 1911 Conrad expressed delight that Dawson had suggested him as a possible contributor to a new French journal called *Progrès*. Never averse to widening his public, Conrad decided to offer his nearly finished "Freya of the Seven Isles," which had seemed to him merely "a silly story" a month before,[4] but at the moment, under new circumstances, appeared "quite good magazine stuff, quite Conradesque (in the easier style). . . ."[5] Toward the end of February Conrad finished "Freya" and sent it off to France. By that time, however, the *directrice* of *Progrès*, Adeline de Lano (Conrad called her "Mrs. de Lano Demachy"), had decided on the safer course of taking a translation of a known work, *Typhoon*, rendered by Joseph de Smet. The table of contents for the May issue of the new magazine was therefore enhanced by an announcement of Conrad's "Le Typhon (Illustrations de R. Berti)"—as well as, incidentally, an "Étude psychologique sur les races noires de l'Afrique orientale (*Avec 10 photographies*)," by Warrington Dawson. Conrad must have been reasonably satisfied. He later wrote Dawson "Just a word to say that the negotiation with Progrès 'a abouti'—thanks to your friendly office, tact, wisdom and diplomacy. What could be more admirable than your speeches to Mme D!"[6] He also conveyed cordial compliments to De Smet for his part in the venture,[7] and De Smet, much taken by Conrad, stepped forth in the May, 1912, *Mercure de France* as the author of a long, encomiastic article on the great Polish-Englishman. As it turned out, however, Dawson may have been a bit embarrassed by the episode, for *Progrès* progressed nowhere. In half of no time it sank out of sight.[8]

3. Archibald B. Roosevelt to Randall, 21 August 1964. Mr. Roosevelt continues: "He also had a peculiarly childlike confidence in his friends which was most appealing."

4. Letter of 12 January 1911 in *Letters from Joseph Conrad 1895–1924*, ed. Edward Garnett (Indianapolis, 1928), p. 222.

5. Conrad to Dawson, 15 February 1911 (No. 8).

6. Conrad to Dawson, 24 August 1911 (No. 13).

7. Letter of 30 November 1911 in *Joseph Conrad: Life and Letters*, ed. G. Jean-Aubry, II (Garden City, N.Y., 1927), 136–137.

8. Roméo Arbour, *Les Revues Littéraires Éphémères Paraissant à Paris entre 1900 et 1914: Répertoire Descriptif* (Paris, 1956), p. 69.

The first visit of Dawson to Conrad's new home took place in early August, 1911. Henceforth Dawson was to associate his Conrad memories with Capel House. Not only was it here that all his visits except the first one to Aldington took place, but also it was here that he first experienced the exhilarating satisfaction of a late night talk with the great man, possible now because the Conrads, even with both boys at home, had room to "put up" a visitor. About a mile from Hamstreet station, "nestling in, perhaps, the most peaceful nook in Kent,"[9] in a countryside where woods were plentiful and seagulls sometimes lighted down in meadows of grazing sheep, Capel was a place which Conrad understandably found "sympathetic," a "charming specimen." From the outside it appeared to be simply a comfortable farmhouse of mellowed red brick, set generously off the road, but actually it was a converted, half-timbered house with a history stretching back for centuries. The pool at its eastern side (where the younger boy, John, was to sail toy boats) was really the remnant of a moat. Conrad's study was at this same end of the house, overlooking the pool on one side and a hedge-enclosed yard on the other. This study—which served also as a drawing room, music room, and library—was a crowded and cozy sort of place with its faded family photographs, its books and fireplace, and Jessie's piano. On one of his visits Dawson made a few notes about it: "The desk people saw—& the special table at which he wrote— The paper-knife made by Borys— The arm-chair in which he rested or smoked, but a straight, hard, uncomfortable chair to write in 'and keep myself awake.' "[10] The rent at Capel House was certainly hard to keep up, sometimes too hard,[11] but Conrad seemed lord of the manor here, and Dawson had come to proclaim his fealty.

Conrad at the time was working on *Chance.* Though not one of his better novels, *Chance* was the turning point, his first popular book, the one which brought him "success . . . in the material sense . . . , after eighteen years of steady writing."[12] Spurred by an

9. Conrad, "Poland Revisited," in *The Book of the Homeless*, ed. Edith Wharton (New York, 1916), p. 77.

10. From an undated fragment in the Dawson Collection (filed under "Commentaries on Conrad").

11. Interview of 5 December 1964 with Sir Roland Oliver, a friend of Conrad and the son of his landlord.

12. Letter of 20 November 1922 to Elbridge L. Adams, in Jean-Aubry, *LL*, II, 283–284.

agreement with the New York *Herald* for serial publication, Conrad managed to write at a good clip once he got started. The first of twenty-four installments appeared in the *Herald* on 21 January 1912, and the entire manuscript was completed 25 March at "3.10 a.m., just as my working lamp began to burn dimly and the fire in the grate to turn black. It's my *quickest* piece of work. About 140 thousand words in 9 months and 23 days."[13] As a matter of fact Conrad had been tussling with the story for a number of years. The history of *Chance* has been pushed back to 1906, even 1905, and now, with some hints from Dawson, it is tempting to push at least the inception of the book further back still. Knowing Conrad's habit of drawing characters and situations from life, his close and curious friend Richard Curle could only guess that De Barral, the swindler in *Chance*, was "a composite picture of several financial swindlers who flourished in London . . . ,"[14] but in the light of Dawson's reminiscences the novel may be traced in part to the sensational Humbert case which broke in the spring of 1902.

Frédéric Humbert, the nineteen-year-old son of Gustave Humbert, Life-Senator of the Republic, had been married in 1878 to a certain Thérèse Daurignac, a plain, portionless girl from a farm in Aussonne, near Toulouse. Thérèse had bad grammar but big ambitions. Moreover, she had early made a habit of success. As *The Idler* put it, she "married off herself, her brother and her sister to the two children and the nephew of a Life-Senator of the Republic who was already at the head of one of the Supreme Courts, and was soon to preside over the entire judicial organisation of France as Minister of Justice."[15] How deeply the elder Humbert was involved in what followed would be hard to say. Certainly it was reported at the time of the trial that he had given substantial help in the early stages of the game, but his intelligence flickered and faded badly as he aged, and he died in 1894, some eight years before the game was up. Though

13. Letter to John Quinn of 27 March 1912; transcript in Vol. I of "The John Quinn Collection of Letters," New York Public Library.

14. *Joseph Conrad and His Characters: A Study of Six Novels* (London, 1957), p. 23. Jocelyn Baines, the best of Conrad's biographers, supposes that "Of all Conrad's novels *Chance* is perhaps the least dependent on a source in his experience or in his reading" (*Joseph Conrad: A Critical Biography* [London, 1960], p. 388).

15. Sterling Heilig and Stoddard Dewey, "The Greatest Swindle of the Century," *Idler*, XXII (October, 1902–March, 1903), 8. For the present summary I have used a variety of contemporary accounts. These contain errors and contradictions, but I have thought it best to convey a sense of the story as it appeared at the time.

Thérèse had never hesitated to use the old Senator's name and influence, the Humberts continued to manage very well after he was gone. By using a variation of the "buried treasure" swindle (a fictitious American *milliardaire* figured in the genesis of their myth), and with the aid of Madame's sister and two brothers, the Humberts rose to wealth and social prominence. Making possible their steam yacht, their seventeen carriages, their chateaux, and their sumptuous mansion at 65 Avenue de la Grande Armée—making possible all these things and more was an immense safe in an upper room of their home. Presumably the safe held 120,000,000 francs in "solid securities." When opened, however, in May, 1902, its contents proved to be an Italian coin, some empty envelopes, a steel button, and "a hundredth part of a share in a mining company worth a few louis. . . ."[16] The *Nation* reported that

> On the strength of phantom millions the Humbert family floated no less than 700,000,000 francs of notes, much of which went in usury and renewals, but 60,000,000 francs of which they actually received in cash. . . .
> By the apparent regularity of their current transactions they put everybody off their guard, from the keenest of their usurer creditors to the humble folk who put their savings into the annuities of the *Rente Viagère*.[17]

The parts played in the case by Thérèse and Frédéric Humbert were difficult to determine even after the swindle broke into the news because Madame always looked like the family cook dressed up in her mistress's finery, and Monsieur seemed merely a fragile, artistic weakling. Who inspired whom was anyone's guess, but the public prosecutor said that Frédéric "reared the framework of the swindle, while Mme. Humbert had sought by every means in her power to amass a colossal fortune out of the scheme."[18] Warrington Dawson, who felt he knew the case "as well as it could be known to anybody" because he had attended "all the hearings before the Paris

16. T. P. O'Connor, *The Phantom Millions: The Story of the Great French Fraud* (London, 1902), p. 201.
17. *Nation*, 10 September 1903, pp. 203–204. The *Rente Viagère* was the Humberts' insurance company. O'Connor's book, dashed off while the Humberts were still a *cause célèbre*, reports that "All France has been supplied with almanacks containing at once a eulogy of the virtues of economy and of safe and sound investment in . . . solid establishments like that of the Rente Viagère . . ." (p. 11).
18. Quoted in London *Daily News*, 20 August 1903, p. 7.

Assizes," agreed with the prosecutor.[19] Toward the end of the trial—
"the reigning sensation of the summer" of 1903[20]—Dawson was
present when finally Frédéric Humbert, "exasperated by the clumsy
heckling of Thérèse by a financial expert . . . , suddenly lost his temper, or perhaps was simply carried away by the overwhelming sense
of his repressed superiority, and rebutted the expert's argument, . . .
[allowing] himself to be drawn on and on in a discussion of the ins
and outs of High Finance." At the end of the trial Thérèse merely
babbled, but "From the very instant when the sensation [of
Frédéric's revelation] broke upon us . . . , he seemed to take pride
in revealing fully who he was and what he was good for."[21]

If there are discrepancies between the facts of the case and Dawson's recollections of it, the latter are nonetheless important here.
Dawson tells us why:

> Perhaps it is not generally known that the Humbert Case
> served Joseph Conrad as background, the essential stuff of
> psychological inspiration, for the De Barral Case in *Chance.*
> This is not mere assumption or even deduction on my part. I
> know because he told me so. Told me so while *Chance* was ac-
> tually in the writing. And he questioned me lengthily about the
> affair as it had broken on the public and its developments in
> Court. He already knew about it and had his own ideas for
> making of it a characteristically English case: a *tour-de-force*
> in which he succeeded admirably while having the artistic sense
> to leave just a touch of Gallicism to it by referring to the part-
> French origin of de Barral as suggested by the name.[22] But
> Conrad in his great artistic conscientiousness always wanted
> more and more information until he felt so completely sure of
> his ground that he felt as much at home there as in his own
> house. And so we talked, we talked for hours on end, we talked
> through many an entire night until dawn.[23] And I had the very
> signal privilege of hearing him read aloud to me some of the
> pages he had freshly written: a thing he but rarely consented
> to do for anybody however intimate with him.

19. From "13 Years—13 Windows," an unprinted work in the Dawson Collection, p. 18.
20. "The Humberts Convicted," *Outlook*, LXXIV (29 August 1903), 1014.
21. "13 Years—13 Windows," pp. 19–20.
22. See *Chance* (London, 1914), p. 63.
23. Probably poetic license.

As I look over those pages to-day, I think that he defined the characteristics of the Humbert-de Barral case as nobody else I have known ever could have defined them: the vivid evocation of what I knew from experience to be absolutely true, concerning a gigantic hoax. . . .

Whole sentences stand out to my eyes from the pages of the First Edition copy which he inscribed to me.

The slogan Thrift—equivalent of *Economies, economies!* so dear to ear and heart of modest Frenchmen in that pre-war period. . . . And those companies to attract the unimaginative eye, named for that purpose and none other: "A pretty fancy in names—nothing else, no other merit." "Fishing out from the depths of the incredible such a colossal manifestation of human folly." "The alacrity of human folly in rising to the bait." "The greed of that absurd monster is so incalculable, unfathomable, inconceivable, it will rise to a naked hook." "No imagination, unable to organize anything to promote any sort of enterprise if it were only for the purpose of juggling with shares." "Nobody knows what he wants to do—what his game is. There was no game, no game of any sort or shape or kind." "Just facilities for taking money."

So it all was, indeed—excepting that Conrad fused in the single person of de Barral the dual Frédéric and Thérèse Humbert who played so well into each other's hands that they were indeed as one in making dupes of the public and the judges too.

Then, the reactions when the scandal broke, and the public realized there were no funds, no securities, no anything—and there had never been anything in those famed Humbert institutions except that facility for taking in money over the counter:

"Not the bottom dropped out—there never had been a bottom to it." "The fury, a mass of people fooled by means too simple to save their self-respect from a deep wound." "What comes with a shock is admitted with difficulty."

Exactly so. Pictures of the Empty Safe had to be published all over France before the common run of people could be brought to accept what those in the know had long believed before daring to say so. . . .[24]

24. "13 Years—13 Windows," pp. 35–36.

Thus Dawson enables us to look at *Chance* with fresh eyes. The strangely ineffectual De Barral, for instance, Conrad's gray, uncertain ghost of a swindler, now seems a reasonable transmutation for a fictional Gustave Humbert, or perhaps for a fictional blend of white-haired old Gustave and Frédéric, or even (as Dawson suggests) of Frédéric and Thérèse. The androgynous Mrs. Fyne is an English incarnation of Mme. Humbert. Though surely no swindler —at least in the realm of finance—she is a woman of firm, masculine ways, a woman of "flint,"[25] altogether a convincingly misogynistic creation to have evolved in a mind saturated with stories about the domineering woman in the Humbert case, a woman who "practically effaced" her weaker husband and brothers.[26] Mrs. Fyne, says Marlow, operates on the feminist doctrine that "no consideration, no delicacy, no tenderness, no scruples should stand in the way of a woman. . . ."[27]

In addition to the several guilty persons who figured in the Humbert affair there also was one made conspicuous by her innocence, the Humbert's daughter, Eve. Because of the centrality in *Chance* of the swindler's daughter, Flora de Barral, it is of interest to find the press of 1902 reporting that "Considerable sympathy is felt by the public for Mlle. Eve. . . . By common consent she is considered to be the innocent victim of the colossal swindlers. . . ."[28] Eve was of only peripheral interest as far as the basic issues of the case were concerned, but she proved to be the object of a certain amount of easy, journalistic sentimentality. O'Connor, for instance, told how she was kept

> always under the eye either of her governess or Madame Parayre [the "watchdog" of the house, equipped with a "freezing and affrighting look"] . . . or of her aunt. She never had read a novel, never received a letter, never opened a newspaper. She was even forbidden to telephone. She had no friend, no balls, no dinners where she could meet girls of her own age. . . . There is something strangely pathetic in this detachment by this gang of criminals of the one pure being in their household from all the soiling things around.[29]

25. *Chance*, p. 47.
26. London *Daily Mail*, 10 August 1903, p. 5.
27. *Chance*, p. 53.
28. London *Daily Mail*, 23 December 1902, p. 5.
29. *The Phantom Millions*, pp. 170–171.

44

In view of the secluded upbringing of Conrad's Flora de Barral it would be a mistake to overlook that Eve Humbert was supposedly reared "with scrupulous care and almost convent-like seclusion and severity."[30] It was Dawson's belief, however, that

> Temperamental little Flora de Barral . . . had nothing whatever in common with pathetic Eve Humbert, either physically or mentally or spiritually—if these two last qualities existed in Eve. . . . She was as uninteresting, colorless, apathetic a bromide as could be imagined, imposing attention only because, first, of her alleged vast *dot* making of her a *parti* which set a noteworthy portion of Paris running after her, and secondly, of her . . . monumental physique. . . . She was a standing jest in Paris, during the first painful days of crisis; until the police found her in her hiding-place and arrested her, and she crumpled up like the helpless little child she was in nature. . . .
>
> No: Flora de Barral was completely, absolutely, fundamentally a Conrad creation.[31]

Dawson overstates himself here. If nothing else, Flora fell heir to the innocence which resulted from Eve's peculiar isolation, and hence she had some of Eve's pathos.[32] In fact, the striking and strangely complementary characters of Mme. Humbert and her daughter both appear to have exerted a major influence on Conrad's *Chance*. As Baines observes, "The role of woman is so chewed over that it might be regarded as a subsidiary theme of the novel."[33]

It may prove difficult to find just what Conrad read about the Humbert swindle because the case was in effect a serialized suspense story in a good many newspapers. It was also the subject of magazine articles, even of books. One is therefore left to ponder about the

30. T. P. O'Connor, "Criminals I Have Known—IV. Madame Humbert," *Harper's Weekly*, LVIII (10 January 1914), 12. For a contrary view of Eve's rearing see the London *Daily News*, 22 May 1902, p. 7.

31. "13 Years—13 Windows," pp. 38–39.

32. Conrad refines on Flora's state. Not "innocence," he says; "that word would not render my exact meaning, . . . but I will say . . . ignorance, or better still, . . . unconsciousness of the world's ways, the unconsciousness of danger, of pain, of humiliation, of bitterness, of falsehood" (*Chance*, p. 91). Conrad's description of Flora would suit Eve well enough: "The clouded brow, the pained mouth, the vague fixed glance! A victim" (*Chance*, p. 41). When the Humberts were finally cornered in Spain, the doctor who examined the prisoners to see if they could stand the thirty-six-hour trip to Paris "found Eve suffering from 'nerves,' but otherwise healthy . . ." (*Daily News*, 30 December 1902, p. 5).

33. *Joseph Conrad*, p. 386.

degree of coincidence in the fact that the old widow of Gustave Humbert was quoted as saying that her beautiful granddaughter—not Eve, but a cousin of Eve, the daughter of Thérèse's flunky brother, Émile—was going to survive and rise above her family's rottenness. In view of Conrad's symbolic name for his heroine, *grand-mère* Humbert's metaphor is especially striking: "On our ruin there grows a little flower."[34] In other words, though Conrad's specific sources may be elusive, it seems reasonable to suspect that some closer looks into the Humbert case should result eventually in a better understanding of *Chance*.[35] After all, Flora de Barral herself knows as much of her father as she does, we are told, because she has gone "through the files of several papers."[36] On the other hand, Conrad clearly suggests that the De Barral case is broadly emblematic. Old De Barral "was a mere sign," says Marlow, "a portent. There was nothing in him." He was simply well attuned. "Just about that time the word Thrift was to the fore."[37] If Conrad in *Chance* may be seen converting history into symbol, therefore, one reason would appear to be that he was struck by the fact that the Humberts were symbols of current history.[38]

34. O'Connor, *Phantom Millions*, p. 207. In Conrad's novel the little "flower" which has sprung from the "barrel" (Barral) of money / offal / corruption is rescued by "The Knight" (Conrad's term for Captain Anthony) and made the "flower" of the "fern-dale" (Anthony's ship is the *Ferndale*).

35. Additional excitement was generated for a time by rumors that the Humberts had fled to England. Presumably the case had been settled, however, some years before Conrad began work on *Chance*. The Humberts were sentenced in August, 1903, and Conrad told John Quinn that the first part of his novel was written in 1906 (letter of 24 May 1912, transcript in Vol. I of Quinn Collection, New York Public Library). Conrad then laid the MS aside until early 1911—the year of Dawson's visit. He told Hueffer on 29 March 1911: "I am just now trying to make a fresh start with a thing called *Chance* I began some time ago . . ." (Berg Collection, New York Public Library). Hence Dawson could have been of real help to Conrad in recalling such aspects of the case as intrigued him.

36. *Chance*, p. 322.

37. *Chance*, p. 66.

38. Augusto Riera observed that "El proceso Humbert es algo así como un signo de los tiempos" (*La Estafa Mayor del Mundo* [Barcelona, 1903], p. 5).

The Idler provided the additional comment that

Although the late Emile Zola was not aware of the fact at the time he wrote the book, the beginning of the Humbert Affair was the foundation of his great novel 'Money.' The climax of the story is the smashing of the Universal Bank of Paris told in the chapter entitled 'The Battle of Millions.' Zola did not know that the bank was ruined by the arrest of its founder at a critical moment, and that this arrest was caused by Gustave Humbert, Minister of Justice, for a bribe of £20,000, which sum enabled the minister to pay the debt of a paltry thousand pounds owed by his daughter-in-law Thérèse. . . .

("Zola and the Humbert Case," XXII [October, 1902–March, 1903], 223.)

Of course Conrad and Dawson found many things besides *Chance* to discuss. In mid-February, 1911, looking forward to Dawson's visit later in the year, Conrad had said that he hoped the two of them might have "a long argumentative talk."[39] As it turned out, race was one of the subjects which the friends took up in the late summer, by letter, surely, and perhaps in person. And race did, indeed, provide fuel for an argument, in fact the most unpleasant disagreement which was ever kindled between the two. Conrad's first letter after the visit begins with an apology: "I am no end sorry to have acted tactlessly."[40]

Though the evidence is extremely sketchy, it seems that Dawson wrote to Conrad about Perceval Gibbon's new novel, *Margaret Harding*.[41] Another novelist-journalist friend of Conrad, Gibbon had come to spend several weeks at Dymchurch, a seaside village just on the other side of Romney Marsh, from where he could easily drop in on the Conrads.[42] Though Conrad had warned Jessie against Gibbon's sharp tongue before she first met him, she, for one, was fascinated by his "intense virility." She found something attractive in his "unconscious brutality," though in later years she, too, could recall well enough that she had "seen people quite apprehensive of some rather malicious attack, which they evidently doubted their power of defending themselves against."[43] The facts are too few to warrant a guess that Dawson was among the people Jessie had in mind, but sparks were certainly struck during August, and perhaps as the result of a Dawson letter to Conrad about *Margaret Harding* —a book which was dedicated, incidentally, to the Conrads. In *Margaret Harding* Gibbon worked quite boldly with the racial problems of Africa, and in just such a way as to irritate Dawson. Margaret Harding is a cultivated English girl who because of lung trouble has gone to the Karoo, and there has formed a secret friendship with Kamis, the son of a rebel Kaffir chief. Far from being a typical native, Kamis has been educated in England as a doctor and now has returned to his homeland to find himself an outcast from both

39. Conrad to Dawson, 15 February 1911 (No. 8).
40. Conrad to Dawson, 17 August 1911 (No. 12).
41. The present paragraph is based entirely on the Conrad letter just cited. So far as I know, *Margaret Harding* is the only book on the Negro question written at this time by a friend of Conrad whose initial was "G."
42. Letter of 18 July 1911 in *Letters*, ed. Garnett, p. 229.
43. "A Personal Tribute to the Late Percival [*sic*] Gibbon and Edward Thomas," *Bookman* (London), LXXVIII (1930), 323.

whites and blacks. When his friendship with Margaret is discovered, the other characters give it the worst possible interpretation, and Margaret, in particular, is subjected to such insults as befall a white woman who has betrayed her kind. Clearly such a statement of the color problem was shaped for special ends. The question might well be asked, how relevant or fair is it to focus a reader's attention on a Kaffir who surpasses most of the story's white characters in mind, training, and feeling? At any rate, Conrad in some way sided with Gibbon. Apparently he tried to make the point that Gibbon was neither a Negrophile nor a sensationalist writing mainly for cash. Dawson was then moved to clarify his own stand in a letter. Though his views were not so extreme as those of his boyhood literary mentor, Carlyle McKinley, who had advocated the deportation of American Negroes to Egypt, Dawson was very much committed to white supremacy.[44] He could not have considered for a moment denying those feelings about race which he had acquired during his youth, rationalized in his maturity, expressed in his fiction, bolstered during his African experience, and now, most recently, reinforced while doing research for a book on the Negro in America. Gibbon's novel was simply too open-minded. Fortunately, however, in his letter of 17 August, Conrad proved anxious to extinguish any temperamental Dawsonian embers which still glowed from the incident. He even offered Dawson the explanation that he had yet to finish reading Gibbon's book at the time that he had "acted tactlessly." Perhaps he refers here to the fact that the end of the novel fails to suggest a solution to the basic problem it has posed. Gibbon simply sends Margaret home to England. In any case, there survives not a single word from Dawson on the quarrel.

Le problème noir was very much on the young Southerner's mind at this period. Following his August visit to Capel House and a brief stopover with friends in Wales he next moved on to Brittany, where he at once proceeded to put his pen to the matter. At Josselin, the medieval chateau where he settled down to work, he was the guest of the Duc and Duchesse de Rohan. (The preceding autumn he had taken his young friend Kermit Roosevelt there, following a chamois

44. See McKinley's *An Appeal to Pharaoh: The Negro Problem, and Its Radical Solution* (New York, 1889). Dawson's father had contended "for white supremacy in the South but for justice and charity to the Negro" (*National Cyclopaedia of American Biography*, XXIII [New York, 1933], 300).

48

hunt arranged by the Austrian Rohans.) It seems that the Duchesse, who herself was something of a poet, took pleasure in encouraging young writers. When in Paris, at L'Hôtel de Rohan on the exclusive Boulevard des Invalides, "Son bonheur était d'avoir dans son entourage des esprits distingués, des savants, des lettrés, des artistes. Son ambition s'était réalisée, elle était devenue l'âme d'un cénacle intellectuel. . . ."[45] *Ancienne noblesse oblige.* Yet Dawson was singled out for particular favor by being offered a special chamber in a quiet tower of the Rohans' Breton chateau. It was a most congenial environment for a literary young Gareth. On 9 September, his research done, he began to write *Le Nègre aux États-Unis.* By March, 1912, the book was out, with a preface by Paul Adam and a dedication, appropriately, to Madame La Duchesse.[46]

In *Le Nègre* Dawson wishes the Negro well, as might have been predicted, but with firmness and fear he goes on to point out the necessity for the white man's maintenance of discipline. Reconstruction should have made it abundantly clear, he presumes, that the ex-slave, drunk with freedom, was prone to insolence. Even after fifty years of liberty the Negro was the same irresponsible creature he had always been. What else could one expect? After the age of about fourteen the average Negro's mind ceases to develop. The white man's best security, it turns out, is the black man's own instinctive respect for white dominance, and to shake that principle is to shake the whole structure of American society. Problems of social, political, and legal equality must be considered, of course, but the basic black-white problem has only one real solution: The two races must remain as they have been in the past, neighbors yet strangers.

When Conrad read *Le Nègre* he had nothing but praise. "I can indeed congratulate you with all my heart," he wrote. The *Heart of Darkness* author even felt that "It wouldn't be bad if you had an organ in England where you could now and then express the

---

45. Hippolyte Buffenoir, *La Duchesse de Rohan avec un Portrait et Six Illustrations* (Paris, 1904), p. 14. See also Sisley Huddleston, *Bohemian Literary and Social Life in Paris* (London, 1928), p. 189.

46. In his preface Adam points out (p. ix) that "Sauf un certain nombre de personnalités, comme les Booker Washington et les docteur Crum, ces dix millions de nègres affranchis sur le sol de l'Union, forment un peuple amoral, fantasque, épris d'indolence et d'alcoölisme, dépourvu de persévérance, et tout à fait inattentif à la saleté vermineuse de ses taudis."

49

Southern point of view on various American questions."[47] As a matter of fact, Conrad's dearest link with France, Mme. Marguerite Poradowska, also wrote Dawson about it. Apparently she had agreed to stand as sponsor so that *Le Nègre* might be eligible for a prize. In script quite as illegible as that which used to frustrate Conrad's Uncle Thaddeus Bobrowski, she assured Dawson of her pleasure in reading his *beau livre*, but she had to report that the prize committee had turned the work down. "Croyez," she assured him, "que je suis désolée de la chose."[48]

Meanwhile, apparently infected by Dawson's enthusiasm, the Rohans read some of Conrad's fiction. Conrad was "no end flattered" to learn that the "Princesse" particularly liked "The Duel" from *A Set of Six* (1908),[49] and to Dawson's hostess herself he later sent a copy of *'Twixt Land and Sea*. The Duchesse replied with gracious assurance of her "grande sympathie littéraire."[50]

Still another matter which Conrad and Dawson discussed during that August of 1911 was the young man's own creative work. Dawson had several stories under way at the time, so it is impossible to say which received most of their attention. One, however, caused a snag in the friendship a short time later. In November, Dawson was piqued by Conrad's refusal to help place a story which they had considered together, and Conrad, in turn, was distressed to learn of Dawson's reaction to the refusal. Dawson, unfortunately, had not been reared in a way to discourage his bent toward petulance. Beneath his Southern charm he always remained a sensitive, proud boy, and in the present situation, though he would have chosen, surely, to avoid unpleasantness, it was lucky for the course of the friendship that Conrad once again saw fit to write a letter of friendly placation.[51]

It was also in August that Dawson first established a bond with thirteen-year-old Borys Conrad. At thirty-three Dawson had considerable worldly experience and *savoir-faire*, as well as boyish buoyancy. Such traits more than once had helped him hurdle the barriers of age, enabling him to impress and yet draw close to those both

47. Conrad to Dawson, 9 April 1912 (No. 22).
48. Marguerite Poradowska to Dawson, 25 February 1913.
49. Conrad to Dawson, 30 September 1911 (No. 14). The allusion is to Princesse Marie, daughter of the Duc and Duchesse.
50. Duchesse de Rohan to Conrad, 10 November 1912 (a letter attached to a copy of Conrad's *Entre Terre et Mer* [Paris, 1929] in the Jean-Aubry Collection, Beinecke Library, Yale).
51. Conrad to Dawson, 25 November 1911 (No. 19).

younger and older than himself. Moreover, Borys was particularly susceptible to Dawson's sympathetic attention just now because he himself was about to embark on a strange new way of life. Despite his nearsightedness Borys was soon to don the uniform of a cadet on the *Worcester*, a nautical training school lying off Greenhithe, Kent. The idea may or may not have occurred to Dawson earlier, but one important result of his interest in the boy was a stronger bond with the entire family. "It is awfully kind of you to write to Borys," Jessie told Dawson; "he values your friendship most highly."[52] Though never really very close, Dawson's friendship with Borys was maintained for a number of years, through World War I and beyond, and in later years Borys even came to feel that he had been closer to their American friend than had Conrad himself.[53]

All things considered, Dawson was proving something of a success at Capel House. In 1911 there had been a couple of disagreements, but certainly no one was permanently wounded. In the following spring Dawson admitted to his Uncle Jimmie, "I appreciate immensely the advantage it is to me to know in intimacy such people as I know among the elderly and world-famous authors and artists of our day; it is of inestimable assistance to me in my work. . . ."[54] Dawson's friendships with the great were real enough, to be sure, but also, and not quite incidentally, advantageous. The touch of cool intellection in Dawson's words here is a revealing and delimiting, if thoroughly human, part of a man whose qualities, certainly including fine ones, seem to have been filtered sometimes through a screen of social sentiment and conventional nicety.[55] Like any shrine, it turns out, Capel House had its practical aspect.

One multi-phased deed of grace which the friendship inspired was a Conrad lecture that Dawson delivered first in March, 1912. Though he reported later from Versailles that he had recently lectured a "good deal" and "with no little success,"[56] and though he was able to compile a collection of favorable press clippings, there

52. Jessie Conrad to Dawson, 11 October 1911 (No. 15).
53. Interview with Borys Conrad, 21 November 1964.
54. Dawson to James Morris Morgan, 17 May 1912.
55. The central characters in Dawson's books are sometimes fairly obvious versions of himself. In *The Crimson Pall* (Chicago, 1927) the hero is Henry Wentworth, "a retired diplomat and . . . man of leisure" (p. 29) who says: "A certain reputation I had for being a talker . . . helped me more than anything else. People weren't on their guard and didn't suspect how much they talked back at me, because I had played on their passions or their vanities" (p. 121).
56. Dawson's carbon typescript of a letter to "My dear Cousin," 16 May 1912.

is reason to think that his success on the platform was modest.[57] On the other hand, he did give the Conrad lecture at least five times. The first was on 3 March 1912 at the St. Geneviève Club, Paris. (On 29 December 1911 Conrad wrote to say that he was "immensely flattered" by Dawson's choice of subject, but felt he must decline an invitation to attend.) On 3 December 1912 Dawson gave the lecture again, this time to the Contemporary Club in Pittsburgh, at the home of Mr. and Mrs. Cornelius D. Scully. On 4 December 1912 he gave it in Llewellyn Park, New Jersey, when Mrs. Herbert Barry "opened her house informally . . . , the occasion being a lecture delivered by her brother, Warrington Dawson. . . ."[58] And on 3 April 1913, a fourth occasion, Dawson spoke to the New Century Club in Philadelphia. The most interesting occasion, however, came in mid-November, 1913, in Worcestershire. The Honorable Ivor Windsor-Clive was standing for Parliament at Wolverhampton, and his sister, Lady Phyllis, arranged for their mutual friend to speak, more or less on her brother's behalf, at a meeting of the local Women's Institute.[59]

In view of Dawson's style in the Conrad lecture it is just as well that he quoted so freely from his friend. His own wording is loose and toplofty, sometimes even confused. For example, concerning Conrad's achievement with form he says, "We should *hail* him with *gratitude* for this at a period when the *very existence* of novels seems threatened by the *over-development of sheer technique* in *rubbishy* current literature which has rendered the *novel-form odious* to a *large & discriminating* element of the *public*."[60] A similar use of language appears toward the close of Dawson's peroration, which suggests reasonably well the temper of the non-quoted passages in the lecture. Here Dawson explains that Conrad writes

57. His repertoire continued to grow, however, until it consisted of ten topics, each in some way significant for anyone trying to understand the man. The topics were: (1) "Unknown Versailles"; (2) "Life on the Paris Fortifications"; (3) "With Roosevelt in Africa"; (4) "Uganda-up-to-Date" (a trip across Lake Victoria Nyanza and a rickshaw journey to the native capital); (5) "French Society To-Day" (the Parisian *Grand Monde*); (6) "The Practical French of To-Day"; (7) "In St. Petersburg During the Russo-Japanese War"; (8) "The Mission of Art"; (9) "The Fresh Air Art Society"; and (10) "A Great Contemporary—Joseph Conrad."

58. Orange, N.J., *Daily Chronicle*, 4 December 1912 (p. 171 of Dawson's Scrapbook No. 67898).

59. Interview of 5 November 1964 with Lady Phyllis Benton (formerly Lady Phyllis Windsor-Clive).

60. "Joseph Conrad," p. 42 (lecture in Dawson Collection). Italics presumably represent Dawson's underlining for aid in delivery.

for those who believe that the *great artist, delving* into the *heart* of *man,* & *understanding* by his *refinement* of *senses* & his *powers of observation* that which *most* men & women in their *struggle for material life,* have not the *opportunity* to *acquire,* —can *help* & *enlighten them* with his *broad philosophy of nature* & his *knowledge* of the *law* of *human consequences,* when their turn of trial comes. In all his works we find overwhelming power of *character portrayal* & of *atmosphere rendering,* & a *vividness* of *verbal expression* which makes each *word* a *tone* & each *sentence* a *picture.* But under this, is a *truth,* almost a *growling menace,* which stuns—a *truth* calculated to *shake* the *selfish* from their *stolid complacency* & *awaken them* to the *realities* of *life.*[61]

Despite its stylistic strain Dawson's lecture certainly demonstrates a genuine appreciation of Conrad. As for content, of course, it is thin, but it was composed fairly early, after all—in 1912—and Dawson, to give him his due, was an alert and reasonably intelligent young man who was among those having the benefit of a closeness to Conrad which no modern commentators can duplicate.[62] Dawson arrived at the shrine before the world beat a path there.

In July, 1912, Dawson was looking forward to another visit with Conrad, inquiring if his friend would care to meet Robert George Windsor-Clive, the Earl of Plymouth. When Conrad replied that he would be delighted for both the visit and the introduction, "if health and other things permit," Dawson proceeded to make arrangements with Lord and Lady Plymouth for what turned out to be a tea-time call on a Sunday afternoon in October.[63]

Dawson had met Lord Plymouth, a "tremendous admirer of Conrad,"[64] through Plymouth's son Ivor, whom, in turn, he had met in Paris through Mlle. Hélène Vacaresco, one of the spheres of influence within the *grand monde.* Ivor was in France at the time to polish his French, and apparently it seemed only natural for him to invite the ingratiating young American to his home. The result was

61. "Joseph Conrad," pp. 90–92.
62. Curle's comments on Conrad's fiction come even closer to voicing Conrad's views. But see pp. 86–87.
63. Conrad to Dawson, 10 July 1912 (No. 24). A letter from Lord Plymouth to Dawson of 16 October 1912 gave Dawson the mission of escorting Conrad on 20 October.
64. Interview of 5 November 1964 with Lady Phyllis Benton.

that Dawson became known to the entire Windsor-Clive family, including Ivor's sister, Phyllis—who was later to arrange for Dawson's Conrad lecture up in Wolverhampton. Dawson and Lady Phyllis, a young woman of considerable beauty, were observed to share a special attraction for each other, but their quiet, well-bred friendship was to remain simply one of several ties between Dawson and the various members of the Windsor-Clive family.[65] To the end of his days Dawson recalled with unfading delight the welcome which the Windsor-Clives extended to him during that long, golden afternoon before the war, when he had gone to visit St. Fagans, Lord Plymouth's Jacobean castle near Cardiff, or when he had stayed at his lordship's princely estate, Hewell Grange, in Wolverhampton, or when he merely had come calling at his town house in Mount Street. Dawson's cup had been filled to overflowing. Not only was Lord Plymouth a man of position and power, but he was also a man deeply devoted to the arts, a man who sponsored weekly concerts in his home during the summer (Casals played there), a man who wrote a life of John Constable[66] and served as a trustee of the National Gallery and chairman of the Tate. In fact, Lord Plymouth may well have been unique among men of his class and time in the value he placed on national culture.[67] Of course he was very interested to learn that his young friend Dawson knew Joseph Conrad. An introduction proved easy to arrange, and a cordial relationship ensued.[68]

From the lodgings he usually took when in London—in a boardinghouse at No. 8 Duchess Street, Portland Place—Dawson could conveniently make excursions to see friends at both St. Fagans and Capel House. In 1912 the first of three or so visits to Capel House was arranged for 18 and 19 August. Apparently Conrad and Dawson laid plans at this time to meet in London a few days hence, when Conrad was to introduce Dawson first to his agent Pinker, and then

65. In two characters of his *Pyramid*, Evelyn and George, Dawson preserved echoes of the friendship.

66. *John Constable, R.A.* (London, 1903).

67. The *Times* of 8 March 1923 recorded that Lord Plymouth "fulfilled with zeal all the duties that fall to a peer and a wealthy landlord in this country, but he will be chiefly remembered for the assistance he gave, almost too unostentatiously, to art, architecture, town-planning, and other departments of . . . national culture" (p. 12).

68. Lady Phyllis still recalls meeting Conrad a number of times, at least once in the family's temporary home on the Thames Embankment. To her he seemed a man of great, quiet force.

54

to Austin Harrison, the new editor of the *English Review*. Having been reconciled with Pinker since about March, Conrad could now approach his old friend on something like the old footing. A Dawson-Pinker contract, however, was another matter, and Conrad said so.[69] Probably Conrad had been acquiring some private reservations about Dawson's literary ability. Pinker was temptingly successful as an agent, however, and Dawson proceeded to ignore Conrad's advice. A Dawson-Pinker alliance was formed, but it never prospered.

The second call arranged for that day, the one at the *English Review*, was especially kind of Conrad. Austin Harrison had expressed interest in having a contribution from Dawson back at the time when *Le Nègre aux États-Unis* came out, but now that Conrad was able to set a date for taking Dawson to meet him, Harrison proved to be out of town. The current sub-editor, however, John Mavrogordato, was available. Perhaps this was just as well. For one thing, Conrad had had a run-in with Harrison earlier that year when he had tried to have *Chance* accepted for the *Review*. For another thing, the simple fact was that Harrison had no eye for literature.[70] According to Hueffer, the *Review* had been founded as a sort of *aube de siècle Yellow Book*,[71] but once out of his hands it rapidly lost both freshness and color. Still, it was to do a friend a favor that Conrad took Dawson to the *Review* office.

After a hot day in the "biggest and the greatest town on earth," Dawson conceivably reciprocated by taking Conrad back to No. 8 Duchess Street. One cannot be sure, but Dawson's old friend Bernard Lytton-Bernard says that "Joseph Conrad used to stay [there] frequently when he was in London," and it is clear that Mary Withey, Dawson's landlady, at least knew Conrad by sight.[72]

69. At least this is the way Conrad remembered the affair (see letter No. 98). If we trust Conrad's memory, though, we are left to conjecture why he agreed to escort Dawson to Pinker's office.

70. Douglas Goldring describes him as an "amiable but colourless man, with little knowledge of literature and small aptitude, even as a journalist" (*South Lodge: Reminiscences of Violet Hunt, Ford Madox Ford and the* English Review Circle [London, 1943], p. 55). Formerly Harrison had been a reporter on the *Daily Mail*.

71. *Thus to Revisit: Some Reminiscences* (London, 1921), p. 58. Conrad placed his two *Titantic* essays in the *Review* in 1912, but by this time, according to Sir Compton Mackenzie, the magazine had fallen "to the bottom of mediocrity," and in 1913 D. H. Lawrence lamented how "piffling" it was (quoted by Frank MacShane, "The *English Review*," SAQ, LX [1961], 318).

72. Bernard Lytton-Bernard to Randall, 22 June 1965. (When Dr. Lytton-Bernard

In later years Dawson took pride in the fact that Conrad "had first knowledge" of the "novelette" which he finally submitted to the *English Review*. It was an allegorical piece called "The Sin," and Conrad knew of it, Dawson said, because "I read it to him . . . one night at his home in Kent; and he laughed until he cried."[73] When Dawson sailed for the States in early November, 1912, he left the manuscript with Conrad. Presumably the younger artist could not bear to amputate anything from the work, though it needed to be trimmed for publication, so Conrad said "he would, if I approved, just cut anywhere, arbitrarily and regretfully."[74] Regretfully in more than one sense, since Conrad was to find the job "odious" before he was through. Despite the pressures of his own work, Conrad took the time to shorten "The Sin" and then to send it on to the *Review* "with the strongest possible letter making its acceptance a personal matter."[75]

The matter did not end here. Dawson reported to a friend on 19 February that "The Sin" had been accepted, but Conrad was still trying to force some sort of action from the *Review* as late as July. By this time he felt so involved that he threatened to withdraw one of his own works from a forthcoming issue. He said that his play "One Day More" simply would not appear in the *Review* "unless you can tell me positively that *the Sin* will be published too—say in October."[76] The cause of the delay is unclear. Maybe the story did not satisfy editorial expectation. It was certainly still too long.[77] On the other hand, Norman Douglas in *Looking Back* recalled that when a manuscript was submitted to Harrison, "Often he could not make up his mind for months and months whether to print or not. . . ."[78]

---

first met Dawson, his name was Bernhard Trappschuh. Beginning in World War I and continuing through most of his career, he anglicized this name to Bernard Bernard. The various references to him in the present work are all grouped in the index under Bernard.) "Frequently" is a relative term, but if Conrad was ever Dawson's guest— and Lytton-Bernard is sure that he was—two of the more likely nights were those following the office call in August and the late-afternoon visit with Lord and Lady Plymouth in October.

73. Quoted from the introduction to the later, longer version published as *The Sin: An Allegory of Truth* (Chicago, 1923), p. 5.

74. *Sin*, p. 6.

75. Conrad to Dawson, 3 April 1913 (No. 36).

76. Conrad to Norman Douglas, 4 July 1913 (No. 44), a letter in the University of Texas Library.

77. Before being printed by the *Review*, "The Sin" underwent more excisions.

78. Vol. II (London, 1933), p. 398.

Perhaps it was fortunate for Dawson that Douglas himself was the new sub-editor of the *Review*.[79] Douglas had had ample occasion earlier to learn "how appreciative and encouraging Conrad could be, and what infinite pains he would take with the work of other writers."[80] Conrad had assisted enthusiastically in the launching of Douglas's own literary career. It was even thanks to Conrad that Douglas had his present job with the *Review*. Furthermore, Douglas was now more than ever committed to the Conrads because he had committed his ten-year-old son Robin to their care. Jessie had become "Mum" to Robin, and Conrad had taken it on himself to teach the boy something about ships and stars and splicing ropes.[81] Though Douglas's hedonism and Conrad's moral sense prevented any lasting, close friendship between the two, it was also to Capel House that Douglas, stricken by jaundice, had fled for help in August, 1911. As Douglas later described the episode, "There came a lucid moment when I thought: this must end. All my friends being out of town, I went to Joseph Conrad near Ashford—or rather found myself, somehow or other, at his house."[82] The result was that the Conrads took care of Douglas for several weeks. By 1913, then, the relationship between Conrad and Douglas was neither casual nor simple. And now Conrad approached Douglas directly and strongly on Dawson's behalf. Douglas, who was "Startlingly disrespectful . . . of anything but the best," a man with "Spartan standards of intellectual discipline,"[83] had to face Dawson's "Sin" head-on. The outcome was that the *Review* printed Conrad's "One Day More" in August, and in October Dawson's "Sin" was made manifest.

Unfortunately, "The Sin" is embarrassingly bad. In the preface to its full-length version, published in 1923 by his friend Bernard Bernard, Dawson explains his theme thus: "There's not one of us who has not seen how a convention of secrecy can surround harmless, and even helpful, acts with unhealthy broodings; and how the

79. He held the position from October, 1912, until April, 1916 (Cecil Woolf, A *Bibliography of Norman Douglas* [London, 1954], p. 145).

80. Douglas to Jean-Aubry, 30 November 1924 (a letter in the Jean-Aubry Collection, Beinecke Library, Yale).

81. "My Boyhood with Conrad," *Cornhill Magazine*, LXVI (1929), 27. See also p. 86.

82. *Looking Back*, I, 33.

83. Muriel Draper, *Music at Midnight* (New York, 1929), p. 113.

sneaking sense of unhealthiness, if not fought out and mastered in the open air, will foster a feeling of guilt. . . ."[84] Clearly there is a Freudian fog dead ahead. Dawson makes use of such figures as The Artist, The Friend, and The Decadent, and, among other matters, shows the difficult position of the creative man in contemporary society: "He stood, a stranger in a strange land." It turns out that everyone in the "strange land" has allegorically bad teeth except "The most beautiful Woman in the land," with whom the Artist promptly falls in love. Love is significantly short-lived in this story, however, for it expires with the revelation that the Artist brushes his teeth and—*chose étonnante!*—carries a toothbrush on his person. What to the Artist seems only healthy and normal seems to the people of the land a grave sin. Hence the title. At the close of "Step IX" (there are eleven in all) the Artist goes into the public square and, like a papier-mâché Raskolnikov, brushes his teeth. The bizarre and rather naïvely questionable humor of all this lies mainly in the basic conception. The handling is simply heavy.

What did Conrad find to admire in "The Sin"? Perhaps the wayward humor. Perhaps even the particular dental form which Dawson's humor took. Ford later reported that in the days of the Conrad-Hueffer collaboration Conrad had staunchly maintained that they should include a description of the teeth of an attractive female character,[85] and Edward H. Visiak has more recently reminded us of the striking fact that "Conrad's women . . . are dentally superb. . . ."[86] Bernard C. Meyer goes so far as to conclude that teeth had for Conrad a fetishistic significance.[87] We need not go that far. Still, Dawson, who had read all of Conrad's work, may have sensed some such thing. Then again, Conrad may have responded well to "The Sin" because of its underlying theme of the isolation of the individual, masquerading here as the isolation of the artist who desires to be different.[88] Most likely of all, perhaps, Conrad responded

84. *The Sin*, pp. 7–8.
85. *Joseph Conrad: A Personal Remembrance* (Boston, 1924), p. 152.
86. *The Mirror of Conrad* (New York, 1956), p. 69.
87. "Psychoanalytic Studies on Joseph Conrad," Pt. II, "Fetishism," *Journal of the American Psychoanalytic Association*, XII (1964), 364. For the psychologically oriented critic there is also food for thought in the subject of brushing.
88. An idea of Albert J. Guerard might take us still further. He speaks of "our desire for brotherhood and our propensity to solitary crime" as being among Conrad's major themes (introd., dated 1950, in *Heart of Darkness and The Secret Sharer* [New York, 1958], pp. 7–8).

to the fact that a very engaging Dawson wrote it and first read it aloud in the companionable, winter's night intimacy of the study at Capel House.

There is no doubt that the company provided part of Conrad's pleasure when he first heard "The Sin." Besides Dawson himself, a remarkable musician named John Powell was present.[89] Dawson had been a close friend of the moody, intense young pianist—all who remember him speak of his magnetic personality—ever since their meeting as schoolboys. In more recent years the two friends had grown closer still as a result of Dawson's extraordinary efforts to present Powell to the public. In 1908 Mrs. Dawson wrote home to the States concerning Powell's first concert in Berlin:

> You ask what Warrington was doing in Berlin: Playing Providence for an improvident youth, as usual. A young musician of marvelous talent had chosen to make his début there, against the advice of his Vienna teacher [Leschetizky]. He was a Richmond boy, to whom we had become attached during a brief stay in Paris. He recognized his mistake, and sent out a cry to Warrington to come, or he was lost. Warrington rushed on and found the dreamer had done Nothing that was essential, had even refused to practice for Six Weeks! Warrington was armed with Political, Journalistic, Artistic, and Social introductions. He brought all the critics to celestial moods, and stood over the genius untill he carried the audience by storm. The youth won his laurels—and then collapsed. Warrington took him to the hotel, and nursed him until he could take him about to be admired. And after twelve days, W. was back in harness, radiant with his achievement.[90]

Within just a few years of this episode, when Powell was coming to Capel House whenever he could to see Conrad and to "play Chopin

89. Born in Richmond, Virginia, in 1882, Powell entered the University of Virginia at seventeen and was graduated two years later with a Phi Beta Kappa key. After studying with Leschetizky and Navrátil in Vienna, he made his debut in Berlin in 1907. Before reaching thirty "he was already recognized by the music world as one of the greatest pianists that America had produced" (David Ewen, *Composers of Today* [New York, 1934], p. 198). He also became the composer of some distinctively American music. His better known works include the *Rhapsodie Nègre, In Old Virginia*, and *Natchez on the Hill*. In later years his name faded from public view, partly because he refused to record commercially and partly because his interests became diversified.

90. Sarah Dawson to Eunice Dunkin, 21 January 1908.

by the hour,"[91] his reputation was firmly established. "On his ability
as a pianist," according to the *Musical Standard*, "there is no need
to dwell, since he is so well known: one can only say that in the last
two or three years he has gained in power and understanding, and
may be reckoned one of our few really great pianists of the day."[92]
Conrad was delighted. To him music was "the art of arts"[93] and his
countryman Chopin one of the greatest of musicians, and yet all
too seldom was he able to gratify his musical tastes. His biographer
Jean-Aubry writes: "On peut donc par cet important aveu, compter
Joseph Conrad aux nombre des grands écrivains qui ont nourri dans
leur coeur un amour profond pour la musique, alors même que les
circonstances ne leur ont pas permis de donner libre cours à leurs
goûts secrets."[94] One of Dawson's greatest gifts to Conrad, then, was
John Powell. Not only did Powell play for Conrad. He also delighted
him with a request for a libretto and, eventually, dedicated to him
one of his most important works, the *Rhapsodie Nègre*.[95] Conrad,

91. Interview with Borys Conrad, 21 November 1964.
92. 6 December 1913, p. 541.
93. "Preface" [for *The Nigger of the "Narcissus"*; *"From the* New Review, *De-cember,* 1897"], privately printed (Hythe, Eng., 1902), p. 4.
94. From an unnumbered MS in the Jean-Aubry Collection, Beinecke Library, Yale. Jean-Aubry had heard of Powell, but relegated him to a brief footnote in "Joseph Conrad and Music," *The Chesterian*, VI (1924), 37–42.
95. In 1933 the *Rhapsodie* was finally performed in Powell's home city, Richmond, after being played by "most of the great orchestras with the composer as soloist." At this time Powell described the origins of the work:

In the spring of 1910, I first read Joseph Conrad's wonderful story, "Heart of Darkness," from the volume "Youth," and was powerfully moved by it, feeling that it cried aloud for musical expression. Shortly afterward, I met Conrad, and he invited me to spend several days at his home in Kent, an invitation which I eagerly accepted.
As my visit was drawing to a close and I had begun to feel more at ease, I became bold enough to suggest that he prepare for me an opera libretto based on the story. To my surprise, Conrad flushed and frowned, started to speak, checked himself, and left the room hurriedly. I was much upset, thinking that my suggestion had annoyed him, and then that he had considered me impertinent. However, when he finally reappeared, a few minutes later, all signs of agitation were gone, and the rest of my visit passed without any further untoward happening.
Several years later when it was suggested that I compose an opera for one of the larger opera houses, I thought again of "Heart of Darkness," and determined to write Conrad about it. His reply was that although he considered the emotional character of the story appropriate for musical setting, he believed it would be impossible to put the whole in dramatic form, and suggested that the material might better be used as the theme of a symphonic poem.
I accepted his judgment perforce, and when in 1917, Modest Altschuler asked me to write a piece for piano and orchestra for New York production, the themes of "Heart of Darkness" which had so long been haunting me,

for his part, made a great to-do over the name "Powell" in his current novel. The sailor in *Chance* called Powell was not modelled on the character of the American musician, to be sure, and yet the musician reminisced years later that, yes, Conrad had borrowed his name.[96] As a matter of fact, Conrad and his wife both remembered the name "Powell" for the rest of their lives.[97]

After the fall and winter of 1912 Dawson continued to write book after book, and Powell proceeded to dazzle audiences and critics alike with his concerts, but of the three men it was only Conrad who was to "reach the shores of fame." The turning point for Conrad came in 1914, thanks mainly to *Chance*, his Humbert book, and thanks in some small part, perhaps, to Richard Curle, his young friend and devotee, whom he met in the autumn of 1912. Conrad at first thought Curle "a queer creature,"[98] he told Dawson, but Curle was eventually to prove his usefulness. Perhaps it is natural that Dawson came to feel resentful of Curle, apparently unbeknownst to Curle himself, but in 1912 and later, too, Dawson had the good sense to realize and the grace to appreciate that his own friendship with Conrad was very well launched.

---

came into shape in the "Rhapsodie Nègre." It had its first hearing in Carnegie Hall in March, and seemed so well to please its audience that I was emboldened to ask Conrad if I might dedicate it to him. He replied in a most cordial manner, accepting the dedication.

Three years [later] when I was visiting the Conrads again at their home in Bishopsbourne, I had the honor of playing it for Conrad. Nor can I ever forget the joy his approbation gave me. Under the influence of his sympathy and praise, I reminded him of the time I had first broached the subject of "Heart of Darkness" and apologized for my faux pas.

"Why, my dear fellow, I was not annoyed at all—how could you think I was annoyed?" he said. "Ever since I began to write, it has been my highest ambition to have one of my stories made into an opera, and when you suggested that use for "Heart of Darkness," I was so moved I could not speak, and had to leave the room to gain my self-possession."

("Pianist Wrote Rhapsody out of Conrad Book," Richmond *Times-Dispatch*, 22 January 1933, p. 4; punctuation has been modified and typographical errors corrected.)

96. For this information I am indebted to Professor Ernest C. Mead, Jr., Department of Music, University of Virginia (interview of 27 July 1966). Mr. John D. Gordan, however, has since examined the MS of *Chance* for me and found that "Charles Powell is called Powell from the very beginning. . . . There is no visible hesitation or any alteration" (10 August 1967). The naming must be a coincidence which simply proved convenient for a little harmless flattery.

97. See *Joseph Conrad's Letters to His Wife* (London, 1927), p. 75. Conrad heard Powell play at public concerts in London at least twice, once on 19 November 1912 and once on 20 June 1913.

98. Conrad to Dawson, undated letter, probably written in 1913 (No. 42).

5

The Height of the Friendship (1913-1914)

Back in the States during the winter of 1912 and 1913, Dawson visited friends and relations, lectured on art and Africa, and met Walter Hines Page, the distinguished publisher. He had the pleasure of introducing Page to the largest meeting ever held by the Charleston Chamber of Commerce. Then in March he sallied forth to Europe again—for the last time, it turned out. In April Conrad wrote a humorous letter to Pinker on the amazing fact that none other than his publisher, Walter Hines Page, was to be the new American Ambassador to the Court of St. James's.[1]

Conrad at about this time was also reading Dawson's novel on the American colony in Paris. "Good! Yes! Trés fort!!" he exclaimed about the part he had seen, adding that he would like to keep it longer "for a second reading."[2] On 4 May, working in his comfortable rue Hardy retreat in Versailles, Dawson finally brought the work to a close. For the time being it was called "The Novel of George," George being a young Southerner who kept reasonably close to Dawson's own footsteps, following him to Paris for voice training and to Wales for some rather bland love interest. Conrad read the whole thing with care ("¾ of the work had *four* readings," he said). Then came his verdict: "Allure trés-belle and well sustained. Subject admirably in hand and the work as a whole . . . extremely interesting."[3] The method, however—"Mind I don't condemn the method"—raised some questions in Conrad's mind "which we must have a little talk about in view of future work." Even qualified thus, the praise was heady, and when Dawson went

1. Letter of 6 April 1913 in *Joseph Conrad: Life and Letters*, ed. G. Jean-Aubry, II (Garden City, N. Y., 1927), 144.
2. Conrad to Dawson, 16 March 1913 (No. 34).
3. Conrad to Dawson, 1 June 1913 (No. 38). By the time it reached print the novel was named *The Pyramid* (London, 1922).

down into Kent that summer, Conrad was as good as his word concerning the "little talk."

For nearly fifty years Dawson treasured a relic of this visit. It consists of three small sheets covered on both sides with Dawson's pencilled scrawl, and it is headed simply "Joseph Conrad dict. to me."[4] The little monologue seems to have been taken down more or less verbatim as Conrad spoke.[5] Its subject is twofold: Conrad's use of form in fiction and the nature of Dawson's talent. Because Conrad expressed himself at ease here, at a time when he was working on *Victory*, one of the last of his better books, his thoughts are worth preserving in full:

> There is a convention that only six or seven novel forms exist, & all writers are expected to adapt themselves to those forms.
>
> If everybody has agreed to look at a landscape in one way, I don't see why we should not look at it in another. It does not hurt for us to stand on our head to see it, if it has grown stale to us when we look at it standing on our feet.
>
> I am the only one in our generation who seems to be seeking a new form. Not that I deliberately sought it—stories came to me so. I had to have a number of different people seeing others from different angles. I had already adopted the form before I had fully realised it. And then I knew it was essentially mine, so I continue in it.
>
> I don't want you to imitate me, but I want you to find a new form to express yourself. I am the only one doing this now; as I look about among my young contemporaries, you are the only one I see able to go on with the idea.
>
> "The Scar" is good sentiment[.] "The Scourge" is good drama, "The Novel of George" is perfect as classical novel form. But thinking over the three very carefully with a view to discovering the qualities in yourself which underlie your work, I think I see at last the new lines on which you might develop.
>
> There can be no question whatever that you possess the cre-

---

4. The document is undated, but I feel reasonably sure it comes from the summer of 1913. In the transcription which follows, the use of quotation marks has been regularized.

5. For a comment on Dawson's ability to take dictation, see p. 25.

ative faculty strongly. You are a gifted creative writer, & you have furthermore command of narrative, particularly in this latest book, which is a novel of action. But apart from this, & without prejudice to it, you have the critical faculty remarkably developed. If *la haute critique* existed in England, if a position exalted enough for you to occupy it in this class of work were conceivable for you here, you might go even farther on these lines than on purely creative lines, perhaps—though you must not think I mean by this that you will not go far as a creative writer! But since la haute critique exists no where but in France, & even there has been discredited, why do you not become the critical novellist? No one has yet fully succeeded there, even in France, & in England it would be totally new. The Bergeret book[s] while being critical were too analytical, & so set off the readers.[6] Anatole France made his reputation in trying for the critical novel, but he always either missed or overshot his mark. Why should you not succeed in doing that which he failed to do in "Le Lys Rouge"? Even in "The Scar," you show promises of this critical faculty, under the strong & pure sentiment which dominates the work; in handling the dramatic plot of "The Scourge" you showed it more markedly, but I was first struck by it in definite form in "The Novel of George," and thinking very earnestly over your work, I said to myself, "Those are the lines for him to follow."

Here, surely, is a good example of Conrad's "oriental" flattery. Conrad tended (perhaps wisely, after all) to praise his friends above their desert.[7] On the other hand, he had obviously spent some time thinking about Dawson's work. He must have felt that Dawson, both as man and man of letters, was worth it. Conrad would have lost patience with anyone unable to contribute something during those "many and intimate conversations."[8]

His dictation to Dawson begins with the idea, developed long before with Hueffer, that a revolt against fossilized art forms is neces-

6. Conrad refers to the four volumes of *L'Histoire Contemporaine* by Anatole France: *L'Orme du Mail* (1897), *Le Mannequin d'Osier* (1897), *L'Anneau d'Améthyste* (1899), and *M. Bergeret à Paris* (1901).

7. As Edward Garnett says, "One must guard one's self against taking his moods, his flatteries, his cries of distress in his *Letters* either too absolutely or too lightly" (*Letters from Joseph Conrad 1895–1924* [Indianapolis, 1928], p. 20).

8. Phrase from a Conrad letter to Dawson, 29 July 1923 (No. 106).

sary. Conrad and Hueffer had searched for something new in novel-writing, and they had experimented with their findings. Moreover, the emphasis on form was, indeed, mainly Conrad's. According to Hueffer, "Mr. Conrad's unceasing search was for a New Form for the Novel, mine for a non-literary vocabulary."[9] Conrad's fiction itself is also proof, of course, that he was usually willing to try a new variety of narrative technique, "to stand on his head" if necessary. As he explained to Barrett H. Clark, "My attitude to subjects and expressions, the angles of vision, my methods of composition will, within limits, be always changing—not because I am unstable or unprincipled but because I am free."[10] If Conrad, therefore, in the privacy of his home spoke of himself as "the only one in our generation who seems to be seeking a new form," he spoke expansively, of course, but not altogether without basis. More interesting is Conrad's recognition here of the role of instinct in his search: "I had already adopted the form before I had fully realised it."[11] One might descant and yet again descant upon the theme of art, and still something about that art would prove at the end as inscrutable as the human mind which created it.

That Conrad had sought—or at least found—new forms was no reason to keep others from seeking, too. He takes an extra step here, however, and suggests a particular direction for Dawson to step. Why not become a critical novelist? Hueffer reports that Conrad's rule of thumb was "*Never state: present!*" And he translates it, "*Never comment: state.*"[12] Yet Conrad's advice to Dawson is, "Do not merely state: comment!" It is itself a striking bit of commentary, given all that Conrad says of his own work elsewhere. Anatole France, who had attempted something of the sort, had "a critical temperament joined to creative power."[13] To Conrad he seemed "the Prince of Prose." But Anatole France failed as a "critical novelist" when he attempted *Le Lys Rouge*. Perhaps Dawson could succeed where France had failed? High praise, indeed!

9. *Thus to Revisit: Some Reminiscences* (London, 1921), p. 40. Hueffer is not always reliable, but this point seems true.

10. Letter of 4 May 1918 in Jean-Aubry, LL, II, 204.

11. Douglas Hewitt, for one, writes of Conrad's changing attitude toward the degree of consciousness brought to the creation of his fiction. In earlier times Conrad acknowledges (to use his words) "things that 'just happen' in one's work," but later (in Hewitt's words) he becomes "far more ready to speak as though he has complete control of the creative process" (*Conrad: A Reassessment* [Cambridge, Eng., 1952], p. 122).

12. "Joseph Conrad," *English Review*, X (1911), 77.

13. "Anatole France," *Notes on Life & Letters* (London, 1921), p. 54.

On 11 August, back in Versailles, Dawson dated the final page of a manuscript entitled "The Grand Elixir." Though the origins of this story went back several years, the "Elixir" appears to be at least in part a response to Conrad's advice earlier that same summer. The story had started out as "The Countess" and then metamorphosed first into "Paris Green" and then into "The Grand Elixir" before it was published at last, in 1925, as *The Green Moustache*; but the nature of the story and Dawson's special efforts on it in 1913 suggest that he may have been trying specifically at that time to follow Conrad's recommendation that he become a "critical" novelist. When it came to the great, Dawson usually was willing to be influenced.

He also delighted in exerting his own influence. In the summer of 1913 he remained in London long enough to join with John Powell in founding a new society for various kinds of artists, mainly musicians as it turned out. Ingenuously aimed at the purification of contemporary art, the Fresh Air Art Society is both a measure of Dawson's aspirations and a key to his limitations. More important here, it furnished the impetus for the most thoughtful letter that Conrad ever wrote to his Carolina friend.

In November, six months after the inception of the Society, Dawson explained its origin and ideals in this way:

> Early in the month of June, 1913, a small group of musicians and writers met together, one night, in London, for the purpose of forming a Society.
>
> Each of them had been fighting for certain ideals and principles in his own expression of life and of art.
>
> All were believers in the laws of universal harmony and evolution; none separated the element of spirit from the element of matter which must combine in human life as in human art.
>
> But while each believed in the infinite variety of forms for expression, none was far enough behind his age to accept the theories of individualism tried out and exhausted half a century before. Their own lives, like their own works, were to them as units, component parts of a greater whole, which greater whole had its allotted place in the infinite Oneness of things.
>
> This sentiment of unity, harmony and evolution in their personal lives and work had led them to the sense of fellowship with all whose ideals and principles were identical. . . .

66

This sense of fellowship . . . brought them to the realization that they must also stand with the world while fulfilling their share of its work. . . .

Two weeks after the meeting of that small group of six workers, the new Society held its first Public Meeting and Concert, on the 23rd of June, at the Queen's (small) Hall, London. The Earl of Plymouth, first Honorary Member of the Society, presided and introduced the spokesman of the group [Dawson himself]. In the audience, men and women notable for their work in various arts had proved their interest by their presence.[14]

Besides Dawson and Powell, the other charter members of the group included Benno Moiseiwitsch, Vernon Warner, Sydney Rosenbloom, and Efrem Zimbalist.[15] Powell, Moiseiwitsch, and Warner had all studied the piano in Vienna under the great Leschetizky, and the friendly feelings generated earlier among the three young men had been reinforced recently as a result of Powell's suggestion that the others join him in working out at the gymnasium of the German Gymnastic Society at Pancras Road, King's Cross. Himself an excellent amateur wrestler, Powell was sure that an artist performs best when in the best of health. With the dual goal of good art and sound health, therefore, a little group began to evolve. The young musicians began going to the gymnasium weekly or even oftener, and afterward, Warner recalls, someone would "drift to a piano," and soon they all would be playing to one another "better than we ever did before."[16] Powell, with his personal magnetism, had provided the force which drew the men together, but now Dawson, the group's man of letters,[17] set to work formulating a "Declaration of Principles." These were drawn up on 16 June 1913, and the Fresh Air Art Society was on its way. Rosenbloom was Chairman and Dawson was Secretary.

14. From a fifteen-page printed leaflet inserted in Dawson's Scrapbook No. 68790, pp. 137–150.
15. Moiseiwitsch, who soon married the violinist Daisy Kennedy, was a Russian-English pianist, already beginning to achieve distinction. Rosenbloom was a pianist, composer, and teacher of Polish-Irish parentage. Warner had earlier scored success as a child pianist and at the time of the Society was continuing what proved to be a long and respectable concert career. Efrem Zimbalist, who had already made a name for himself as a concert violinist, was to become the most famous of them all. He eventually forgot the Fresh Air Art Society, however, perhaps because his connection with it was never more than casual (letter of Zimbalist to Randall, 10 August 1964).
16. Interview of 4 November 1964.
17. Dawson had also studied voice and written some songs.

In his lecture of 23 June 1913, after making it clear that the Society hoped to shake off "the shackles of *arbitrary convention,*" Dawson explained that "we declare ourselves for *fresh* in preference to *vitiated* air," the metaphor coming from an Ibsen play "which every theatre-goer is supposed to know."[18] He continued:

> We are conscious of our *audacity* in pleading today for the principle *of mens sana* in *corpore sano.* . . . But let me say *distinctly & explicitly* for those who really wish to understand that by 'sound body, nerves, heart, & mind,' we do *not* mean that physical infirmity *should* or *could* debar a man from *great art.* . . . That against which we *do protest* is the *encouragement & exploitation* of the idea of *physical* morbidity because the idea of *mental* morbidity is a well-paying investment with the public.

The main point, of course, was that art should be buttressed by health. "Perhaps the most *resentful objection* raised against the principle of *healthiness* as connected with *art* is inspired by the old *fetish* of Art *for* Art's *sake* which would make of art an end *in* itself." Art for Art's Sake, Dawson felt, is much too close to Sensation for Sensation's Sake. He denounced that "art" which is a "pretext for *irresponsible exploitation* of the *senses.* . . . To the artist of *high ideals*, the senses are a means for arriving at *great human verities* from which science is *separated* by its *abstraction.*" The function of the true artist is

> To exercise his selective faculty in order to know WHAT is true in all he has seen, WHEN he must use it, & HOW he should present it. . . . If he goes beyond & offers solutions devised from his own appreciation of facts, then the evanescence of the flesh enters into what he has done, & its chance for endurance vanishes.

Dawson's conclusion offered an aphoristic formula: "To attain greatness, art must commence in truth, continue in sincerity, & thrive in enthusiasm"; and the entire lecture rolled to a complimentary close with a sentence borrowed from Conrad: "Leaves must follow upon one another as leagues used to follow in the days

18. Dawson's unpaginated MS.

gone by, on and on to the appointed end, which, being Truth itself, is One—one for all men and for all occupations."[19]

Dawson, in a word, was exercised about decadence and aestheticism, along with any of their unwholesome progeny which might be lumped under the name of "modernism." The notion that contemporary culture was in some way decadent had been evolving in Dawson's adopted country since about 1830, so long, in fact, that by the close of the century many French writers had grown immune to it.[20] Meanwhile the virus of decadence (Conrad's friend Symons called decadence a "beautiful and interesting disease")[21] had crossed the Channel to England. It came in the sixties, along with Baudelaire's *Fleurs du Mal,* and for a while, to some young Britons, the revolt from respectability seemed smart. Once art was relieved of a moral or ethical burden, it had some of the attractiveness of a green carnation. As a matter of fact, however, the decadents' aim of shocking and the aesthetes' absorption with sensation and form at the cost of morality and ethics were never very popular in England, and such vogue as they attained was damned along with Oscar Wilde in 1895.

In that same year Max Nordau's reactionary *Degeneration* fairly burst upon the English.[22] A big, strong, ridiculous book, *Degeneration* was attacked by most of the critics on both sides of the Atlantic, including the conservative William Dean Howells and the radical George Bernard Shaw.[23] Acidly but accurately Shaw summarized Nordau's "message to the world" as a foolish warning "that all our characteristically modern works of art are symptoms of disease in the artists, and that these diseased artists are themselves symptoms of the nervous exhaustion of the race by overwork." Conrad himself,

19. *A Personal Record* (New York, 1912), p. 40.
20. It reached a memorable externalization with the founding in 1886 of Anatole Baju's *Le Décadent* (A. E. Carter, *The Idea of Decadence in French Literature 1830–1900* [Toronto, 1958], p. 21).
21. "The Decadent Movement in Literature," *Harper's New Monthly Magazine,* LXXXVII (1893), 859.
22. Published in Berlin as *Die Entartung* (1892). Nordau (originally Südfeld) was a Budapest-born Jewish physician and writer.
23. Howells, "Degeneration," *Harper's Weekly,* XXXIX (1895), 342; and Shaw, *The Sanity of Art* (New York, 1908). The Shaw passage cited next is from p. 21. Of particular interest among other sources are "Nordau's Theory of Degeneration," a symposium in *The North American Review,* CLX (1895), 735–752; and Grant C. Knight, *The Critical Period in American Literature* (Chapel Hill, N. C., 1951), pp. 70–76.

in *Chance,* created a misguided character who "seized with avidity upon the theory of poetical genius being allied to madness, which he got hold of in some idiotic book everybody was reading a few years ago."[24] But whoever denounced him, Nordau was for a while a forceful figure on the cultural scene. He also became a friend of Dawson in Paris, and it just may be that his wrongheaded diagnosis of the times had some influence on Dawson's thought.[25] Though public interest in *Degeneration* had subsided before 1913,[26] Dawson's thinking was rather in the Nordau tradition. When he spoke out against decadence and aestheticism on behalf of the Fresh Air Art Society, it was because he, too, considered them the unholy parents of "modernism." Modernistic art, as opposed to "healthy contemporaneous art," had all the old, bad traits—hysteria, artificiality, morbidness, fragmentation, and decay.

Dawson and his friends meant to throw the windows open. A few days before their first public meeting they printed an announcement headed "REASON AND SANITY IN ART." The sheet announced not only Dawson's forthcoming address on "Fresh Air Art," but also the illustrative music which would be played at the meeting, including compositions by Powell and Rosenbloom. On the reverse side the ideals of the Society were presented under fourteen headings, interesting both in themselves and for the reaction Conrad had to them:

    I. We believe in the Oneness of Life.
    II. We believe in the Oneness of Art.
    III. We believe in the Eternity of Art as standing for Life.
    IV. Wherefore Art is a means, not an end.
    V. Before the End can be conceived, Life must be understood.
    VI. Before Life can be understood, its responsibilities must be acknowledged.
    VII. That the End pursued by Art's means may be true, the Life which Art represents must be true.

24. *Chance* (London, 1914), p. 168. Of Conrad, however, "Dr. Max Nordau . . . has expressed the opinion that no other living writer possesses so just a sense of word values and coloring in English" (Warrington Dawson, "Joseph Conrad," New York *Times,* 2 February 1913, p. 51).

25. According to Anna and Maxa Nordau, Dawson "intensely interested Nordau. He first came with his mother, who being in ill health, had to consult the physician, Nordau" (*Max Nordau: A Biography* [New York, 1943], p. 106).

26. It was not altogether dead; the book had a London edition in 1913.

VIII. Wherefore Life and Art must alike be founded upon conditions of sound body, nerves, heart, and mind.

IX. But such a foundation must itself rest upon the great Laws which have promoted the evolution of Life.

X. That Art may be controlled, it must contain qualities of reason and of construction beneath all forces or subtleties of appeal.

XI. That Art may not only exist, but may wax strong in the harmony which is Infinity, it must, like Life itself, obey the laws of health which combat decay.

XII. The great facts of human history have been those which bespoke the culminating spirit of a race; the great works of human Art have been those which expressed the highest spirit of their own age.

XIII. To acknowledge that exploiters of superficial emotions or seekers after sheer eccentricity represent the spirit of our age, is to pronounce this age unworthy to be a link between the past as we know it and the future as we have the right to desire it.

XIV. Wherefore we declare ourselves for the Art as for the Life which rest upon a respect for Nature's laws in the Fresh Air of Health and the clear Light of Truth.

Conrad received his copy of the notice a couple of days before the meeting. Though he had never formulated a set of rules for his own use, the appeal from Dawson and Powell was sufficient to bring him to "the Queen's (small) Hall." Hence the special appropriateness of Dawson's quotation in his lecture from Conrad's *Personal Record*. The only trouble was, Conrad chose not to join. Feeling as he did and guessing the disappointment his refusal would entail, he prepared the way for his London trip with a sympathetic but dissenting letter concerning the Fourteen Articles. This letter, dated 20 June 1913, was to be the most vital commentary he ever wrote to Dawson, throwing light both on his involvement with the young American and on his own "credo" as an artist.

Clearly Conrad had read Dawson's Articles carefully (Powell is brought in for politeness), but the man who held that "Theory is a cold and lying tombstone of departed truth"[27] was not likely to

27. Letter of 15 March 1895 in Garnett, p. 34.

embrace such a code as Dawson set forth. "The question of *art*," Conrad had written to William Blackwood,

> is so endless, so involved and so obscure that one is tempted to turn one's face resolutely away from it. I've certainly an idea— apart from the idea and the subject of the story—which guides me in my writing, but I would be hard put to it if requested to give it out in the shape of a fixed formula.[28]

Conrad professed to believe "that the world . . . rests on a few very simple ideas,"[29] but he was not the man to list them one-two-three, much less subscribe to another man's list.

Probably Dawson felt, as Conrad feared he would, that "this man has disappointed us." Probably Dawson thought that when he wrote, "We believe in the Oneness of Life," he was parallelling reasonably closely what Conrad had in mind when he said in the preface to *The Nigger of the "Narcissus"* that the job of art is "to render the highest kind of justice to the visible universe, by bringing to light the truth, manifold and one, underlying its every aspect."[30] In his lecture Dawson even quoted the passage in which Conrad had said that "Truth . . . is one."[31] But now Conrad demurred. Perhaps the point to be made is that for Conrad "Truth" was not only "one" but also "manifold." Truth was "one," yet expressed in a life of "infinite variety." In the letter to Dawson, at any rate, Conrad put the emphasis strongly on life's variety. The artist works with life's differing forms, colors, and lights because these are what he sees and responds to. These are the only "Truth" he knows. Fifteen years before, Conrad had tried to explain the same matter to Galsworthy, emphasizing then, too, the importance of external forms and even pleading innocent—as he does to Dawson—on the score of shallowness. The force of Galsworthy's current book, he wrote, was "in the fidelity to the surface of life, to the surface of events,—to the surface

28. Letter of 22 August 1899 in *Joseph Conrad: Letters to William Blackwood and David S. Meldrum*, ed. William Blackburn (Durham, N. C., 1958), p. 64.
29. *A Personal Record*, p. 14.
30. "Preface," privately printed (Hythe, Eng., 1902), p. 1.
31. One school, of course, says that Conrad is a great intuitive artist but a murky thinker, and that it is beside the point to try to solve problems created by such passages. Support for this stand is given by Conrad himself. In his preface to Ada Galsworthy's translation of De Maupassant he refers to the latter's "philosophy, which in the case of so consummate an artist does not matter (unless to the solemn and naïve mind) . . ." (reprinted in *Notes on Life & Letters*, p. 34).

of things and ideas. Now this is not being shallow. . . . It is not your business to invent depths. . . . Most things and most natures have nothing but a surface."[32]

In the *Nigger* preface, which Jean-Aubry calls Conrad's *ars poetica,* Dawson had read that the artist's "appeal is less loud, more profound, less distinct, more stirring—and sooner forgotten" than that of the thinker and the scientist. "Yet," Conrad had added rather ambiguously, "its effect endures for ever."[33] Art has a certain timelessness because it appeals to man's timeless capacities. Now in 1913 Conrad refused assent to Article III: "We believe in the Eternity of Art. . . ." What reservations did he have? Ostensibly, simply that art and the earth will be conterminous. In fact, as if to fortify his stand, he proceeded to link the termination of both art and earth with a rejection of hell and heaven, or at least a rejection of what he referred to as "the eternity of pain" and "eternity of love." Whether or not Conrad at the moment remembered all the details of his *Nigger* preface, he may have shifted his position a bit. Surely the later Conrad "had no illusions as to immortal fame," says Curle. "He thought that his books, like all others, would be forgotten in due course, and it did not worry him in the least. The desire to express himself was a stronger urge than the hope of applause. . . ."[34] As a matter of fact, Conrad himself recorded a similar view—and in terms of the old *bête noire,* temporary "formulas":

> No secret of eternal life for our books can be found amongst the formulas of art, any more than for our bodies in a prescribed combination of drugs. This is not because some books are not worthy of enduring life, but because the formulas of art are dependent on things variable, unstable and untrustworthy; on human sympathies, on prejudices, on likes and dislikes, on the sense of virtue and the sense of propriety, on beliefs and theories that, indestructible in themselves, always change their form— often in the lifetime of one fleeting generation.[35]

At least Conrad's contrast of the artist and scientist in the *Nigger* preface has a fairly close echo in the letter to Dawson. In each the scientist comes off second best, and especially so in the letter. Con-

32. Letter of 16 January 1898 in Jean-Aubry, *LL,* I, 224.
33. "Preface," p. 2.
34. *The Last Twelve Years of Joseph Conrad* (London, 1928), p. 122.
35. "Books," *Notes on Life & Letters,* p. 6.

rad makes the contrast here, however, partly in order to say that neither the scientist *nor* the artist has the answers.[36] For this reason, "Art for me *is* an end in itself." In the *Nigger* preface he had reflected how sometimes "the supreme cry of Art for Art, itself, loses the exciting ring of its apparent immorality. It sounds far off. It has ceased to be a cry, and is heard only as a whisper, often incomprehensible, but at times and faintly encouraging."[37] Dawson had been much concerned about this matter, and, by the time of the Fresh Air Art Society, spoke of "the End pursued by Art's means." Conrad was willing to say that art must have a moral purpose, but he felt that this moral purpose was itself bound closely to the artist's "remorseless fidelity to the *truth of his own sensations*"— a phrase he uses twice in this letter.[38] This is neither didacticism nor Art for Art's Sake, but something more subtle than either. Frederick Karl states the case well: "In trying to travel the rocky literary path between an 1890's 'code' of artistic anarchy and a Victorian code of professed didacticism, Conrad took refuge . . . in that devotion to craft wherein art and morality meet in commitment, responsibility, and lawfulness."[39]

Informal though it is, and dependent for its clarity on the Articles of the Fresh Air Art Society, Conrad's letter to Dawson of 20 June 1913 belongs somewhere within that circle of documents which are central to an understanding of Conrad's art. In it Conrad graciously but firmly refuses to endorse Dawson's views and, in the process, he proclaims his "whole Credo" as an artist.

36. In the New York *Times* of 24 August 1901 (p. 603) he gave still another of his variants on the topic: Art does not pronounce conclusions; conclusions and teaching are left to science; science discovers laws—but they are true only for a while.

In later years Conrad stood by the *Nigger* preface. He thought less well of it than formerly, he told Rollo Walter Brown, "But that bears only on the expression. My convictions in the main remain the same" (letter of 9 September 1919 in Houghton Library, Harvard).

37. "Preface," pp. 5–6.

38. To Blackwood he had written on 31 May 1902 (Blackburn, ed., pp. 155–156):

My work shall not be an utter failure because it has the solid basis of a definite intention—first: and next because it is not an endless analysis of affected sentiments but in its essence it is action (strange as this affirmation may sound at the present time) nothing but action—action observed, felt and interpreted with an absolute truth to my sensations (which are the basis of art in literature)—action of human beings that will bleed to a prick, and are moving in a visible world.

The word "fidelity," of course, is central in Conrad.

39. "Joseph Conrad's Literary Theory," *Criticism*, II (1960), 332.

On 28 November, back in England again, Dawson spoke at another public meeting of the Society, announcing that "The total active membership has more than trebled in these six months, strict as are the rules according to which none may enter save workers in the arts who subscribe to the [Society's] Declaration of Principles in its entirety."[40] By now the members were a mixed lot. One early enrollee was a young wrestler named Bernhard Trappschuh, who in later years became Dawson's publisher. Helen Sanderson also joined. So did the New Orleans writer Grace King and Lady Phyllis Windsor-Clive, and so did the astronomer Camille Flammarion. Even Jessie Conrad joined. But the biggest catch of the little group was clearly Rodin. "When I recently approached Monsieur Auguste Rodin," Dawson told his audience,

> and asked him to become an active foundation member of the Society, I was asked by him to explain our aims fully and translate into French our Declaration of Principles. When I had finished, he said, "Your principles are those on which I have always worked. Not only do I know them to be true, but they appear to me so evident that I fail to see how they could possibly be disputed. I am happy to become an active member of the Fresh Air Art Society."[41]

During this same month the news of a Rodin-Dawson collaboration was made public. As a newspaper correspondent in search of a story, Dawson had first called on Rodin back in 1899, when he was preparing for the Paris Exposition of 1900. Now the *Observer* of 16 November 1913 reported that Rodin and Dawson would "travel through Italy together, noting its cities and churches and treasures of art. And Rodin will pour out his ideas and Mr. Dawson will write them down."[42] With Dawsonian prompting, it may be assumed, the *Observer* added that "Mr. Dawson's own novels have been influenced, no doubt, by his contact with this superb artist in marble who teaches the unity of art and life and the importance of mathematics in the construction of any work. Some of these ideas have

40. P. 10 of undated printed document, Dawson Collection.
41. P. 9 of document cited in preceding note.
42. From a clipping in Dawson's Scrapbook No. 67898, p. 198. The nature of the project altered, however. On 25 October Dawson had reported that Rodin asked him to collaborate in publishing his notes on art. See also Dawson's letter to Pinker of 6 November (No. 55).

found expression in the Fresh Air Art Society. . . ." Though Nordau had damned him as decadent, Rodin, ironically, may have served as a sort of spiritual godfather of the Fresh Air Art Society.

The press response to Dawson's second lecture for the Society was severe. On 29 November the *Morning Post* reported that "A rather dull and long 'short address,' designed to enlighten the hearer on the subject of 'the principles of Fresh Air Art,' did not serve to attune one exactly to a right appreciation of the first of a series of three concerts. . . ."[43] Music there was, beginning with a performance by Powell and Rosenbloom of Mozart's Sonata in D for two pianos. The *Globe* attacked the Fourteen Articles and then continued thus:

> Nor did Warrington Dawson, who delivered a lecture on the Fresh Air Artists' aims, make matters much better. His earnestness was as evident as his dislike of homely language, and one could only feel sorry that an ardent apostle of a new school should feel so confident in the strength of his own cause, and so scornful of the views of his adversaries, that he could not bring himself to state his case simply and modestly.[44]

Earnest, ardent, and proud. The *Globe* reporter saw Dawson clearly, if not whole.

Perhaps the most striking detail in the subsequent history of the high-minded little Society was its formation of an Austrian branch. On 30 March 1914, "in den Kleinen Saal des Wiener Konzerthauses," Dawson gave an address on Fresh Air Art in French. Before the next summer was over, though, the holocaust had come, and the little Art Society quietly expired.

Conrad's letter of 20 June stayed in Dawson's mind and files a long time. He knew it was good, and in 1927 he included parts of it in the foreword to *The Crimson Pall,* a novel dedicated *"To* JOHN POWELL / *In Memory of Our Night-Talks / On Life and Art and Letters / With Joseph and Jessie Conrad."* The foreword consists of three letters, two ostensibly by Conrad and one by Dawson. On

43. From a clipping in Dawson's Scrapbook No. 67898, p. 199.
44. From a clipping of 29 November 1913 in Dawson's Scrapbook No. 67898, p. 199.
   In *The Pyramid* Dawson presents a fictional counterpart of a Fresh Air Art Society meeting. He describes the music as "full of melodic qualities, as free from eccentricity as from conventionality," and he tells how a "short address [is] placed, not apologetically but as the crux of the whole affair, in the very midst of the programme" (p. 358). The speechmaker, George Alayn, is throughout the book a thinly veiled alter-ego of Dawson.

examination it becomes clear that the two Conrad letters are really patchworks, both considerably better than life. Not that Dawson was betraying his late friend. It turns out that Conrad had long before given Dawson permission to try his hand at epistolary collage. On 2 June 1922 Conrad had written from his last home, Oswalds, in Bishopsbourne, Kent, that he was constitutionally incapable of writing a "literary appreciation," but that Dawson was welcome to quote from any of his letters "if you think that the publication (whole or in extracts) of what I have said to you in the open intimacy of our friendship may be of any use. . . ." Over a year later, on 20 July 1923, Dawson wrote to Conrad:

> In connection with "THE PYRAMID", I shall publish our correspondence. But there is so much of my own expression of opinion in it that I am wondering if you would let me add to your reply to my letter these lines of what you told me after reading "THE PYRAMID". . . .
>
> They would make a real and even thundering reply to my letter. . . .

Conrad again granted Dawson permission to proceed as he saw fit, with the result that the second Conrad letter in Dawson's *Crimson Pall*—not, as it turned out, *The Pyramid*—is a monster for a bibliographer's nightmare.[45]

Dawson's motive is clear. He gives it himself at the conclusion of his own letter in the foreword: "There has . . . been one thing I have wanted earnestly during these years of writing. I have wanted your readers to know you think kindly of me."[46] As Dawson saw literary success receding farther and farther before him, even while he was writing his heart out to reach it, he sometimes had to salve his pride. Not here, though. Complete with its tinge of pathos, this passage shows Dawson at his honest, straightforward best.[47]

Back at work in Versailles after the flurry of founding the Fresh

45. The first paragraph is from the 2 June 1922 letter from Conrad just cited (No. 99); the next seven paragraphs are from Conrad's dictation to Dawson, probably made in 1913 (see pp. 63–64); the next four are from the letter of 20 June 1913 on the Articles of the Fresh Air Art Society (No. 40); and the final three are from a letter of 29 July 1923 (No. 106), in which Conrad comments on his meeting with Powell in the States—an appropriate closing because Powell is the dedicatee of the book.

46. *The Crimson Pall*, p. 22.

47. See pp. 108–109 for relevant comments on Conrad's foreword to Dawson's *Adventure in the Night*.

Air Art Society, Dawson was soon putting the final touches on his introduction to an edition of his mother's girlhood diary. Conrad finished reading the proof of the book—whose value he seems to have glimpsed—as early as 23 July 1913, and at Dawson's request he sent it on next to Dawson's old friend Grace King, who was visiting for a while in England.

Meanwhile, with the diary off his desk, Dawson was free to devote himself to the fantastic work which in manuscript he called "The Grand Elixir." Whether or not this was an attempt at a "critical novel" such as Conrad had recommended, it was surely a work which Conrad had discussed with Dawson earlier that summer. Conrad had suggested the names "Evlampia," "Sidor," and "Ossip" for characters in the story, and, according to Dawson, had even sketched out "the architectural appearance of the haunted Castle of Sarovinia."[48] When the book was finally published in 1925, its full title, *The Green Moustache: A Fantasy of Modernism*, clarified the fact that Dawson was continuing to attack in fiction what he had attacked in his Art Society lecture, modern manifestations of decadence and aestheticism. Green had been the special color of the decadents, and a green moustache was quite satisfactorily "unnatural." It would seem that Dawson's intent may have been to emulate not only Anatole France's *Lys Rouge*, as Conrad had suggested, but also Robert Hichens' *Green Carnation* (1894), a witty, lively, and popularly successful satire on the excesses of aestheticism. Whatever its models or innovations, however, Dawson's book was dated, slow, and unclear.[49] Those who think that Conrad was incapable of anything but flattery for the writing of his friends should consider his letter on Dawson's *Green Moustache*. Conrad makes the unmistakable point that "You want something to steady you artistically."[50]

In July, 1913, Dawson tried to arrange for a series of lectures dur-

48. Letter of Dawson to Arnold T. Schwab, 18 March 1954 (from Dawson's carbon typescript). See also Conrad to Dawson, 2 August 1913 (No. 49).

49. One difficulty was that Dawson found much that was congenial in the elegant international society he tried to criticize. For collateral evidence one may turn again to his *Pyramid*, where he writes of "Soft voices—subtle phrases—graceful movements;—impeccable clothes on the men, dresses of exquisite hue and perfect line on the women;—and over the whole an atmosphere of charm, of wit, of refinement, of fascination, which roused a deep yearning in any outsider" (p. 301). These last words tell the story.

50. Conrad to Dawson, 24 October 1913 (No. 53).

ing his visit to the States the next winter, but engagements were hard to come by, and in late August he cancelled the entire 1913–1914 lecture season, explaining that he simply could not afford to take time away from writing every winter.

October brought forth the first American edition of *Chance* and Dawson's long-repressed "Sin," and in November came the announcement of the Rodin-Dawson collaboration. Rodin was now the most famous sculptor of the day, a stolid victor over poverty, scorn, and neglect. Unfortunately, however, his wrangling with the world had left its wounds. According to his friend Judith Cladel, "after a long career of beating off attacks, he had acquired a touch of persecution mania, [and] was always unconsciously on the defensive and suspicious, even of a friend. . . ."[51] For this cause or some other (there was never a public explanation) the Rodin-Dawson collaboration fell through, leaving Dawson with a few notes and some precious recollections of days at Meudon, but without a subject he could use.[52]

Meanwhile, things were looking better for Conrad. To be sure, Jessie reported on 19 January 1914 that the Conrads were afflicted with "a sick house," but Conrad, working on *Victory*, had energy enough to read the manuscript of a book which young Richard Curle had written about him. And it was a gratifying experience. Conrad

51. *Rodin*, trans. James Whitall (New York, 1937), p. 242.
52. Dawson later said darkly that the relationship "ended with a tragedy . . . , in which just he and I were the players, and which I have not yet been able to bring myself to discuss . . ." (from carbon typescript, letter of 31 March 1926, Dawson to Theodore D. Jervey).
Dawson's finest hour with Rodin was probably that when he suggested the angle at which the *maitre* placed the arm of his "Woman Centaur." Charles A. Reopell describes the episode in "A Man of Three Careers," an essay in Dawson's MS volume called "A Man and His Work," p. 63 (original in the Ralph Foster Museum, School of the Ozarks):

> The arms, as far as the shoulders, had been made separately, and they and the rest of the statue had stood for years on a shelf at the Meudon studio because Rodin had not been able to put them together to his satisfaction. When Warrington Dawson found the angle and line Rodin had been seeking, the sculptor exultantly fixed the arms with wax while his young friend held them, and the statuette was immediately sent to be moulded. . . .

Léonce Bénédite relates a fact in *Rodin* (London, 1924), p. 20, which makes the story seem plausible, viz., that Rodin habitually "experimented with arrangements of lines and groupings of bodies, using the remains of old figures, arms, legs, feet, hands— 'ses abattis,' as he used to call them—in order to simplify his work and with the hope of arriving at new combinations." Plate 51A of Bénédite's book depicts Rodin's *Centauresse*.

also had cause to be pleased by the reception of *Chance*. The cheeriest of all his letters to Dawson was written on 17 February 1914, after it had become clear that *Chance* was to be a success: "who knows if the hour of justice is not about to strike!" he wrote. "I have just heard that Doubl: Page have bought . . . ['my poor Nigger'] from Dodd Mead and are going to publish it uniform with *Chance* this very year!"

In March Dawson was off to Munich and Vienna, and in April came the publication of Curle's panegyrical analysis. Now about five months had slipped by since Dawson's last visit with Conrad, and the younger man began to think of another pilgrimage to Kent. This time, however, he had the idea of combining work with pleasure. He would stay someplace different in the countryside, not with the Conrads, and for a longer time than usual. When Conrad responded to this suggestion on 25 April, he extended the family's love and welcome, and reported that Jessie already had in mind a suitable nearby farmhouse. Thus began the planning for the best and longest of Dawson's visits. No one knew, of course, that it was to be the last.

Jessie arranged for Dawson to stay at Gill Farm, a pleasant old red-brick-and-tile place tucked away at the end of a long lane. It was altogether a good retreat for writing, and Jessie even offered to send over such little items as would add to Dawson's comfort. When Dawson arrived, all went very well, indeed. On 11 June 1914 he wrote to Ambassador Walter Hines Page at the Embassy:

> Since the day after I had the pleasure of lunching with you, I have been down here, in the farmhouse next to Conrad's[,] he working on the novel he is finishing, & I on the one I am beginning, each day, & in the evening I go over to dine with him. It has been a very wonderful experience.[53]

The luncheon to which Dawson alludes here was no casual affair. The Ambassador had been "most anxious" not only to meet Conrad, but to bring him together once more with F. N. Doubleday, Page's partner in publishing. Just two months earlier, on 12 April, Conrad had written to Galsworthy that "Doubleday was talking to me about getting a license from my other publishers for a uniform set of my books . . . , but he talked vaguely."[54] Obviously matters could not

53. Entire letter in Part Two (No. 69). Original in Houghton Library, Harvard.
54. Letter in Jean-Aubry, *LL*, II, 145.

profitably remain thus. Page's first move was to invite the Conrads to dinner on 2 June, but Conrad declined. Whatever further tactics Page may have tried, he eventually wrote a note to his fellow Southerner, Dawson, requesting that somehow he "induce" Conrad to come to luncheon on 28 May.[55] One cannot always make out the shadowy line between matter and art in Dawson's recollections, for facts sometimes give way to impressions, but in later years he remembered his mission to capture Conrad as follows:

> by inducing him to accept a certain luncheon invitation in London which he had temperamentally declined in writing and in no uncertain terms,[56] I, armed with a special mandate from Ambassador Walter Hines Page who regarded me as the only man with enough influence on him to make him reconsider, succeeded after two other informal ambassadors had only managed to make matters worse. Throughout an entire night the battle raged, beginning between nine and ten o'clock with a terrific explosion in Conrad's study, and continuing with the same broken but by brief interludes when I fled to Jessie's sitting-room for secret consultations (she being on my side), after which there would be yet more of the same battle with multifold intensity, continued until between seven and eight next morning when, both of us being at the uttermost limits of exhaustion, but I showing just a Troy Weight pennyworth of endurance more than he, Conrad capitulated and we faded away to bed. Some days later, I triumphantly convoyed Mr. and Mrs. Joseph Conrad to London, where over a particularly brilliant luncheon at the Embassy the personal contact was established assuring the signature of an important literary agreement on which Conrad's entire material future turned.[57]

Dawson was not the man to underplay an account of his role. The dragons he slew were always big ones. On the other hand it is true that Walter Hines Page was very much a man of literary interests.[58]

55. Page to Dawson, letter of 16 May 1914 (No. 65).
56. In a letter of 25 March 1954 to Schwab, Dawson speaks of the luncheon as "a preliminary for patching up a virtual rupture between Conrad and Mr Doubleday which had sidetracked negotiations . . ." (from Dawson's carbon copy).
57. From a Dawson typescript entitled "A Joseph Conrad Reminiscence," pp. 3–4.
58. Not only was he himself a sometime novelist (*The Southerner* [1909]), but, in succession, he had been editor of the St. Joseph (Missouri) *Gazette*, and the

The entertaining he most enjoyed as Ambassador was his private entertaining of men and women of letters. And, as Retinger observes, Page eventually became one of those Americans who made the pilgrimage down to Capel House.[59]

As for the relationship between Conrad and Doubleday, which later became quite warm,[60] it is significant that in July, a couple of months following the Embassy luncheon, Conrad was able to refer to Doubleday as "(in America), my future publisher."[61] At least Doubleday, that early, was no longer talking "vaguely."[62] But the

---

Forum, Atlantic Monthly, and *World's Work;* and in 1899 he had become a partner of Doubleday, Page & Company. He was the sort of publisher, furthermore, who held that a book of "sterling quality—a real book—ought never to have the imprint of a publisher who is not really a sharer of its fortunes, a true partner with the author. For only with such a book can he do his best" (*A Publisher's Confession* [New York, 1905], p. 48). See "Walter Hines Page" in Supplement No. 1 of *Library of Southern Literature,* ed. Edwin Anderson Alderman, Charles Alphonso Smith, and John Calvin Metcalf (Atlanta, 1923), pp. 425–454.

59. *Conrad and His Contemporaries* (New York, 1943), p. 96.
60. See F. N. Doubleday, "Joseph Conrad as a Friend," *World Today* (London), LII (1928), 145–147.
61. Conrad to Curle, letter in *Conrad to a Friend,* ed. Richard Curle (London, 1928), p. 8.
62. So far as I have been able to determine via correspondence, the records of Doubleday & Co. preserve nothing of the episode. Deposited at the New York Public Library, however, are some relevant papers of the Macmillan Co. On 28 March 1914 Conrad wrote to George P. Brett of Macmillan that his connection with Doubleday, Page & Co. was "an old one. It has been dormant for a few years but of late it has been renewed." On 17 July, about seven weeks after the luncheon, Doubleday himself wrote to Brett, asking particularly to buy *Almayer's Folly.* On 22 July, nevertheless, Conrad wrote glumly to Curle that he had been talking to Pinker about copyrights of his books: "This is the psychological moment when, he thinks, we ought to get hold of all the copyrights and work them ourselves to the best advantage according to a plan he has in his head"; but he added, "Unfortunately I haven't the money, and neither has he, and this is a business one can't go to a cold capitalist with . . ." (*Conrad to a Friend,* pp. 28–29). A month later, on 25 August, a Macmillan memorandum noted that the *Almayer's Folly* transaction had been successfully completed.

Conrad's own most extended commentary on the matter may be that in a letter to John Quinn of 10 August 1916 (transcript in the John Quinn Collection, Vol. I, New York Public Library). Peeved by recent actions of Doubleday, Page & Co., Conrad wrote that

the idea of the Collected Edition is not D. P. & Co.'s idea at all. P[inker]. and I planned it long before we got into touch with Mr. Doubleday in 1913. P. went to work, and by the display of perseverance and diplomacy brought my various publishers (and some very hostile, too) to accept it; *and without it's costing me a penny.* No mean feat, I assure you, for trade jealousy came into play at every turn, very fierce indeed. However, by infinite patience we got them all soothed at last.

It was then that Mr. Doubleday came to London and made overtures to me. Pinker advised me strongly to accept them (there were others at the same details of the luncheon episode remain obscure.

On 10 May 1914, at Duchess Street, Dawson had finished a novel called *The True Dimension* (published in 1916). When reading Dawson's previous manuscript, the fantastic affair about the green moustache, Conrad had suggested that it might "be rather good for you to throw your next fiction into the autobiographical form, which gives certain facilities and also imposes certain restraints."[63] Whether or not Dawson proceeded at once to strive for the kind of control that Conrad indicated, he did narrate *The True Dimension* largely in the first person, and he did build the events of the book on his experiences during the Spanish-American War, when he had sailed as purser on the *Sam Handford*. In fact, Dawson's ports and ships in the story are fairly firmly anchored to actual circumstances, with the partial result that the story is the most Conradian work he ever produced. He spoiled it all, however, by trying to imbue his material with a significant theme. The "true" dimension of the title turns out to be the Fourth Dimension of psychism.

The next work he turned to, now that he was settled in Kent, was "The Rock." He had planned this novel several years earlier, during the Roosevelt expedition to British East Africa. It was to remain incomplete, however, until January, 1922, at which time Dawson said that he had tarried so long because of his sense of the "overwhelming greatness in *Heart of Darkness.* . . ."[64] The plot of "The Rock" would remind no one of Marlow's trip up the Congo, and yet its main point sounds familiar enough: "when the mask of civilisation is stripped off, men and women are shown as they are."[65]

Conrad, meanwhile, was still hard at work on *Victory*. Not that the two men worked all the time. Some of their evenings were spent in talk, as were those afternoons "when we happened to have finished our day's work by tea-time."[66] According to Dawson,

time). Among other things he pointed out to me that it was an excellent firm to take in hand eventually the Collected Edition in the U.S. But, he said (his textual words), "we won't talk about it to him yet. We must see first how your next two books go." The books went well. We opened the matter to D.P. & Co.—and then the war broke out.

63. Conrad to Dawson, 24 October 1913 (No. 53).
64. From p. 3 of the introductory matter to the typescript of "Border-lines" in the Dawson Collection. ("Border-lines" was a variant title of "The Rock.")
65. "Border-lines," p. 45.
66. Letter of 30 January 1933 (No. 118), Dawson to David McCord, from Dawson's copy at Duke.

We made none of the conventional restrictions about "not talking of our work." Quite the contrary, we kept our liberty of thought to talk about everything which passed through our minds. I was one of the extremely few people to whom Conrad ever talked of his work while engaged on it, and he would even read to me passages from his unpublished manuscripts. . . .

Looking back much later, Dawson called this springtime in Kent "the happiest period in my life. . . ."[67]

One of the best days was a Sunday when Ellen Glasgow came down to Capel House. Although a native of Richmond, Virginia, Miss Glasgow as a girl had made her debut at a St. Cecilia's Ball, so she knew a little about Dawson's Charleston milieu. As a matter of fact she and Dawson had not only been acquainted for a good many years, but they also had certain things in common. Most strikingly, both had concerned themselves with interpreting Southern social history in fiction—though Miss Glasgow, with a number of solid books behind her, had far outdistanced Dawson as a literary artist.

In 1914 her brother Arthur, "who had made a brilliant reputation as an engineer," was living with his wife in Berkeley Square in a "charming house . . . with window boxes of running pink geraniums."[68] Miss Glasgow herself was staying at the Hotel Curzon nearby. Thus she was also conveniently close to the ambassadorial residence of Walter Hines Page. Page was a man whom she had regarded as one of her "close friends ever since he had discovered *The Descendant* [1902] . . . ."[69]

Social contacts were made easy for Miss Glasgow not only by her brother and the Ambassador, but also by her travelling companion, Louise Collier Willcox, who had lived in England for a time. Mrs. Willcox, of course, was more than a mere social asset. According to Miss Glasgow, she was "a brilliant woman who wrote able criticism."[70] She had been an editorial writer for *Harper's Weekly* and *Harper's Bazaar*, a member of the editorial staff of the *North American Review*, and a reader for the Macmillan Company, and at the

67. "At the Crossroads" (MS from the Ralph Foster Museum, School of the Ozarks), p. 3.
68. *The Woman Within* (New York, 1954), pp. 117, 207.
69. *Woman Within*, p. 207.
70. *Woman Within*, p. 204.

moment she was a reader for E. P. Dutton & Company. Unfortunately, however, wherever she went she "was addressed, respectfully, as 'Ella Wheeler Wilcox.' "[71] This was the cause for some mild distress. Ella Wheeler Wilcox was the current vexation of the literary intelligentsia, a Wisconsin woman who was very busy churning out an impossible series of popular books—*Poems of Passion* (1883), *Poems of Pleasure* (1888), *Poems of Progress* (1909), *Poems of Problems* (1914), etc. At a literary luncheon given by Ellen Glasgow, when Dawson was placed next to Louise Collier Willcox, he made the usual mistake of confusing Willcox with Wilcox. Miss Glasgow quoted her friend's lament: "If only . . . I might enjoy Ella Wheeler's international reputation, without being held responsible for her verse!"[72] But there was poetic justice in the case of Dawson's error. Mrs. Willcox thought *he* was Coningsby Dawson, the author of a recent and rather torrid best-seller called *The Garden without Walls*.

Much later Miss Glasgow recorded in her autobiography how she and Mrs. Willcox went "everywhere in England" that summer. Of course she remembered vividly that "everywhere" included Capel House, but she neglected to mention that her visit was made possible by Warrington Dawson. Having just described a successful call upon Thomas Hardy, she went on to record that

> Another perfect day was the one we spent with Joseph Conrad and his family at Capel House in Kent, where they were then living. Although Conrad's work, with the exception of *Heart of Darkness*, has not, in my judgment, lasted so well, at the time of my visit to him I was familiar with every book, and with almost every line, he had written. And I found the man very attractive, with a lovable personality, capricious and fascinating. His dark, animated face, with the prominent cheekbones and the narrow chin, held a shy woodland charm of its own. . . .
>
> From the first instant of meeting, I felt we were friends, and I was gratified when he told Louise Willcox that he thought I was doing better work than any other American woman novelist.[73]

71. *Woman Within*, p. 204.
72. *Woman Within*, pp. 204–205.
73. *Woman Within*, pp. 200–201.

This last was a silky bit of flattery. Conrad could not have named many American woman novelists.

Another sign that Conrad was in good form that day is the fact that he let Dawson record the visit with his camera. The two principals posed together rather formally on Conrad's "quarter-deck," the gravelled place in front of the house. Miss Glasgow was prim, well-bedecked, and self-contained, and Conrad melancholy and rather rumpled, but every inch a gentleman. Probably the picture which caught this moment is the best of the lot, for its subject is the *raison d'être* of the occasion.[74] Others, however, show Conrad slumped at ease in a canvas deck chair, in the shade of a little sumac tree; Jessie, amiable and ample, her two canes close at hand, by the tea things over which she has just presided; and Borys with knickers and thick glasses, not "beautiful, poor boy," as Conrad said, but "a good fellow."[75] Most touching of all is a picture of the Conrads' little "sprite" John, dressed for the occasion in a white sailor suit and standing in the tall grass out beyond the hedge (but within calling distance of the old folks), leaning against a tree with young Robin Douglas. The Conrad biographers are rather quiet on the subject of Robin Douglas, though Robin himself explained later— and with marvellous objectivity—that his father, Norman Douglas, had a "knack of getting on with all manner of people [which] was the means by which Conrad was induced to help in the task of bringing me up, during the years when my father was travelling in far-away places." Robin "spent many years in . . . [Conrad's] happy household, almost a member of the family."[76] Thus he was there on the day when the lady novelist from America came down into Kent to see Conrad.

Immediately after he returned to London, Dawson wrote a review of Richard Curle's *Joseph Conrad: A Study*. Curle was one of the most ardent of Capel pilgrims by this time, and Conrad, it is generally acknowledged, thought highly of his work. Dawson's review, however, datelined 24 June and printed in both the Boston *Evening*

74. It is reproduced in the present volume as illustration No. 10.
75. Conrad to William Rothenstein, letter of 2 August 1913 in the Houghton Library, Harvard.
76. "Norman Douglas," *Cornhill Magazine*, CLXVIII (1955), 153. At any rate, to quote Jessie Conrad, Robin "used to make his holiday home with us" (*Joseph Conrad and His Circle*, 2nd ed. [Port Washington, N.Y., 1964], p. 100.

Transcript (3 July) and the Charleston *Sunday News* (5 July), is headlined in the latter paper with a blunt "Mr Dawson Exposes Errors in New Book about Conrad."[77] The subtitle is scarcely more kind: "Richard Curle's Study of Noted Author Not Without Value, But Some of His Generalizations Are Grotesquely Mistaken." In the article itself, though he also says some kind things about Curle's view of Conrad, Dawson asks ironically, "What . . . is this alleged sardonic and pessimistic philosophy of futility, built up on a sympathetic warmth for beautiful lines [i.e., lives], and on ideas of duty, sincerity, courage, compassion, honor and endurance?" Furthermore, Dawson denounces Curle's "tendency to exclude Conrad from English literature, although he is now generally accepted as one of its greatest masters." Much has been said of Conrad's approval of Curle's book, yet Dawson claimed that his own critique refuted those passages by Curle "which Conrad resented particularly as 'throwing him out of English litera[t]ure' as Conrad himself expressed it to me."[78]

Correctly or not, the review came to seem especially important to Dawson. For some reason he felt that Curle held it against him. Curle probably would have resented a bad review less, however, if he ever saw it—and it was only one of several—than he would a young rival for Conrad's favor. Curle felt increasingly possessive about Conrad, and at worst was rather predatory about the man he seemed to venerate.[79] Still, he had little to fear from Dawson. Dawson's position was strong enough to begin with, but it was to become much less enviable with the passing of the years, so much less enviable that finally he felt a need to explain why he played no role in the things that men wrote about Conrad. Somehow he hit upon Curle as the chief censor and villain. But even if Curle considered the possibility of rivalry in the person of the South Carolinian from Versailles, Dawson's disappearance from the scene became so complete that forty years after Conrad's death Curle could reminisce, with complete equanimity, "I often heard the

77. P. 23. The Bostonian headline is more discreet: "Justice for Joseph Conrad" (p. 12).
78. From a Dawson note dated 24 May 1959.
79. Curle returned from Oswalds to London on the day that Conrad died and turned out an article on Conrad's last hours which was printed the very next day in the *Daily Mail*.

name of Warrington Dawson [in Conrad's home] and always, within my very vague memory, pleasantly spoken," but "I never met him."[80]

Between the time Dawson wrote his Curle review and the time it was published, the Archduke Francis Ferdinand and his wife were shot by a young Serbian student in Sarajevo, the capital of Slavic Bosnia. The event seemed remote in every way to Conrad, so he and his family proceeded to carry out the plans they had made to visit Poland. On 25 July the Joseph Conrads and the Joseph Retingers left Harwich for Hamburg, then pushed on toward the "academical town of Cracow," where Conrad had attended school just forty years before.[81] Three days after their departure on this sentimental journey, Austria-Hungary declared war on Serbia. Then on 12 August, less than three weeks after they had left, a notice released to the United States diplomatic and consular offices in Europe identified Mr. Warrington Dawson as a representative of the United Press "in Europe as a war correspondent."

80. Curle to Randall, 11 August 1964. The simplest explanation of Dawson's absence from later discussions of Conrad is that he figured so slightly in earlier discussions, and later scholars have had nothing to build on. The most remarkable omission of Dawson is that of Jean-Aubry, who knew of Dawson and printed letters referring to him, yet neglected to identify him either in his two-volume *Joseph Conrad: Life and Letters* or in his *Lettres Françaises* (Paris, 1930).
81. Jean-Aubry, *LL*, II, 155.

6

The War Years (1914-1918)

Early in 1913 Dawson had contracted with his old syndicate, the United Press, to become a war correspondent whenever hostilities began.[1] Once the time came, though, journalistic opportunities seemed too restricted to him, and censorship frustrating. At least this was the way he later spoke of the situation. At the time he confided to his friend Bernhard Trappschuh that "the conditions were hard enough, but the dishonesty of the methods used by other journalists made even an effort at competition impossible."[2] Whatever the reasons, the upshot was that Dawson decided to break away from the syndicate once more, and devote himself mainly to gathering materials for a history of the war. Soon again, however, his energies were deflected, and the history was never written.

For one thing, according to his fragmentary memoirs, he served for a while as a counterespionage agent. Though Dawson's recollections can be relied on not to underdramatize his various roles, it appears that one day in Paris he was approached for help by Georges Ladoux, at that time in charge of telegraphic censorship, a sorter of telegrams in clothes baskets, but eventually the head of French intelligence and the French counterespionage service, the man who ordered the arrest of Mata Hari.[3] More pertinent here, Dawson later reminisced that in September, 1914, just before the Battle of the Marne, Ladoux cracked a code being used by German spies in England. To take immediate action and bypass sluggish channels of

1. Charles A. Reopell, "A Man of Three Careers," in the unprinted collection called "A Man and His Work," p. 58, in the Ralph Foster Museum, The School of the Ozarks.
2. Letter of 7 January 1915, in Bernard Lytton-Bernard Collection, Duke.
3. See Jean Bancaud, "Une Figure de l'Espionnage: Le Commandant Ladoux," *Revue Mondiale* (Paris, 1933), pp. 30–31, and Georges Ladoux, *Marthe Richard the Skylark: The Foremost Woman Spy of France*, ed. and trans. Warrington Dawson (London, 1932), esp. p. 39.

British protocol, he presumably called on Dawson. Dawson's assignment was to write his friend Lord Plymouth an urgent secret message which was to be rushed to British Intelligence. In *Mes Souvenirs* (*Contre-espionnage*) (Paris, 1937) Ladoux rather strangely attributed this and other adventures to an American aviator identified as *l'agent R. . . .*[4] According to Ladoux's account, Lord Plymouth proceeded at once to transmit R . . .'s message to "M. F[rederick]. E[dwin]. Smith (ultérieurement Lord Berkenhead), chef du Bureau de Presse britannique. . . ." The question is, then, was agent R . . . really Dawson?

Dawson later told also of a journey which he made in September to deliver a special message to "The Tiger," Georges Clemenceau, at the provisional capital in Bordeaux. The actuality of this interview was confirmed by Ladoux himself in a letter to Dawson printed in 1932.[5]

More striking still were the events which Dawson said occurred in Switzerland during the following month. On a night train to Zurich he was presumably given restricted enemy information by a pro-German Swiss, then invited to the German sector to investigate conditions for himself, in hopes that he could be lured into *verboten* territory. Dawson avoided any such trap, but claimed later that the announcement of his death had already been released, apparently because the enemy was sure that he would come and be shot by sentinels.[6]

What is one to make of all this? Some of the secrets which R . . . learned were learned by Dawson and scribbled in his notebook in October, 1914, and yet surely there is cause to doubt part of what

---

4. *Mes Souvenirs*, pp. 13–14. See also Marguerite Steedman, "Charleston's 'Secret Agent R—' The Incredible Life of Warrington Dawson," Charleston *News and Courier*, 7 September 1958, p. 1-C; 14 September, p. 1-C; and 21 September, p. 1-C.

5. *Marthe Richard*, p. 246.

6. In the *Souvenirs* of Ladoux (p. 24) one finds the name of the ostensible villain and a description:

> Rudolph Laemmel, Autrichien de naissance, naturalisé suisse, docteur ès sciences et professeur de chimie, qui s'attribue le faux titre de Direktor du Reform Gymnasium de Zurich où il a été attaché comme professeur, mais où il ne l'est plus depuis longtemps. Ce Rudolf [*sic*] Laemmel est considéré de source certaine comme un des chefs de l'espionnage allemand en Suisse.

In the *Vorwort* to Laemmel's own *Reformation der Nationalen Erziehung* (Zurich, 1910) he is described as "Gründer und Direktor des Züricher Reform-Gymnasiums." The *Neue Schweizer Biographie* (Basel, 1938) lists him as *Lehrer* at the Reform Gymnasium from 1902 to 1914 (p. 303).

Dawson later recalled. As time passed, perhaps he took the black-and-white facts of the case, enlarged them, and colored them. Eventually, perhaps, it was no longer so important what the bare facts themselves might have been. His touched-up picture of the past may have become, then, in a very real sense, more meaningful than the past itself. In any case, it was his picture that he lived by.

The most important of the incidents which Dawson later reported is one he assigned to a misty October afternoon when he had been persuaded to go to a little roadway *estaminet* among the hills outside Zurich. Here the same pro-German Swiss had him served a glass of coffee topped with "evil-looking greenish froth."[7] Dawson was clever enough merely to pretend to drink the brew, he said, but he made the mistake of touching it with his lips before pouring it out on the ground. That night he fell into a "raging fever" with "nightmare visions."[8] Meanwhile his Swiss acquaintance moved out of the rooms where he was staying, leaving behind in his laboratory two freshly cleaned test tubes. The whole affair was too melodramatic to be put into fiction, Dawson admitted, and yet he maintained to the end of his days that it happened just as he told it.[9] Whether or not it was all true, the poisoning story was the explanation he gave for his subsequent long paralysis. The doctor he saw back in Paris on 3 November said that his trouble was "nervous exhaustion,"[10] but for the rest of his life Dawson claimed that during World War I he had suffered bacterial poisoning at the hands of German agents. Though sensitive about talking on the subject, he confided to intimates that his poisoning in October, 1914, had led to rhizomelic spondylosis.[11]

7. From an unpublished Dawson memoir, "Think It Not Strange," p. 61.
8. "Think It Not Strange," p. 64.
9. The problem is to determine the boundaries of authenticity in Dawson's accounts —quite apart from how hard he tried to keep within them. It is surely plausible that he was at least watched closely, even if his connection with Ladoux was unknown to the enemy. Not long after the period in question Nicholas Everitt wrote that "The stunt . . . most in favour with the Intelligence Departments of all nations is journalism; thus it has been worked threadbare. Every foreign newspaper man on the Continent in recent years has been suspected, marked, and watched from the start, simply because he is what he is and for no other reason" (*British Secret Service During the Great War* [London, 1920], p. 170).
10. "Think It Not Strange," pp. 85–86.
11. This is a progressive disease, however, sometimes arrested but never reversed. Had Dawson been afflicted by it so as to prevent walking, he never would have walked again—as he did (interview with Dr. John M. Rhoads, Duke University Hospital, 20 October 1965).

That same October, with Mrs. Alexander Montgomery Thackara, wife of the American Consul-General in Paris, Dawson managed to found the Urgent Fund for Serbian Wounded.[12] Plagued now with erratic but failing health, he managed also to turn out a series of newspaper articles called "France in War-Time."

Conrad, meanwhile, was sufficiently recovered from the trials of his Polish trip to begin writing "Poland Revisited," and Jessie, little dreaming how vastly Dawson's life had changed, wrote on 14 December to say that she looked forward to telling him all about the Conrads' "wierd experiences."

In January, 1915, Dawson went up into Northern France to aid a boyhood friend from Charleston, Lucien Memminger, who was facing a heavy barrage of problems as United States Consul in Rouen. Engaged as a "Special Clerk," Dawson set to work helping Memminger with the task of "straightening out the files of the German prisoners of war placed under the care of the United States in the Rouen area."[13] This was Dawson's first taste of official work. After only a few weeks, however—and about five months after his Swiss adventure—he awoke one morning unable to move his legs or to see more than a dense white mist before his eyes. His stint as Special Clerk was over.

In retrospect Dawson's condition in early 1915 appears to be explicable not only in terms of his 1914 "poisoning," but also, and more strikingly, in terms of his prolonged hospital stay back in 1897. From his youth to his very old age, in fact, it appears that Dawson reacted to unmanageable situations—and never knew why—with an invalidism which served to shelter his unusually tender ego. As a child he had been safeguarded like a cherub in a glass case, but as he grew older that early kind of shelter was impossible to maintain, and, once shattered, impossible to replace. Invalidism was a partial answer. What might have been merely a passing, self-protective gesture in another man (a headache to avoid an interview) became so exaggerated in Dawson that at last it determined the very structure of his life. Despite intelligence and ability, his pride was so great and his goals so high that there was often something that he had to repress or avoid. There had been scholastic difficulties at school (which would have seemed tragic both to him and his mother had

12. He and Mrs. Thackara were decorated by King Peter with the order of the Serbian Red Cross.
13. "Think It Not Strange," p. 87.

they not been able to rationalize them); there had been disappointments in his career (though Mrs. Dawson did not live to realize it,
her son was never a successful novelist nor even a very well-known
journalist, a fact which menaced both his self-esteem and his economic success); and if a good many stray clues may be totalled to
make an hypothesis, there had been chronic erotic frustration, quite
probably the result of repressed inversion. Dawson's plight on this
last score may have been made more bearable by a rather underpowered libido, but this would have been cold comfort in the long
run, for he carried his problems along with him into advanced old
age. More immediately, in the midst of World War I, there was the
utterly dismal prospect of subjecting himself to military discipline.
Aside from physical discomfort or even pain, which he could meet
on his own terms, the rigor and discipline of army life, with its inevitable, vulgar collectivism, would have been particular hell for
Dawson. In a later autobiographical sketch he provides the key to
what may be considered his solution to this last problem: The trip
to Switzerland in the fall of 1914 made him "unfitted for military
service."[14] Despite its suspiciously obscure origins, Dawson's disability provided him at least partial escape.[15]

The price he paid—the extremity of his physical affliction—is the
best clue we have to the intensity of his inner conflicts. Dawson described quite clearly but never understood the symptoms of hysterical blindness. Almost equally drastic were his motor disturbances,
most notably the paralysis of his legs, and eventually even the
"freezing" of his back.[16] (In his youth the physicians of St. Luke's

14. From an undated autobiographical sketch.
15. That Dawson was escaping from something is more clear than what that something was. He himself may not have known. To Lady Phyllis he wrote on 18 December
1915: "I must confess I should be discouraged with the way this illness is lasting, *if*
[italics added] it weren't for the work I continue to do. . . . I have never found pain
to interfere with my thinking, & *often it has rendered me a service* [italics added] by
cutting me off from uninteresting & superficial people."
16. Bernard Bernard, in his physical culture magazine called *Health & Vim* (March,
1916, p. 69), gives an interesting insight into Dawson's own view at the time of his
health breakdown. There is nothing here of coffee topped with green froth. Instead,
with Dawson as his source, Bernard attributes his friend's condition to fatigue complicated by a fall from a horse. Dawson had been as frank as he could with Bernard:
"You see, I am ashamed of my inactivity at such a time, & feel that unless some
reason for it were made clear, the effect upon your readers would be bad" (letter
of 12 January 1916 in Lytton-Bernard Collection; see also No. 79, n. 1). Dawson,
after all, was Vice President of the *Health & Vim* Association of Honour! On 26
January 1916 Dawson wrote of the same riding incident to Mrs. J. Smith Brockenbrough: "My doctor thinks that while exposure & overwork are directly responsible,

in New York had been successful in using hypnosis to relieve him from paralysis.)[17] After 1915 he suffered periodically from aphonia. Mysterious skin troubles began in 1916 and plagued him to the end. Relevant also are some of the psychic phenomena which he claimed to experience, though the latter he himself would not have regarded negatively. Of all his symptoms, in fact, the psychism and paralysis were perhaps the most conducive to mental composure, at once the means of escape and, in different ways, the means of enhancing his self-esteem. The psychism was the more private of the two phenomena. For one thing, he could think of it as an inheritance from his mother, and therefore as a sort of link between them. For another, it was a fairly sure means of setting himself apart from most other people. The paralysis was from the outset the more public matter, its authenticity reinforced for himself as well as others by various kinds of treatment over an extended period. In fact, the desuetude of his back—his father, he held, had been shot in the back, and his mother's back had been injured by that fall from the buggy —the desuetude of his back became in time a symbol of fortitude under martyrdom, a symbol which could not be overlooked by even the most casual caller.

But this is looking ahead in Dawson's story. After he was stricken with lameness and temporary blindness in the early part of 1915, his health improved somewhat, and, back in Paris, he put his wide knowledge of France at the informal service of the new American Ambassador in Paris, the Ohioan William Graves Sharp. Between 1915 and 1918, dependent on his wits, a brace, and a cane (or sometimes a couple of crutches), Dawson undertook numerous missions to the front, gathering confidential news for Sharp and public news for the *News and Courier* and the Boston *Evening Transcript*.

Even in circumstances like these, Dawson was unwilling to let his fiction slide. In fact, he somehow found the time to progress fairly well on what was to prove his best novel, *The Gift of Paul Clermont* (1921). In 1916, in the magazine *Health & Vim*, Bernard Bernard

---

the secret to my present neuritis & like illnesses of recent years lies in my back, an injury long ago by a fall from a horse. *I like to believe that is true*" (Powell Collection, Alderman Library, University of Virginia; italics added).

It is of interest and perhaps significance that in Dawson's early novel called *The Scourge* (1908) the male character who best represents the old, genteel aristocracy, now enduring bad times, suffers an apoplectic stroke, injures his spine on a chair in falling, and consequently suffers paralysis of the legs.

17. When his treatment began, he was unable to walk without a cane.

printed excerpts from *The Pyramid,* Dawson's old, autobiographical "Novel of George," which Conrad had long since read and approved. Furthermore, 1916 was the year of Dawson's *True Dimension.* Jessie wrote to tell him that the story was being well reviewed in the *New Statesman.*[18]

Meantime Conrad's nerves were beginning to fray again. He had managed to get *Victory* out in 1915, and young Borys, impatient to be in service, was in the army rather than complaining at home, but Conrad fretted and strained. He wrote to Dawson on 12 February 1916, "my mentality seems to have gone to pieces. I can do nothing. . . ." Matters were to grow still worse for him in May, however, when the indispensable Arthur Marwood, the "Wise Man of the Age," joined the ages.

At least Borys was lucky enough to see Dawson fairly frequently in Paris, thanks in part to a lady. At a time when aviation was young the beautiful journalist-aviatrix Jane Anderson Taylor (known as "the American flying girl") had gone down to Capel House, played Jessie's piano, and sung songs of the cotton fields far away. Altogether, she had succeeded very well in arousing the interest of Conrad *père.*[19] Now, over in France, she proved to have the happy knack of acquiring military passes for Conrad *fils.* Though Borys never learned Jane's secret, he was grateful and delighted. Sometimes when he saw Dawson in Paris it was with his parents' friend Retinger.[20] Sometimes he saw Hueffer, too, though never with Dawson. Hueffer was very kind to Borys during the war, despite his quarrel with Conrad and despite the fact that Borys himself was put off by Hueffer's apparently professional bohemianism. Warrington Dawson did not put him off. Dawson he found pleasant and charming.

During the war Dawson renewed his ties also with the Roose-

18. In July the *Atlantic Monthly* printed his non-fictional account of a train trip from Rouen to Paris, "Refugee: The Experience of a War Correspondent," CXVIII (1916), 131–137; and that December the same magazine published his "Man on the Altar: An Experience in Petrograd," pp. 777–786.

19. In any thorough study of Conrad's complex attitudes toward Americans one would certainly have to include this young lady. In *Joseph Conrad and His Circle,* 2nd ed. (Port Washington, N.Y., 1964), pp. 206–208, Jessie half tells and half withholds the story of the friction Jane caused at Capel. See Robin Douglas, "My Boyhood with Conrad," *Cornhill Magazine,* LXVI (1929), 20-28, and Jocelyn Baines, *Joseph Conrad: A Critical Biography* (London, 1960), p. 408.

20. Interview with Borys Conrad, 21 November 1964. Retinger, not quite by the way, also knew Jane. After the war, in his words, she "caused a certain estrangement between [Joseph] Conrad and myself" (*Conrad and His Contemporaries* [New York, 1943], p. 98).

velts. It pleased him in later years to be able to say that he had repeatedly been the guest of Lieutenant Colonel Theodore Roosevelt, Jr., and Captain Archibald Roosevelt, and the latter still recalls the day when "Warry" introduced him with pride to Joseph Jacques Césaire Joffre, Marshal of France.[21] Joffre was French Commander in Chief until 1916, Chairman of the Allied War Council from 1916 to 1918—and he was also Dawson's friend.

Conrad and Jessie naturally had constant cause to be fretful. The guns used for practice firing "at Dover, in Sheerness, and in the estuary of the Thames" shook the very earth that Capel House stood on, making its windowpanes shudder.[22] Troops passed continually down their road. Then in the autumn of 1916 Borys was gassed and shell-shocked during the advance of the Second Army on the Menin-Cambrai road.

Perhaps in response to the general disruptive violence of the war, Conrad made more room in his life for action than there had been for many years. As Baines puts it, he entered into "a scheme, sponsored by the Admiralty, to visit certain British ports and observe the various naval activities. Thus in September he went off to Lowestoft and joined the minesweeper *Brigadier* on one of her patrols."[23] (On 30 October he was already finishing a timely short story on submarine warfare, "The Tale.") He went up in a plane from the Royal Naval Air Station at Yarmouth. In November he even took a brief turn on deck again. He took a post on board the seventy-year-old brigantine *Ready*, hunting for U-boats in the North Sea.[24] In his honor the *Ready* sailed under the wartime alias of *Freya*, and Conrad, after a good many years, stood again sometimes at the wheel. But he was pushing his luck by this time, and had to be put ashore, sick, at Bridlington.[25]

In the following January Jessie "snatched the fearful joy" of having Borys home for eight days. The strain then, said Conrad, was

21. Interview, 9 September 1964. Ambassador Sharp said that Dawson provided liaison "of utmost value" between himself and Joffre (*The War Memoirs of William Graves Sharp*, ed. Dawson [London, 1931], p. 279).

22. Jessie Conrad, *Joseph Conrad as I Knew Him* (Garden City, N.Y., 1926), p. 91.

23. *Joseph Conrad*, p. 408.

24. The episode is recorded by J. G. Sutherland, *At Sea with Joseph Conrad* (Boston, 1922).

25. Jessie Conrad, "Joseph Conrad's War Service," *The Blue Peter*, XI (1931), 255.

"telling," and when the United States entered the war in April, he could speak only with quiet bitterness.[26] It was a "piece of luck," he wrote Dawson, a strange event to issue from the American "mist of words[,] the years of reserve so impartial (officially) as to be almost dreadful. . . ."

In that same month the French Ministry of War granted Dawson permission to follow certain courses at the St. Cyr Military Academy. Then on 17 September he became attached to the United States Embassy as a sort of confidential assistant to Ambassador Sharp. At last his talents had a suitable outlet. Sharp in his *Memoirs* described Dawson as "a very capable member of the staff."[27] Not only did Dawson prove to be a valuable assistant, but he also founded and became chief of an Embassy press bureau. Though by this time a permanent cripple, he still was able to get about with his brace and cane, and even to go on a number of war missions, sometimes with Sharp. He was under bombardment at Verdun, Reims, Pont à Mousson, Nancy, Baccarat, Lunéville, Dunkirk, Bailleul, Lunel, Poperinghe, the Valley of the Serre, and Saint-Quentin, as well as in Paris itself.[28] Later he recalled in particular the hours immediately following the German evacuation of Saint-Quentin, when "the ruins were still smoking from the fires started by the retiring enemy."[29] This was 7 October 1918. It was his "last trip under fire, and the last walk of any length which my legs have ever allowed me to take. . . ."[30]

Whatever Dawson lacked, it was not moral strength. He clung doughtily to his Embassy post, and when the new Ambassador, Hugh C. Wallace, took over after the war, in the fall of 1919, he acknowledged Dawson's previous two years of semi-official service by formalizing his position. Wallace had the Department of State appoint Dawson as Special Assistant to the Ambassador. Eventually Dawson acquired a staff of some seven to nine stenographers, typists, and translators, and, even when confined to his couch at home, he managed to carry on. It was with justifiable pride, then—and greater brevity than usual—that forty years later he could write: "I . . .

26. Conrad to Dawson, 22 April 1917 (No. 84).
27. *Memoirs*, p. 34.
28. Dawson, *Paul Clermont's Story and My Own Followed by The Gift of Paul Clermont* (Chicago, 1928), p. xxvii.
29. "Think It Not Strange," p. 134.
30. *Paul Clermont's Story and My Own*, p. xxx. Sharp makes much of this trip in his *War Memoirs*.

served under Ambassadors Wallace, Herrick, Edge, Straus, Bullitt, in the Administrations of Presidents Wilson, Harding, Coolidge, Hoover, and Franklin D. Roosevelt."[31] It was a record which any man could be proud of, especially since he had done the job so well.

From a literary standpoint the friendship of Dawson and Conrad produced little of significance during the war. Dawson sent Jessie a copy of his mother's *Diary*, and the Conrads sent him both *Victory* and *The Shadow-Line*. Dawson also planned for the *Bookman* a series of articles which were apparently to treat, at least in part, the subject of Conrad. News of the articles made Conrad "very pleased," according to Jessie, but Conrad himself failed to write, leaving Jessie to explain that "Since the war poor Conrad has seemed quite unable to write letters. . . ." She added kindly, "He knows that you th[o]roughly understand him,"[32] but the articles never appeared.

The most interesting insights of the period come from letters touching on Dawson's *True Dimension* and Conrad's *Arrow of Gold*. Conrad begins a letter of 22 April 1917 with a compliment for *The True Dimension*: The book is built upon "une belle idée." Immediately, however, he adds the reservation that "your metaphysical connections with the subject-matter of the F[ourth]. D[imension]. are not graspable to *my* mind."[33] One might at first suppose that the occult Fourth Dimension itself and not Dawson's "connections" would puzzle a nature such as Conrad's, but the fact is that Conrad himself had once regarded the Fourth Dimension as a topic suitable for fiction. *The Inheritors*, an experimental *roman à clef* of 1901, had been mainly the work of Ford Madox Hueffer, and yet the name of Conrad, too, was affixed to the title page, and the "inheritors" of the story were emphatically Fourth Dimensionists. They were "a race clear-sighted, eminently practical, incredible; with no ideals, prejudices, or remorse; with no feeling for art and no reverence for life; free from any ethical tradition; callous to pain, weakness, suffering and death, as if they had been invulnerable and immortal."[34] Hueffer later recorded his revised opinion that all this

31. "Think It Not Strange," p. 149½.
32. Jessie Conrad to Dawson, 30 December 1917 (No. 86).
33. For a definition of Fourth Dimension see the *Dictionary of Mysticism*, ed. Frank Gaynor (New York, 1953), p. 66. Concerning *The True Dimension*, see also p. 83.
34. *The Inheritors* (New York, 1901), pp. 11–12. Regarded less antagonistically, people who develop "higher dimensional" or "cosmic" consciousness might "inherit"

was "queer" and "thin," a "farrago of nonsense."[35] And he was quite right. The real wonder, after all, is not so much that Conrad was perplexed about Dawson's "connections" with the Fourth Dimension as that he himself once toyed with it. Dawson, as a matter of fact, who had read all of Conrad's works, may have thought that he was following the lead of his friend. Be this as it may, Dawson himself was, as we have seen, inclined toward psychism. It is not simply that he was an *imaginatif*.[36] He had even studied psychic phenomena with a sort of tutor, and in the early days he had been able to furnish his friend Flammarion with a personal instance of transatlantic extrasensory perception.[37] In later years this side of the man assumed much greater proportions. In a single letter of 18 October 1951 he told of his contributions to *Psychic News*, of his golden-hued vision of the Virgin (which had formed itself in his mantel mirror), and of the Thibetan who was his father in his first important earth-life thousands of years ago.[38]

Apparently Dawson's psychism touched Conrad but slightly. During one of his visits in Kent, however, while walking alone through the moonlit countryside, Dawson had one of his more memorable psychic experiences. Above the soft, southwest sea-wind, which swept over the fields to the crossroads where he stood hesitating,

---

and "regulate human affairs by reason of their superior wisdom and power" (Claude Bragdon, introd. to P. D. Ouspensky, *Tertium Organum: The Third Canon of Thought, A Key to the Enigmas of the World*, trans. Bragdon and Nicholas Bessaraboff [New York, 1938; copyright, 1920], p. 5).

35. Quoted by John A. Meixner, *Ford Madox Ford's Novels: A Critical Study* (Minneapolis, 1962), p. 101. See also Paul L. Wiley, *Novelist of Three Worlds: Ford Madox Ford* (New York, 1962), pp. 140–142.

36. The word is used by his friend M. Alfred Vicher in a letter of 22 May 1963 to Lady Phyllis Benton (Dawson Collection).

37. Flammarion duly recorded it in *La Mort et Son Mystère* (see *Death and Its Mystery*, Vol. I, *Before Death*, trans. E. S. Brooks [New York, 1921], pp. 130–132).

In *The Guardian Demons* (London, 1928), pp. 20–21, Dawson relates an experience which occurred shortly after Flammarion's death, but before Dawson was informed of it: "I was aware of a light surrounding me in the darkness as I lay with closed eyes; not a flash but a clear, diffused, steadfast radiance of intense power but of immense beauty and complete serenity. It was suggestive of an immaterial presence high and pure and noble. . . ."

Three incidents pertaining to Dawson's psychic abilities were included by Walter Franklin Prince in his *Human Experiences* (1931), a volume issued by the Boston Society for Psychic Research.

38. The letter itself is something of a mystery, since both it and another of the same month are addressed to "My Dear Mr Leslie Howard." The famous actor of this name had a daughter named Leslie, but he himself died in a plane shot down by German fighters in June, 1943. No other Leslie Howard has appeared in my research.

there came to him—or seemed to come—the sound of a spirit's voice. Immediately he hurried back to Capel House, snatched up a pencil, and began to scrawl. The result was a long piece of verse which he called "At the Crossroads." It was not very good. "Mortals, as a general rule," it says at one awkward point, "have not learned the voiceless language / Of other spheres. . . ." The next night Dawson read Conrad as much as he had finished of the poem, "as I have read or sent to him, and discussed with him, everything I ever wrote. . . ."[39] Conrad's specific reaction is unrecorded, but his attitude may be surmised when Dawson adds that "What he [Conrad] invariably called Metaphysics always made him rather uncomfortable, unless approached on the bias; he claimed not to understand them, while being fascinated by them."[40] Conrad was big enough and good enough to consider that most men need a certain number of illusions in order to survive. "Every one must walk in the light of his own heart's gospel," he had written long ago to Edward Noble. "Another man's truth is only a dismal lie to me."[41]

On 14 July 1918 Jessie informed Dawson that "your dear Conrad has finished another long book called 'An Arrow of Gold.' " It was the autumn of 1919, however, before Dawson procured a copy, read it, and mailed off his response. Conrad's counter-response, written 22 September 1919, conveys a characteristic sense of weariness and melancholy, and touches directly on the pervasive subject of his fiction, man's inevitable isolation. Here the isolation is nakedly Conrad's own: "Through my fault," he says "—or is it simply Fate? —I have missed all along the chances of closer contacts." The real purpose of the letter, however, is to thank Dawson for his appreciative comments on *The Arrow of Gold.* "Nothing has given me greater satisfaction," he says, "than your good words about the Arrow. You were often in my thoughts while I wrote. It was unavoidable." Understandably so, since a central character in the novel is a South Carolinian.

It is possible that the negative aspect of Conrad's feeling for Americans may be traced in part to certain experiences which he had in the late 1870's. It was then that he joined a little "syndicate"

39. From Dawson's typescript entitled "A Joseph Conrad Reminiscence," p. 4.
40. "A Joseph Conrad Reminiscence," p. 5.
41. Cited in "The Intimate Letters of Joseph Conrad. . . ," *World Today,* XLIX (1926–1927), 138.

which had been formed to smuggle arms, the purpose presumably being to assist Don Carlos de Bourbon in his try for the Spanish throne. Actually the smuggling may have had little to do with the Carlist cause. In any case, Conrad wrote in his autobiographical *Mirror of the Sea* (1906) about the oldest, most imposing member of the syndicate as "a North Carolinian gentleman" whose initials were "J. M. K. B."[42] This American Southerner was memorable in Conrad's life not only as a companion in adventure, but also, it seems, as a rival for a lady. Whatever may have happened between them—and we will never know the whole story—Conrad for the rest of his life carried a scar on his chest which he claimed was the result of a duel with "J. M. K. B." It is fairly clear now that his wound was really the result of a suicide attempt. Nevertheless, it still may have been, at least in some sense, a memento of his conflict with "J. M. K. B." Regardless of its source, however, the wound was an ever-present emblem for Conrad of his brush with death in February or March of 1878—the year that Dawson was born.[43]

Granted his penchant for using real-life characters and names in fiction, it is not surprising that Conrad finally put his American antagonist in a novel, nor that the initials "J. M. K. B.," which he included in *The Mirror*, were fleshed out in *The Arrow of Gold* to reveal one "J. K. Blunt." In his letter to Dawson about the *Arrow* Conrad's words suggest clearly the actuality underlying the Blunt of the book. He says that "The antagonism of feeling had of course to come out. . . ." Jerry Allen, furthermore, has shown in *The Sea Years* that the historical Blunt was John Mason Key Blunt, not of North Carolina (as *The Mirror* said) nor of South Carolina (as *The Arrow* said), but of Maryland. In fact, he was the grandson of Francis Scott Key.[44] That the Blunt of the novel is from Dawson's home state is of course not likely to represent a lapse in Conrad's memory. It is, indeed, a partially understandable and intriguing bit of obfuscation.

42. *The Mirror of the Sea* (London, 1906), p. 266.

43. See Baines, "The Affair in Marseilles," *The London Magazine*, IV (November, 1957), 41–46, and Zdzislaw Najder, ed. *Conrad's Polish Background: Letters to and from Polish Friends*, trans. Halina Carroll (London, 1964), pp. 20, 196. One would like to know if Conrad ever learned that Dawson's father was knighted for his stand against the *code duello*.

44. His mother, Mrs. Ellen Lloyd Key Blunt, was the daughter of Francis Scott Key (Jerry Allen, *The Sea Years of Joseph Conrad* [Garden City, N.Y., 1965], pp. 63 ff., *passim*).

When Conrad and Dawson wrote to each other about *The Arrow of Gold*, the war had been over for ten months. In March, 1919, the Conrads had moved from Capel House to Spring Grove, Wye, and now they were waiting to move again, this time to Oswalds, in Bishopsbourne, Kent, which was to be their "real home where we hope to stay a long time."[45] Oswalds was even to have central heat and electricity. The more simple Capel House, with its good food, good talk, and camaraderie, its cozy, low-beamed rooms and its well-seasoned warmth, belonged already to the past—a past which Dawson had marvellously shared. To the Conrads, however, the "sympathetic" character of Capel had now been qualified. Jessie wrote that

> It was a bit of a wrench to leave poor old Capel but the last year there holds so much pain and anxiety that I really was glad to leave it. The terrible months of the war and our great anxiety about dear Borys seem to belong somehow to the house. Then nine months ago I had a very serious and painful operation on my knee and again, the house seems to have had some share in the nightmare.

Pain and suffering could not be left behind in the past, but Capel House, like the war, was consigned to memory.

45. Jessie Conrad to Dawson, 31 March 1919 (No. 88).

7
The Decline of the Friendship (1919-1924)

In Conrad's last years the friendship waned. As Curle wrote in one of his essays, "by and large it is hopeless to try to keep up friendships by correspondence alone. . . ."[1] Then, too, Dawson had never materialized as a novelist, while Conrad, though creating less well these days, had obviously moved out into the mainstream of English letters. Even if the two men had been able to meet once more, it could never have been the same. Though he still had a pleasant, boyish look, Dawson was now over forty, no longer the fair-haired youth setting out to slay giants. And while Conrad might continue to brood and to fret that his life's course somehow ran in a place apart, the failure of the public to buy his books was a less valid complaint every year.

Of course the war had been hard on Conrad. When he emerged from it he still was able to write, but he told André Ruyters, "I am over sixty and . . . a sick man—I work very slowly. . . ."[2] He himself had come to realize that his major work lay behind him. "Of course, *mon cher*," he wrote to Walpole of *The Rescue*, "it is not very good. I did my best work long ago."[3] In fact he had the feeling that it was time to put his "literary affairs in order."[4] He felt the need for rest: "I want some time to myself to do nothing—just do nothing."[5] Meanwhile Jessie's condition, among other private problems, added to his strain. Since 1904 one of Jessie's legs had been more or less crippled, and though the surgeon's "knife" enabled her to walk almost normally for a while (to return "à la vie perpendiculaire,"

1. "Rare Characters and Stray Thoughts," *Caravansary and Conversation: Memories of Places and Persons* (New York, 1937), p. 307.
2. Letter of 8 June 1919, Beinecke Library, Yale.
3. A notation made by Walpole for 18 July 1920, quoted by Rupert Hart-Davis, *Hugh Walpole: A Biography* (London, 1952), p. 195.
4. Letter of 24 November 1919 to Sir William Rothenstein, in the Houghton Library, Harvard.
5. Letter to Ruyters, cited above.

Conrad said),[6] she was usually in pain and sometimes in great pain. The two elder Conrads did manage a trip to Corsica early in 1921, and Conrad even made it to America in 1923, but everything was harder now. Despite the good which came to them in the 1920's, including relief, at last, from financial pressures, his biographer Baines concludes that "The last two years of Conrad's life were rather melancholy. He was constantly feeling ill, physically and mentally, and death was creating gaps among his friends and acquaintances."[7]

After 1920 the Conrads' crippled American friend was confined to his Versailles apartment. Somehow, though, he managed to carry on his Embassy work. Officialdom at one point, at least, considered that perhaps his status of absentee attaché should not be allowed to continue, but, unknown to Dawson, the members of the Theodore Roosevelt family "chipped in" to pay his salary for a while. Thus he was able to keep working for the Embassy long enough to demonstrate the continuing value of his knowledge and devotion.[8]

Always a creator, he began in these years to evolve a distinctive aura for himself. Not that there was anything totally new in it. Even his dwelling place, emblematic in retrospect, was a setting which he had chosen long before. A genteel, literary American in historically aristocratic Versailles, far removed from the vital Parisian spheres of Stein, Pound, or Hemingway, or even Ford Madox Hueffer—now Ford Madox Ford—Dawson created his own cultural and diplomatic sphere.[9] A steady stream of callers was drawn eventually to his chairside. Many were awed by his knowledge of France and the world, and charmed by his enduring warmth, which somehow gained in value now that it was bestowed from an increasingly great altitude. Archibald Roosevelt recalls, not unkindly, that the atmosphere in Dawson's parlor became rather like that of a throne room. Dawson received his guests in a special invalid chair, surrounded by his treasured books and artifacts and *objets d'art*, which were all so

6. Letter to André Gide of 1 February 1920, included in *Lettres Françaises*, ed. G. Jean-Aubry (Paris, 1930), p. 151.

7. *Joseph Conrad* (London, 1960), p. 426.

8. Interview with Archibald B. Roosevelt, 9 September 1964.

9. In his lecturing days Dawson had protested that Versailles was "No more dead than France, or than the principle of conservatism in the world!" ("Unknown Versailles," p. 8, from the Dawson Collection). Now, by determining who entered his apartment, he could exercise considerable control over his sanctuary-within-a-sanctuary. Retreat brought a sort of tragic victory.

many clues into the labyrinth of his personality. Along with his father's magnolia-wood armchair, from the Charleston home of his youth, he kept the throne of the Prime Minister of Uganda, a relic of his trip to Africa. Perhaps most prominent of all in his rooms, however, was his beloved collection of old paintings. That the pictures were of dubious origin is and always was beside the point. Dawson's conviction of their value conferred value upon them.

As Dawson's image took shape—and it came about gradually in the 1920's and the early 1930's—he began to receive more and more homage from old friends, awed young people, and peripheral celebrities. He would greet them in a velvet robe of gold or garnet, worn over what Mr. Roosevelt recalls as a dazzling white nightshirt.[10] All through the years Dawson had had a certain well-bred theatricality, a discreet sort of flair. Now these became increasingly manifest. Perhaps in a way they served as expressive yet protective wrappings for his psychic wounds. At any rate, it began to be clear that Dawson's greatest creation as an artist was himself.

The most gratifying creation of his literary life was *The Gift of Paul Clermont.* Conrad had wished the book godspeed as early as 30 December 1920 (in the same letter he told Dawson of the coming trip to Corsica), and it was published in New York by Doubleday, Page & Company in September of the following year. Rather strangely Dawson had begun writing the book back in 1913, and yet it was in every sense a war novel, composed mainly during the war and sometimes even within cannon range. Captured in it were many of the sights and sounds which Dawson himself had experienced. An autobiographical piece from the *Atlantic Monthly* of July, 1916, called "Refugee: The Experience of a War Correspondent," became the basis for the story of young Paul's captivity in Part Four, and the various soldiers' narratives given in Parts Two, Three, and Four were drawn directly from factual accounts which had been printed under Dawson's name in the columns of the Charleston *News and Courier* and the Boston *Evening Transcript,* between 1913 and 1918. What is more important, Dawson put his factual material to moderately effective fictional use. Later on he claimed that he had needed Rudyard Kipling's encouragement to persuade him to finish the book, but if this was true, Dawson was himself

10. Interview with Archibald B. Roosevelt, 11 September 1964.

unaware that *Paul* is better than anything he had written earlier.[11] It is not really good, and yet Dawson put some of his most skillful work into it. With the character of young Paul he symbolized his concept of the ever-fresh spirit of France, and with Paul's friendly attachment to an American named Henry Aubret (the Dawson-figure in the novel) he suggested the friendship between France and the United States. As for story, Dawson traced Paul from a village childhood through his initiation into war, and finally to death in battle. All this is moderately interesting. The London *Times Literary Supplement* cannily observed, however, that the most intriguing thing about the book is Dawson's experimentation with point of view:

> Mr. Dawson uses, in turn, the impersonal narrative, a personal narrator, or reporter of events, and the direct narrative of the principal character, and he passes from one to the other, at times, in an almost bewildering way, loosely linking up the impersonal with the personal narrative by some such phrase as 'all this Paul told me,' &c. The personal narrator, M. Aubret, an elderly American philosopher, does not appear until a little way on in the book.[12]

It was a natural kind of experiment for a Conrad devotee. In any case, Dawson was proud of the novel, and when it was finished he dedicated it to his distinguished friend from war days, Marshal Joffre.

Three and one-half years later, as a sort of foreword to the French version, *Le Sacrifice de Paul Clermont* (1925), there appeared a laudatory—and posthumous—"*Lettre de M. Joseph Conrad à M. Warrington Dawson.*" Essentially this is a French translation of the praise which Conrad wrote on 30 November 1921, after receiving his copy of the first edition. The letter was to appear again in a somewhat abbreviated English version on the jacket of *Paul Clermont's*

---

11. *Paul Clermont's Story and My Own Followed by The Gift of Paul Clermont* (Chicago, 1928), p. xi. Kipling even wrote to F. N. Doubleday about the book. On 24 November 1920 Doubleday sent Dawson some of Kipling's comments:

> Your firm either has had or will have soon submitted to them a novel called 'Paul,' by Warrington Dawson. I want you to look at it. It is about the only book I have ever read in typescript for a quarter of a century which strikes me as good—good as a novel, good as work, good as a study of France and French ideas from the inside. . . . Warrington Dawson may be a good man.

12. *TLS,* 1 December 1921, p. 787.

Story and My Own (1928). Fortunately for Conrad's reputation, he was not alone in his praise. In fact, J. J. Jusserand, member of the *Institut de France* and former Ambassador to the United States, chose to link himself specifically with Conrad in a quotation used on the jacket: "All readers will share the opinion of Mr. Conrad and will be deeply moved." And the New York *Times* reviewer found the book to be "beautifully written," "vivid," and "thrilling."[13] Although modern literary excavators, even students of the war novel, have completely overlooked *The Gift of Paul Clermont*, the book seemed sufficiently worthy in its day to pass muster with the Académie Française. Marshal Joffre himself came out to Dawson's apartment on the afternoon of 6 December 1926 to present Dawson with a gold medal on behalf of the "forty immortals." Like Conrad, the immortals felt that "France has in you a wonderful friend."

On 23 January 1921 the Conrads left for Corsica by car, accompanied by Borys as far as Rouen, and by Jean-Aubry from Rouen to Lyons. Borys turned back because he was soon to begin work on a new job in London. On his way home, however, he paused briefly to visit Dawson in Versailles. For a while the elder Conrads considered stopping at Dawson's, too, on their return trip, and if Conrad had been very determined on the subject, the visit probably would have taken place. On 27 June 1922, long after they returned to Oswalds, Jessie could only write to assure Dawson that "I should certainly have managed to find you out but I was so very much a cripple. This November we mean to try to get to the South of France and, who knows, we may come through Versailles as we shall go by car." Jessie did finally make it to Versailles some seven years later. But by then she had to come alone.

Now as always Dawson continued to be plagued with an inexhaustible creativity. He wrote almost constantly, groping sometimes at the idea that perhaps he might really launch his novels if Conrad would tug them out into public view. Naturally Conrad refused. He told Dawson pretty much what he had told Gerald Cumberland earlier: "I have no critical faculty."[14] Though on rare occasions Conrad had managed to say a few words about someone else's books, literary commentary came hard to him, and he knew that he was not

13. *Times Book Review and Magazine*, 20 November 1921, p. 30.
14. Letter of 20 November 1919, in *Joseph Conrad: Life and Letters*, ed. G. Jean-Aubry, II (Garden City, N.Y., 1927), 235.

good at it. In terms which are relevant both to his work as a novelist and his character as a man, he explained the matter to Dawson:

> I don't believe in my own wisdom, and I shrink from putting forth my opinions to the general public. I am like that. I cannot help it. It is temperamental; and it is closely associated with the unliterary complexion of my mind.[15]

Thus the creator of Marlow.

One thing that Conrad could do, nonetheless, was allow Dawson to quote from the letters which Conrad already had written him. Dawson's *Adventure in the Night* (1924) was therefore not merely dedicated "To My Friend Joseph Conrad," but also equipped "With a foreword by Joseph Conrad."[16] This "foreword" was a single-page letter which praised the work in hand. It was even garnished with a facsimile of Conrad's signature. But it was not a letter which Conrad had written. Though Conrad had approved its publication (whom could it hurt?), it was a Frankenstein hybrid. The first two sentences were taken from a commentary that Conrad had made on Dawson's plans for "The Rock" some thirteen years earlier (24 August 1911); the third, from something he had said of *The Pyramid* (undated letter); the fourth, fifth, and sixth from views he had conveyed to Dawson concerning *Le Nègre aux États-Unis*—! (9 April 1912); and the final four from another letter discussing "The Rock" (2 June 1922).[17] Most painful of all, Conrad's words on the color question were presented here as if they had been meant to praise *Adventure in the Night*: "*one cannot help feeling with you,*

15. Conrad to Dawson, 2 June 1922 (No. 99).

16. The wording was suggested by Conrad himself, who had been flattered but disturbed by the high-flown, ambiguous phrases of an earlier dedication, probably that which Dawson wrote for *The Pyramid* (1922). The latter work was addressed to "The Prophet of Two Continents / Who Looks with True Vision on the World / Yet Keeps His Faith / and with Wise Words / Strengthens Faith in Others." As a matter of fact, the "prophet" here was probably Kipling, who had corresponded with Dawson about the book in general and the dedication in particular. Kipling had said that in some circles it would do Dawson no good to link Kipling's name very specifically with *The Pyramid* (8 April 1921). Then again, Dawson may have been thinking of his old friend Bernard Bernard, who had his own place in the history of the book because he had first printed parts of it in *Health & Vim*. Bernard, said Dawson, was "known throughout America and England as the great apostle of health and rational living. His books and his *Health and Life* magazine have helped many to preserve the strength they had, and many more to build up strength they had lost" (*Paul Clermont's Story and My Own*, p. xxxiii). In short, Dawson may have got triple mileage from this particular dedication.

17. I.e., respectively, letters No. 13, 50, 22, and 99.

all the way with you—even apart (in my case) from the complete accord of thought. . . ." Frustration and desperation, and a chronic need to reshape the hard lines of reality had driven Dawson into an egregious commercialism. To give him due credit, it was foreign to his background and, at least in its grossness, untypical of the man.

Granting permission for the foreword to *Adventure in the Night* was perhaps Conrad's last gesture on his friend's behalf. Dawson's *Crimson Pall* (1927), published three years after Conrad's death, contained still further scraps of Conrad's prose, but Dawson had received permission long before to print them. Taking as a cue Conrad's hints that he try to be a "critical" novelist and that he try to write a "critical exposé" of his philosophy, Dawson manufactured three letters on literary matters and presented them as an introduction to the *Pall*. Two, as we have seen, were presumably by Conrad, and one was by himself.[18] The first he created of patches from four actual Conrad documents;[19] it praises Dawson's abilities, offers him encouragement, and invites him to compose the "critical exposé." The second and longest letter is the one by Dawson, in which he explains what he has tried to achieve as a writer. Third and last is another Conrad patchwork, cut largely from the commentary which Conrad had dictated to Dawson back in 1913, but making use also of three actual letters, including the "credo" letter of 20 June 1913.

All this put Dawson's best foot forward. The literary world, however, took little note. Readers of *The Crimson Pall*, a murder mystery set in Pittsburgh, were likely to be the sort who would skip introductory matter, and Conrad enthusiasts, even scholars, could scarcely be expected to know about the book. Bernard Bernard, the old friend who brought it out, did the best he could by Dawson, and yet the simple truth was that Dawson's best talents, despite his desires, were not for creative writing. As the years slipped by, he came to an increasingly clearer realization of this fact, and still, as he told Conrad on 20 July 1923, when asking permission to create the *Pall* introduction, "I must go on writing, or I'll just die stupidly like anybody else, and I don't want to do that!"

18. Pp. 76–77.
19. Par. 1 from part of par. 1 of letter of 22 April 1917 (No. 84); par. 2 from part of par. 3 of same 1917 letter; par. 3 from par. 4 of same letter; par. 4 from part of par. 1 of undated letter (No. 50); pars. 5 through 10 from pars. 1 through 5 of letter of 1 June 1913 (No. 38); and par. 11 from par. 5 of letter of 2 June 1922 (No. 99).

Toward the end of the second Conrad letter in *The Crimson Pall,* Dawson included what Conrad had written to him of their mutual friend John Powell—the dedicatee of the *Pall*—after the novelist and the pianist had met in New York. Conrad had sailed from Glasgow on board the *Tuscania* on 20 April 1923, and on 4 May, visiting in the Oyster Bay home of his publisher, F. N. Doubleday, he wrote to Jessie about seeing Powell: "Imagine, my dear, Powell was there too! Mrs. D. asked him to call, and he dined here yesterday and then played Beethoven and Chopin."[20] Conrad was genuinely pleased. At the end of May, shortly before he returned to England, he found time to convey Jessie's "very special love" to Powell, and to assure him that his was one of the Conrads' "precious friendships."[21] Perhaps the high point of the American visit, however, was Conrad's talk in the palatial home of Mrs. Arthur Curtiss James. Though Doubleday later recalled that Conrad "was in a state of nervous collapse, and I was not far behind,"[22] the event was one of the most gratifying in Conrad's entire career. To Jessie he wrote on 11 May, "I would have given anything for you to have been there and seen all that crowd and all that splendour, the very top of the basket of the fashionable and literary circles."[23] In September, after returning home, he told Bruno Winawer how the whole trip had gone: "I felt all the time like a man dans un avion, in a mist, in a cloud, in a vapour of idealistic phraseology; I was lost, bewildered, amused— but frightened as well. . . . I have feelings of great friendship towards many people there."[24] Still, it was of John Powell that Conrad wrote to Dawson, telling how they had

> talked of old times, mostly in affectionate reference to yourself, and with genuine sorrow at the heavy trial that fell to your lot. You were very much in my thoughts over there. From that land

20. Jean-Aubry, *LL*, II, 307. Powell had recently given a highly successful all-Chopin concert at Æolian Hall.

21. Conrad to Powell, Alderman Library, University of Virginia. Asked to write something about Conrad for the New York *Evening Post,* Powell turned out an article which was printed under the headline "Conrad and [Roger] Casement Hut Mates in Africa: Writer Told Friend of Sinister Impression Made at First Sight of Ill-Fated Irish Sympathizer, Then an Ivory Trader" (11 May 1923).

22. "Joseph Conrad as a Friend," *World Today* (London), LII (1928), 146.

23. Jean-Aubry, *LL*, II, 309. See Arnold T. Schwab, "Conrad's American Speeches and His Reading from *Victory,*" *MP*, LXII (1965), 342–347.

24. Letter of September in Zdzislaw Najder, ed., *Conrad's Polish Background: Letters to and from Polish Friends,* trans. Halina Carroll (London, 1964), p. 292.

of novel experience and generous kindness I turned my eyes more than once towards Versailles where my second American friend (Crane was the first, in time) gave us all—as I told J.P.— a great object lesson in serenity, courage, and undaunted fortitude.[25]

Dawson had written to Conrad just a few days earlier, recalling how they once had planned to go to the States together—"And I am here on my back, more helpless than ever. . . !"[26] Conrad must have remembered, too: "My greatest regret was not to be able to visit the South. . . . Perhaps if you had been by my side—who knows! But this doesn't bear thinking about." In the same letter he also expressed hope of coming over to Paris "in a not distant future," and, of course, seeing Dawson. There was to be no such visit, however, and apparently no more letters. Conrad had his secretary, Miss Hallowes, write twice in the following year, once to accept Dawson's dedication of *Adventure in the Night* and once to say thanks for the book when it arrived. Then early one Sunday at Oswalds—the morning of 3 August 1924—after an especially bad spell, Conrad slipped quietly down from a chair in his room. In the next room, her crutches out of reach, Jessie heard him gasp, "Here . . . you." Then the great man was gone.[27]

25. Conrad to Dawson, 29 July 1923 (No. 106).
26. Dawson to Conrad, 20 July 1923 (No. 105), quoted from Dawson's carbon.
27. Jessie Conrad, *Joseph Conrad and His Circle*, 2nd ed. (Port Washington, N.Y., 1964), p. 276. Apparently he died of a coronary thrombosis.

8

After Conrad's Death (1924-1962)

Jessie, plagued with sorrow and pain, continued to correspond with Dawson. The death of her husband was followed a year later by that of her mother, and she herself faced a series of operations that seemed to be endless. Then on 18 May 1926, explaining that "You my dear Warrington have proved yourself a real interested friend," she broke down and told of Borys's secret marriage back in September, 1922. From this time on, she was able to derive a certain comfort from confiding some of her problems to Dawson. She had known him a long time, he was a sympathetic listener, and he lived far away. In some ways he made an ideal confidant.

The year 1927 brought both Jessie and Dawson some very bleak days. Jessie could walk with a single stick now—for a while, at least—and John was in "architectural college," but still she was full of worries. When Ellen Glasgow came to call, things went badly. "Tea with Mrs. Conrad was rather dismal," Miss Glasgow reported. "She has become enormously stout, and so very complacent, poor soul, clinging to the shadow of fame which he shed over her."[1]

Dawson, meanwhile, was continually turning out dispatches and weekly reports and confidential memoranda for the Embassy in Paris, though at times he was too weak to sit up for more than two or three minutes at a stretch. Moreover, he had at last faced squarely the fact that as a novelist, despite his gold medal, he was not a success.[2] Of course he continued his creative writing. It was as natural to him as breathing, and, all things considered, he managed to put a fairly good face on a very sad situation. To his friend George Clough Sharp, son of the former Ambassador, he could even say: "I have fulfilled all I had aspired to do. I could die to-morrow—no,

1. Letter of 25 August 1927 to Anne Virginia Bennett, in *Letters of Ellen Glasgow*, ed. Blair Rouse (New York, 1958), pp. 87–88.
2. Draft of letter to Kipling dated 16 July 1927.

but literally within a month and not before two weeks have passed—and I should have completed the task allotted to myself in childhood."[3] At the time he wrote this he had thirty-five more years to live.

The last of Jessie's homes, like the last of Conrad's ships, was named "Torrens." It was "a jolly little place about a mile from Canterbury,"[4] and from here she wrote on 17 February 1929 that she had had "yet another" operation on her knee; "I have faced the knife just a dozen times now." Yet early the following autumn she was sufficiently better to go touring in Wales and the Lake District, and even to contemplate an American tour. Something of what Ellen Glasgow had found in her is to be seen in her letter to Dawson of 15 September 1929: "My idea would be to have some rooms in New York and be at home there to all Conrad's friends and admirers for a month." She adds, "I might be able to give talks if not actually lecture." Even her surgeons were favorably disposed toward the idea, but on 24 October she reported that "The Trustees [of the Conrad estate] decided that the season was too far advanced. . . . I am coming over to France instead and intend coming to see you on Tuesday next. ! ! !"

Jessie's visit to Dawson was long anticipated and long remembered. Earlier she had written how she always regretted "that J. C. would not let me make further efforts to discover you when we came from Corsica in 1921,"[5] but now the two old friends were to meet face to face once again. Jessie brought with her a copy of *A Little Less Than Gods*, Ford Madox Ford's Napoleonic novel of the preceding year. She inscribed it "To dear Warrington / With love from his old / friend Jessie Conrad. / On a memorable occasion / October 29th 1929." Doubtless she chose the gift because Conrad at one time had planned to collaborate with Ford on the subject of the book, and, indeed, had tackled it in his own unfinished *Suspense*. Certainly Jessie was not a Ford fan. In a distorted sort of way, she probably regarded Ford's novel as a last, sad bit of Conradiana.[6]

3. Draft of letter dated 6 October 1927.
4. Jessie Conrad to Dawson, 24 August 1928.
5. Jessie Conrad to Dawson, 18 May 1926.
6. On 9 November 1928 Ford had written to George Oppenheimer of The Viking Press on receiving a publishing sheet for *A Little Less Than Gods*: "For myself I should have preferred a little less of dwelling on Conrad and a little more as to the sterling romantic qualities of the book, for I am a little tired of being tacked on to

In any case, the long-deferred meeting with Dawson was charged with nostalgic reminiscences of the good old times and of the great man whom they had, to some degree, shared. The next day Jessie scrawled hastily, "It was such a mixture of plain [*sic*] and pleasure yesterday and I shall carry the mental picture of you with me always."

Jessie in any important sense had nowhere to go in these years. She had long since fulfilled her duty of cushioning Conrad from the thousand natural shocks of life that he, more than others, was heir to, and she sorely missed the call on her maternal capabilities. Dawson, meanwhile, early in the 1930's, began to come into his own again. On 15 October 1930 he was awarded the cravatte of a *Commandeur de la Légion d'Honneur* (having been made *Chevalier* in 1921 and *Officier* in 1925). In 1931 he was made a *Citoyen d'Honneur de Versailles*. In 1932 he was made *Commandeur de l'Ordre de St. Sava* and *Commandeur de l'Oeuvre des Vieux Militaires*, and was awarded the *Médaille de la Société des Sauveteurs de la Seine* and the *Swastika d'Argent*. Though a cripple confined to his apartment, he rationed out his energies so astutely that he was able to achieve wonders. On 13 February 1932 he was warmly congratulated for the issue of his Special Report No. 1000. His research on behalf of the restoration of Williamsburg, Virginia, was extensive and fruitful; among other things, he turned up maps of the Revolutionary War, an eyewitness account of the siege of Yorktown, and "le chapeau de La Fayette." In May, 1932, after an eighteen-year intermission, he even returned to singing. After all, he had studied "for some years" with Manoury, Juliani, Pizzarello, and Georges Lantelme.[7] He announced to one friend, "I am planning to reserve the second Sunday afternoon in each month, beginning in October, for receptions where there will be a musical programme. I shall sing, but I shall want to have also other artists who are willing to volunteer their services." And he adds: "Having been a Wagnerian tenor at my recital in the early part of July, I intend to appear as an Italian

---

C's coat-tails and I don't believe the public cares a damn about it" (*Letters of Ford Madox Ford*, ed. Richard M. Ludwig [Princeton, N.J., 1965], pp. 181–182). See also Jessie Conrad, *Joseph Conrad and His Circle*, 2nd ed. (Port Washington, N.Y., 1964), p. 221, and Paul L. Wiley, *Novelist of Three Worlds: Ford Madox Ford* (New York, 1962), pp. 123–124.

7. From Dawson's carbon of a letter to M. Maurice le Tellier, written 17 October 1931.

'tenor gracieux' in October."[8] As many as eighty people crowded into his apartment to see and hear this prodigy. There were "streams of visitors and an overwhelming correspondence,"[9] and, perhaps to suit the image better to the action, there was even a new haircut which made Dawson "look very grand and important," though it left "little of the W.D. of yore."[10] In the New York *Sun* of 13 January 1931 Bob Davis took note of the fact that Dawson was fenced off from his visitors by

> an oak railing perhaps a foot and a half in height, which prompt-
> ed the illusion that the tenant was seated on a makeshift throne.
> "Touch me lightly," said he, extending a white, thin hand.
> "Any shock to my spine is to be avoided."[11]

In January, 1935, Dawson moved to No. 2 rue de la Paroisse, where his windows looked out over the gardens of Versailles. When the trees to the south shed their russet in autumn, he could even see the northern façade of the palace itself. More immediately at hand was the splendid *Bassin de Neptune*. Now his musicales had only to be switched to the first Sunday of the month in order that his guests might have the added delight of viewing the spectacular *Grandes Eaux de Neptune* from his windows after tea.

Jessie's life was far removed from all this. She could share with Dawson certain parts of a great memory, and, despite their mutual physical disabilities, she could even go so far as to plan a book on Conrad with him. But Jessie was a far simpler soul than Dawson, and as the bridge between them receded farther into the past, their gestures of friendliness were offered over a gap that was always widening. When their collaboration fell through, Jessie went on alone to write *Joseph Conrad and His Circle* (1935). Whatever comforts and pleasures came to her in these later years—she was a grandmother now—she was sometimes "desperately lonely," she told Dawson.[12] Involved to the limit of his capacity in various projects, Dawson, who had always been kind to her, failed now to write for what seemed " a ter-

---

8. From Dawson's carbon of a letter written 20 July 1932 to Fräulein Christl Kerry.
9. From Dawson's carbon of an unsigned letter written for him on 21 March 1933 to his sister, Ethel Barry.
10. Lilian Segonne to Dawson, letter of 28 September 1931.
11. From "Bob Davis Recalls: The 'Prisoner of Versailles' Receives His Decorations."
12. Jessie Conrad to Dawson, 1 August 1932 (No. 116).

ribly long time."[13] He was increasingly able to magnetize to his apartment the friendly and the curious—too many of both, sometimes. Sometimes he was even able to rise from his chaise longue and, with great care, to shuffle about his rooms a bit. But Jessie's world and activity were contracting. "I get more of a fixture than ever," she wrote to him on 1 May 1934. "It is now three years since I have been in London and almost a year since I have passed the garden gate." Two years later, in a letter of 2 January 1936, she wrote, "My powers of walking get less and less. . . ." Yet there lingered the hope of coming to see Dawson once more: "if only I can get the necessary funds together I have still the car and a keen spirit of adventure left." It was a doomed hope. Jessie died on the night of 6 December 1936, in Guy's Hospital, London.

Dawson's activities continued unabated. For a while they even expanded to include the writing of plays. *Beaumains*, for one, his five-act Arthurian drama for children, was produced at the nearby Théâtre Montansier (he liked to think of it as Marie Antoinette's theater) on 17 May 1936.[14] In 1937, when he retired at last from the Embassy, he was merely freeing time for other kinds of work.

Several years before giving up his Embassy post, in fact as early as 7 February 1933, Dawson had reported that Japan's "preparations for war were aimed directly at the United States."[15] In other words, Dawson had detected some of the earliest danger signals, rumblings similar to those which he first had heard in March, 1913. It was no fatuous compliment that his friend Hugh Gibson offered when he wrote to Dawson on 3 June 1940 that "All seems like a bad gramophone record of something we have already lived thru once, and you will understand that more than most people." Dawson was to remain in his Versailles apartment throughout World War II. From his magnificent windows overlooking the *Bassin de Neptune* he watched the parade and review of German soldiers, and in his journal he wrote: "I don't think that ever in my life I've felt so utterly alone and helpless, here in this house which I am physically unable to leave, tended by two women. . . ."[16] He was completely cut off.

13. Jessie Conrad to Dawson, 1 May 1934.
14. Dawson wrote a handful of plays for the Éclaireurs de France (the French Boy Scouts), with whom he became much involved.
15. Noted in Dawson's obituary, New York *Times*, 27 September 1962, p. 37.
16. Quoted by Dawson in an unpublished MS called "At Neptune's Gates," p. 215.

"No letters or telegrams are accepted for Paris, nor telephone calls.
. . ."[17] When the bombs came, he took refuge in what he called his
"secret cabinet," a tiny room set in the wall of the Louis XIV part
of the house. At the sound of whistling projectiles he learned to slide
quickly from his pouf to the floor. German officers from the *Kom-*
mandatur took over the apartment above him. And still Dawson
kept up his writing. "I do what is natural for me, continuing in my
solitude to talk out things in writing for my own relief and satisfaction. . . ."[18] The Rohans' beloved Josselin was occupied. Word
came through that Kermit had died in Alaska—"Dear, wonderful
Kermit!"[19] Then at last it was over. On the night of 26 August 1944
Dawson hailed from his window the first American soldiers to come
walking down the rue de la Paroisse, shadowy forms lighted by sheet
lightning. For a while he had thoughts of ending his long exile, but
it was too late now. Though he still spoke with the Charleston accent
of his youth, Versailles was his permanent home.

Already in his later sixties at the close of World War II, Dawson
somehow regained much of his old spirit. The journalist Marguerite
Steedman called on him for an interview in 1955 and was amazed
at what she found:

> his complexion was as clear and almost as smooth as a girl's.
> He was wearing sandals of leather and the velvet robes that so
> became him[,] and his hair was a cloudy, silvery white. His eyes
> were blue, or blue-grey, very penetrating and immensely kind.
> . . . There was something absolutely royal about him. . . .
>
> I cannot sufficiently emphasize the vitality, the agelessness
> of the man. I have never seen anybody like him. Born in 1878,
> he was—let me see—77 when I saw him. I give you my word, he
> had the reflexes and perception and alertness of a teen-ager,
> almost. . . .[20]

Dawson delved with renewed enthusiasm into psychic phenomena.
He began turning out newsletters for the *News and Courier*; the
reporter who had covered the Paris Exposition of 1900 was writing
now of flying saucers and the Cold War. And on 23 April 1957 he

17. "At Neptune's Gates," p. 250.
18. "At Neptune's Gates," p. 370.
19. "At Neptune's Gates," p. 402.
20. Marguerite Steedman to Randall, letter of 20 August 1964.

told his old friend Bernard Bernard that he had at hand "some *ten* unpublished books."

That was the rub. Though Dawson continued to write to the end, much of what he wrote was refused. At last, at eighty, he made himself stop writing. To his old friend Lady Phyllis he reported on 22 June 1958 that he was feeling somewhat better physically——

> But having laid aside the creative writing which has been my animating force since childhood, I seem to have outlived my life itself. . . . I don't believe I have lost creative power. It is that the mere idea of producing another useless book is inexpressibly abhorrent to me. I want never to try to produce anything again. Or "try" is not the right word. Creative work is the one thing which requires no effort from me. Its rather that I must resist a weakness—the weakness of doing anything again and all to no purpose. It becomes a question of self-respect.
>
> I devote my time and such strength as I have to cleaning up— destroying a great deal.

The decision to stop writing was painful and could not be carried through. The sorting of papers was set aside, and the writing was resumed.

Physical infirmities closed in at last, however. There was a return of the old aphonia, there were skin troubles, and, worst of all, there was fading eyesight. His good friend Alfred Vicher reported to Lady Phyllis that Dawson had lost sixty per cent of his vision, and that his doctor advised him to read very little, for him a catastrophe.[21] Still, because he was very proud, because he did not wish to be pitied, he never complained. The friends who had filled his apartment on those Sunday afternoons before the war had died now or moved away or forgotten him. There was an occasional visitor still, but no more crowds and no more songs. What had once been a torrent of letters now shrank to a trickle.

Four weeks before Dawson's death in the fall of 1962 the younger son of his sister Ethel—who herself had died in 1956—brought his family to Versailles, and Dawson managed to impress them even yet with his keenness, his energy, his creativeness.[22] Against the

---

21. Vicher to Lady Phyllis Benton, letter of 17 February 1963, Dawson Collection.
22. Stuyvesant Barry, Charleston *News and Courier*, 28 September 1962, p. 8-A.

doctor's advice, he had returned to his writing once more. In the very year of his death, which came within a week of his eighty-fourth birthday, he published a little anthology called *Contes et Merveilles*. He simply had to do something with himself, and writing was what he liked best. Besides, he found that sleep came with increasing difficulty. Toward the end he took to getting up in the middle of the night and coming to sit in his armchair in the parlor, where he could be among his books and *bibelots*. Here he could switch on the lights beneath certain of his paintings, his well-loved Raphaels and Van Dycks and Leonardos, genuine at least in his mind's eye, and he could dream his dreams while still awake. The questing and the tilting of the gentle old *commandeur* were clearly coming to an end now. His journey had taken him through richer gardens and deeper sloughs than most men ever see, but now it was drawing to a quiet close. In his armchair, early on the morning of 23 September 1962, a servant found him dead.

"I do not regard myself as having accomplished anything particular in life," he had written as he approached seventy. "The most I can say of myself constructively is that I have laboured very hard and very earnestly, never giving up whatever the difficulties against which I had to contend."[23] He had never become a good writer, and yet, take him for all in all, perhaps he underestimated himself at the end.

23. Dawson's carbon of "Answers to New Series of 40 Questions" (1946), written for S. Frank Logan, p. 17.

9

Conclusion

Looking back over the years, Warrington Dawson saw his friendship with Joseph Conrad as "one of the very greatest things in my life."[1] Reared largely by his mother and instilled at an early age with a sense of his own position and abilities, Dawson as a young man had tended to seek out older men of stature, men of achievement, character, and fame whom he could respect and admire. There were Camille Flammarion, Auguste Rodin, and Theodore Roosevelt before there was Conrad. The murder of his father, the "Czar of South Carolina," had robbed Dawson early of something fine and strong that he needed. Like most men, and perhaps to a greater degree than most, Dawson required example and approval. To Conrad he admitted quite openly, "I need not say how much every single word of approval from you means to me."[2]

In a letter of 27 April 1911 to a friend, Miss Alice Dukes, Dawson had earlier commented on the same subject from another angle: "I can't help trying to influence everyone about me, or trying to be influenced when I am dealing with a nature or an intelligence which has anything to give me." Dawson himself, as the older man, established friendships with John Powell and Bernhard Trappschuh, as well as with numerous others. He helped to bring up a young English cousin, Ethelbert White, in fact to supervise the boy's "education and general development."[3] And in the case of Kermit Roosevelt and Borys Conrad and, later, George Clough Sharp, the friendship with the son helped to reinforce the friendship with the father. In each of these latter cases Dawson was a two-way success.

1. From Dawson's unpublished "13 Years—13 Windows," p. 67.
2. From *The Crimson Pall* (Chicago, 1927), p. 11.
3. Dawson to Mrs. J. Smith Brockenbrough, a letter of 20 July 1908 in the Powell Collection, Alderman Library, University of Virginia.

Jessie told Dawson, "You do not know how much your kind friendship to the boy, means to Conrad and I."[4]

Yet Dawson never saw, or perhaps never admitted to himself, a fact which Lady Ottoline Morrell grasped at once: Conrad's "apparent frankness had a great reserve."[5] The truth may be that Conrad's friendliness toward Dawson, after his first warm response, was tinctured by indulgence. Dawson to Conrad was *un bon garçon*, an earnest young man whose friendly offices were for many and complicated reasons more easy to accept than refuse. There was the episode in which Dawson offered to find Conrad a French outlet in *Progrès*. There were the Conrad lectures that Dawson delivered— not many, in fact, but all coming at a time before Conrad was widely known.[6] There was the matter of the Page luncheon and the Doubleday contract, and, of course, the friendship with Borys. Sometimes Dawson became a trifle too importunate, perhaps, but there was also the fact that Conrad had committed himself to a certain degree by saying that the main thing he disliked about Americans was "the irresponsibility with which people are used and dropped."[7] The correspondence between Conrad and Dawson might run thin at times (Conrad, Jessie apologized, was "a terrible person to write letters"),[8] but it was never allowed to run dry.

Whatever its low spots, moreover, the friendship had many things in its favor. For one thing, thanks to Valentine, Dawson "had not only read Conrad" when the two first met, "but, according to Conrad, 'understood' him—a thing which, in his ultra-sensitiveness, he rarely admitted."[9] Then there was the timing. Dawson first appeared on the scene when Conrad had a special need for reassurance. "One requires a fund of belief in oneself to do any artistic work," Conrad had explained to Rothenstein three years before, "and you pay a generous contribution to that account which is always on the verge of being exhausted."[10] In May, 1910, when he met Dawson,

4. Jessie Conrad to Dawson, an undated letter headed "Tuesday" (summer of 1913?).
5. *Memoirs of Lady Ottoline Morrell: A Study in Friendship 1873–1915*, ed. Robert Gathorne-Hardy (New York, 1964), p. 235.
6. On their basis Dawson deemed himself "the first lecturer on Conrad and his work in the US" (Dawson's carbon of a letter dated 15 February 1954 to Arnold T. Schwab).
7. Dawson to Schwab, from carbon of a letter of 11 March 1954.
8. Jessie Conrad to Dawson, 15 September 1919 (No. 89).
9. Dawson to Schwab, from carbon of a letter of 11 March 1954.
10. Conrad to Rothenstein, 21 August 1907, letter in Houghton Library, Harvard.

Conrad's entire being—physical, mental, and emotional—was shaky in the extreme, and Dawson's strong admiration may have helped a bit to restore Conrad's equilibrium. There were other bonds, of course. For one thing, Dawson was a novelist. Though not a good one, he was, nevertheless, a novelist. (He was also a journalist, which would not have endeared any man to Conrad, but Dawson was far more highly refined than any mere run-of-the-mill newsman, and, besides, such friends as Crane and Gibbon had demonstrated earlier that not all journalists were bad.) Then, too, both Conrad and Dawson were Francophiles. Both, like their fathers before them, were expatriates. Both came from cultivated backgrounds. Both had been raised in the aura of the Roman church—and Dawson, like Conrad, might have said that "dogma sits lightly on me."[11] And both had had their experiences at sea and their insight into Africa. Whatever the obstacles—Dawson's psychic interests, his somewhat childlike enthusiasm, his delicate ego, his constant offering of manuscripts—Conrad's last letter to him still conveyed "warm sympathy and love," as well as admiration for Dawson's "undaunted fortitude."[12] Both the love and the admiration were reciprocated. Lady Phyllis remembers well how Dawson "used often to talk of Joseph Conrad[,] whom he loved & admired . . . intensely."[13]

Jessie's place in the picture was at first confined mainly to the kitchen. After Dawson's stay at Gill Farm in 1914, however, he became "Dear Warrington" to her, and throughout the war she took over the bulk of the correspondence from Capel House. From after the war until 1924 Conrad wrote more than she did. Then, with Conrad gone, it became Jessie rather than Dawson who did most to keep the friendship alive, writing out of her loneliness, offering news and asking for news. Jessie was never much interested in things cultural and intellectual, but she responded to Dawson in the way she knew, to the man rather than the artist. Dawson's boyish good nature would not have been lost on the woman who believed that "the most lasting affection is that which partakes of the paternal or maternal quality."[14] Conrad himself had thought it "extraordinary

11. Conrad to Gordon Gardiner, 8 October 1923, letter in Houghton Library, Harvard.
12. Conrad to Dawson, 29 July 1923 (No. 106).
13. Lady Phyllis Benton to Randall, letter of 12 August 1964.
14. Jessie Conrad to George T. Keating, a note dated 24 March 1924 in a copy of Conrad's *Some Reminiscences* (London, 1912), now in the Beinecke Library, Yale. Cf. No. 102.

how that woman understands you."[15] When Dawson had come down to the Aldington cottage, of course it had been to find Conrad, but Jessie was there, too, and Dawson's Southern charm won her over. As Jessie wrote in 1929, "Warrington Dawson has made me feel that I had a real place in his affections, that I did indeed share in his friendship with Conrad. . . ."[16]

Dawson was never a second Galsworthy for Conrad, nor a Sanderson, a Crane, or a Curle. But he did become a friend, and he must be reckoned with in any complete understanding of Conrad's life and character. Certainly the Conrad-Dawson letters expose no startling new character traits, but they do bring to light a number of new details in Conrad's life. They demonstrate Conrad's kindness in new forms. They show his forbearance to rather better advantage than usual. They show at once his graciousness and his melancholy. Furthermore, despite circumstances that were sometimes difficult, they show his fidelity.

In his Humbert novel, *Chance,* Conrad wrote that "Dark and, so to speak, inscrutable spaces being met with in life there must be such places in any statement dealing with life."[17] At the very least his letters to Dawson cast a handful of sparks into some of the dark spaces of his own life. They help to answer just a bit better the plea "I want to be understood,"[18] which to Conrad seemed the universal aspiration.

15. Undated letter (No. 50).
16. From "Friendship's Friend" (see p. 35).
17. *Chance* (London, 1914), p. 93.
18. *Under Western Eyes* (London, 1911), p. 36.

Part Two

The Friendship in Letters

1. *Theodore Roosevelt to Mrs. Theodore Roosevelt*

No 31   Lake Naivasha,[1]
July 18th 1909

Darling Edie,

Here on the lake we have done well enough. Kermit[2] got one hippo, and I another; both of them were obtained under interesting circumstances, Kermit's giving us a regular chase in the steam launch, while mine charged us while we were in a rowboat—Kermit, with characteristic nerve and coolness, taking a series of pictures of the hippo as it came open-mouthed at us through the shallow water, while I was shooting. Now that we are out of the lion country (or rather, of the country where lions are most plentiful) I am again thoroly enjoying Kermit; he is a dear boy, and a fine fellow, too.

Warrington Dawson is out here with us. He has been a friend of real value to Kermit, and will tell you all about him; he is a clean, honorable fellow, whom I like to have with Kermit. I really greatly like him; and it is a relief, among my beloved hunters and naturalists, to meet a man of literary cultivation! He has been more than kind in taking dictations of letters &c, & has gone over my Scribner's articles (I have now finished 8; and do not expect to do more than 6 for all the remainder of the trip). He will bring the "Louves de Machecoul" to you.[3]

I have had a slight attack. . . .[4]

1. Lake Naivasha, northwest of Nairobi in British East Africa (now Kenya).
2. Roosevelt's oldest son.
3. *Les Louves de Machecoul*, by Alexandre Dumas and G. de Cherville. "I took Dumas's cycle of romances dealing with the French Revolution, because I had just finished Carlyle's work thereon—and I felt that of the two the novelist was decidedly the better historian" (*African Game Trails*, II [New York, 1910], 517).
4. Here Roosevelt reached the bottom of the sheet on which he was writing. Whatever became of the rest of the letter, this first part was doubtless given to Dawson because of its complimentary allusion to him.

2. Dawson to Mrs. J. Smith Brockenbrough[1]

1 bis rue Hardy, Versailles, France.
17th May, 1910.

Dear Betty:—

I wish I could write you a good long letter, but I am stealing time from the SCOURGE proof sheets to write you even these few lines!

John went back to London yesterday only, and I follow him to-morrow. I shall be visiting the McMillans, of East Africa;[2] they were here last week, I got them to invite John to lunch with them and me at their hotel, and they are going to help arranging for John to play for Mr Roosevelt by proposing that it be at their house, while I am there. Isn't that fun?

The lunch with Mathot the publisher went off splendidly.[3] The suite "In the South" will be on sale within a month; the Hahr Variations have gone to the printers, but the type-setting will be slow.[4] John played his wonderful Violin Concerto for Mathot who sized it up—as well as other people's music—by remarking "It is new and powerful—BUT melodic!!" The expense of publishing will be so heavy that Mathot will have to think up some scheme for launching it too; but he is so interested that he is going to try to do it.

John made ten-strikes with Marchesi and with the Princesse de Polignac. I think the old Marchioness Marchesi fell in love with him! At all events he can count on her influence, which is immense, for his concert. At Max Nordau's, he made a big hit.[5] Both the Dr and Madame were lovely to him; he met several notabilities there, including De la Nux, composer of the opera "Zaïre" and head of the Composition department of the Paris Conservatory;[6] also Jean Finot, editor of the Paris Review of Reviews. He played the F sharp and B flat Impromptus delightfully, and then at Max Nordau's request he played his "Erotique" and "Negro Elegy" which the Dr

1. Mrs. Brockenbrough was the sister of Dawson's pianist friend John Powell, with whom the letter is largely concerned. Original MS in Alderman Library, University of Virginia.

2. Originally from St. Louis, William Northrup McMillan was an explorer, rancher, and big-game hunter in Africa.

3. A. Z. Mathot is identified by Dawson in a letter of 23 March 1908 to Mrs. Brockenbrough as "a friend of mine . . . who recently founded a musical publishing house on lines of honesty towards composers" (Alderman Library).

4. Frederick Charles Hahr had been Powell's second piano teacher in the States. Mrs. Brockenbrough herself had been the first.

5. Max Nordau was a well-known physician-author of the day. See pp. 69–70.

6. Paul Veronge de la Nux, Zaïre (1889).

pronounced "remarkable". When I was going, both Dr and Mrs Nordau said to me separately, but almost in the same words:

"I thank you for the pleasure you gave us in coming this evening, but I thank you even more for the pleasure we had in hearing Mr Powell!"

I think John in better health and spirits than I have ever known him to be. I wish you could see him now! But you will see him this summer, and I know he will still be as well for it is a good solid reliable sort of health he is enjoying.

Much love from us both.

Warrington.

3. *Conrad to Dawson*[1]

ALDINGTON,/HYTHE,/KENT.

21 May 1910

My dear Sir

Les amis des [sic] nos amis etc but as a matter of fact I had your name laid up in a cell of my brain for some time now. It is (I mean my brain) a rather crazy structure with rusty-hinged doors and dark corners—and all dusty with ashes of good intentions. Thus I haven't as yet obtained either of your novels.

Let us meet without any more delay than may suit your convenience. Only you must understand the situation. You find here a man who has just got out of bed after a long illness: an attack of gout, literally from neck to ankles. You'll find him lame, grincheux and stupid—more than usual. And you must come to see him. He can't come to you in London. Like figures in a bad novel l'animal ne tient pas debout—at any rate not yet.

But this is not the worst. We have been living here in part of a cottage where we piled in a year ago with the idea of making it a centre for house hunting in this part of Kent—farm-house hunting. That sort of game is scarce; but we brought down a charming specimen only last week after no end of wearisome stalking. That's very well, but meantime (we can't enter till June) we have no bedroom to offer you and you must be prepared for a most primitive

---

1. This first Conrad letter to Dawson was sent c/o McMillan, Berkeley Square.

reception. Something like the rude and unaffected hospitality of cave-men—with this difference only that the meat shall be cooked.

None but les intimes have been allowed to come near us here. Will you have the courage to join their rank, to undertake a horrid railway journey of 2 hours (11 to 12.58) and the horrors of the return trip by the 8.20 up. Will you? The hardships of the caravan track are as nothing to the enterprise I am inviting you to. I have been frank; but if, in the pride of youth and recklessness (perhaps) or your disposition, you won't take the warning, why then—we shall be *very glad* to see you. Name your day (except Tuesday next) and I'll try to meet the train or shall send a dependable native. We shall have an afternoon together; and if I quarrel with you after the manner of une vieille ganache more than is becoming (as between two brother-craftsmen) you can always report me to dear old Ted[2] who no doubt will do justice by shooting me next time he comes home on leave. Voilà! Meantime believe me very

Sincerely yours
J. Conrad.

Pardon this variegated scrawl; I am writing on the knee.

2. Conrad's friend Edward Lancelot Sanderson, whom Dawson had visited in Nairobi.

4. Conrad to John Galsworthy[1]

Aldington, Hythe, Kent.
Tuesday

Dearest Jack,

Thanks for your letter. I am trying to work as fast as I can without knocking my feeble brain silly.

I'll report to you soon how I am *really* getting on. All that went before, mere trial runs so to speak. I have been also interrupted. Hugh Clifford returned from Ceylon, turned up last Friday. On Sat. a young American writer who has been with Roosevelt in S. Africa arrived for the day.[2] The greatest news is that Mrs. Ted

1. This letter, which should be dated 31 May 1910, is reproduced as it appears in G. Jean-Aubry, *Joseph Conrad: Life and Letters*, II (Garden City, N.Y., 1927), 107.
2. Conrad's confusion of "S. Africa" with B.E.A. is understandable; his friends the Sandersons had lived in the former a number of years.

Sanderson has discovered in herself a talent for writing and that the Ex-President has been so struck that he placed three of her S. A. sketches with *Scribners' Magazine*.[3] They seem very well and happy over there.

Same young man brought a formal message from the only Teddy.[4] He would have invited himself to come and see me only too busy with official festivities.

Many, many thanks, my dear best Jack. Our dear love to Ada.[5] How is she? This weather is not very good.

3. Published as "African Sketches and Impressions" under the name "Janet Allardyce" in *Scribner's Magazine*, XLVIII (1910), 627–632. "More African Sketches" followed in LI (1912), 103–110.
4. Not Sanderson, but Roosevelt.
5. Mrs. Galsworthy.

5. *Conrad to Dawson*

ALDINGTON,/HYTHE,/KENT.
4 June 1910.

My dear Sir

Thanks for all you say. I've ordered the Secret Agent—which, by the by, has begun to appear in French as feuilleton of the Temps.[1]

Let me in my turn remind you of the promise you have given me of sending me one of your books. Les bons comptes font les bons amis.

Give my love to the boy who has read *Youth* and expressed so artistically his reason for liking my prose. I can send him no less than that. Before he acquires a boy of his own I shall be no longer here—on this earth of fine sights, honest endeavours and kindly hearts. But I like to think that my memory may be kept green by the youngest of the generations now existing.

Marwood was here yesterday and wishes to be remembered to

1. *Le Temps* presented *L'Agent Secret* in thirteen installments between 31 May and 8 July 1910 (not noted by Kenneth A. Lohf and Eugene P. Sheehy, *Joseph Conrad at Mid-Century: Editions and Studies, 1895–1955* [Minneapolis, 1957]). The translator was Henry D. Davray, a notable man of letters, born in Paris and educated at the Sorbonne and the University of London. Among other achievements Davray established and managed the collection of foreign authors by the *Mercure de France*, and translated numerous works by English authors.

you.[2] We talked of you a good bit. You have awakened his sympathy and interest.

I don't speak of myself; on that you must form your own judgement. Let me only say that I hope our acquaintance shall not be allowed to die out wherever you are—in the New World or the Old.

Yours cordially
J. Conrad.

2. Conrad's good friend Arthur Pearson Marwood had been present when Dawson came calling the previous Saturday.

6. *Conrad to Dawson*

CAPEL HOUSE,/ORLESTONE,/N^R ASHFORD.
27 Sept 1910.

My dear Dawson.

I didn't dare to look at your book till I finished a rather long thing which I was writing.[1] It is really complimentary; I am shy of reading a man whom I credit with *power* while busy with my own prose. I have not been disappointed. Yes, certainly. There is *power* to begin with, and a great charm of style, a soberness of presentation which appeals to me extremely, l'œil artiste as to details, with a large conception of the whole. In short, mon cher, beaucoup de talent. Talent, I mean, of the sort that is on the way of becoming *exceptional*. Voilà. That is, concisely stated, my impression corrected by some conscientious meditation; for as you may imagine I am not writing this after one reading only.

The first was rather rapid on account of the intrinsic interest of the story which carries one on finely. A great quality that! The second was au point de vue du métier. You know what I mean. All this holds together excellently and all the figures stand square in surroundings which are rendered completely. The tragic atmosphere (because it *is* that) does not oppress one—these are human affairs and one feels them to be in life not on a stage. My congratulations —and my thanks for very real pleasure combined indeed with instruc-

1. Conrad probably refers to his own "A Smile of Fortune," published in *The London Magazine*, XXV (1911), 801–836. He had now found time to read Dawson's *The Scar* (London, 1906; Boston, 1910).

tion; because as you may imagine all this—so removed from the ordinary convention—is quite new to me.

I had two letters from Sanderson who is now in Scotland. I hope to see him here in October. I am on the eve of tackling a long novel without a purpose but which I hope shall show some artistic sense.[2] But it will be a devil of a job. Do believe my dear fellow in my thorough appreciation of your friendly letters if I don't answer them as quickly as decency would demand. And whatever you do don't forget us when you come over.

My wife sends her kind regards. She enjoyed the book immensely. Marwood wishes to be remembered to you. He was very captivated by your novel which we have been talking over together only the other day.

Tout à vous
J. Conrad

2. *Chance.*

7. *Dawson to Mrs. J. Smith Brockenbrough*[1]

1 bis rue Hardy, Versailles.
30th Sept, 1910.

Dear Bettie:—

What has become of you and John all this time? Never a line since your letter from the country saying you would write from Richmond. I don't even know when John is coming back.

When you reached Richmond, you probably heard of the dastardly means the Times-Dispatch found for maligning me and killing the SCAR among Virginians—by alleging it was an attack upon Virginian qualities of HOSPITALITY! I wrote a protest for publication, which Mr Hemphill, the editor, who for twenty-three years was living off his News and Courier salary paid largely by me, wrote to me that he would publish, but I have reason to believe he never did.[2]

Is not the accompanying letter from Joseph Conrad about The

1. Original MS in Alderman Library, University of Virginia.
2. James Calvin Hemphill, city editor of the *News and Courier* under Dawson's father, became managing editor after Captain Dawson was killed. In 1910 he resigned to become editor of the Richmond *Times-Dispatch*. Dawson here exaggerates both the nature and the possible effect of the review, which appeared on 25 July.

Scar delightful?[3] I have immense admiration for Conrad, and his opinion is one which really counts with me; besides, he is considered practically the only English author of the day who has kept his whole grip on his public and is forging steadily ahead instead of losing ground.

My plans are now changed, and I expect to spend the winter over here, so don't bother about the Woman's Club just for the present.[4] When I do come to America, however, I shall make a particular point of wanting to come to Richmond so as to face my treacherous enemies.

Affectionately,
Warrington.

3. Dawson enclosed a copy of Conrad's letter of 27 September (No. 6).
4. Mrs. Brockenbrough was to have arranged for Dawson to lecture in Richmond.

8. *Conrad to Dawson*

Capel House,/Orlestone,/Nr Ashford.
15 Febr '11.

My dear Warrington Dawson

Thanks for your friendly letters. I feel remorseful towards you in this matter of correspondence; but I've grown so shameless that I have forgotten even how to apologise in fitting terms. I prefer to brazen it out and ask for forgiveness as a sturdy beggar asks for alms —with a sort of unholy leer confessing his unworthiness at the very moment he asks for charity.

It is jolly of you to beat my little drum "en bon camarade." I should be delighted to appear in the new magazine. If she[1] wants something of mine *complétement inédit* I am putting finishing touches to a story, (which I think I'll call *Freya of the Seven Isles*), length about 20000 words (3 or four instalments) of which I could send her the typescript in say a fortnight. It's quite good magazine stuff, quite Conradesque (in the easier style),—"no blush to the cheek of the young person" sort of thing.[2] Perfectly safe. Eastern

1. Adeline de Lano Demachy, *directrice* of *Progrès*.
2. Conrad uses here the words of Mr. Podsnap, Dickens's embodiment of narrow Victorianism in *Our Mutual Friend*.

134

Sea setting, but not too much setting. I would be glad to hear from the lady.

Tell me mon bon—should Mrs de Lano Demachy write to me—whether I can ask her for 1000 frcs for giving her the *English text* in advance of publication here? I mean that she should get the translation done herself. But I would revise it if she wished it. Qu'en pensez-vous? Of course in confidence. I ask you only because I don't want to do anything outrageous. I should think she could get the translation done for 200–250 frcs. Altogether say the stuff would cost her about £50 which does not seem much?

It's good news to hear that you are coming over. We can put you up now. So you must come for the night—a night at least—and we shall have a long argumentative talk. I am looking forward immensely to seeing you. My wife sends her most friendly remembrances. Au revoir. A bientôt—then.

Yours ever sincerely
J. Conrad

9. *Conrad to Henry D. Davray*[1]

Capel House
[1911]

Cher Davray,

Je vous écris ce mot tout de suite pour ne pas avoir l'air de manigancer des affaires derrière votre dos. Un ami à moi Dawson (journaliste, romancier Américain—peut-être vous connaissez?) m'a mis en relation avec madame Demaché, Revue: *Progrès*, pour une œuvre de moi. Je suis en train de finir une nouvelle (24.000 mots) qui fait l'affaire. Je lui ai cédé (serial rights) le texte (inédit) Anglais pour mille frcs. Elle fera faire la traduction. Voilà. Vous concevez mon cher, que je ne suis pas allé chercher cela. Je l'ai fait pour D. qui est un bon garçon et voulait me rendre service.

Dans les circonstances, je propose que nous partagions—c'est-il juste, croyez-vous? Mais comme j'ai diablement besoin d'argent peut-être voudrez-vous bien me débiter les frcs 500 que vous prendrez en

1. This letter is reprinted from *Lettres Françaises*, ed. G. Jean-Aubry (Paris, 1930), pp. 107–108. It was probably written about mid-February.

compte en réglant ce qui pourra me revenir sur les livres publiés par le "Mercure". Voulez-vous?

Nous espérons de tout notre cœur que la convalescence de Madame a été heureuse.

Mille amitiés.

Tout à vous.

10. *Conrad to Dawson*

Capel House. Orlestone/N^r Ashford.
28 Mch 1911.

Cher ami.

Just a word to let you know, in view of your promised visit, that unfortunately in the month of May we shall be in London. It has been decided that another operation is necessary on my wife's knee. What must be, must be.

I'll send you the address in London as soon as I know myself where we shall hang out that troublous time. But we expect to be back here by the first of June. Anyway we must see each other either here or in town.

Mrs Demachy prefers to take the *Typhoon*[,] de Smet's translation—I hope good.[1] Would you mind, when you see the lady, asking her to return me the MS of *Freya* if she still has it in her possession. It may be she has given it to Davray who has arranged with her for the Typhoon.

But don't give yourself any special trouble over the matter. It is not particularly important. Only if occasion offers.

Wife's kindest regards.

Yours cordially
J. Conrad.

1. Joseph de Smet was a Belgian man of letters. In his edition of Conrad's *Lettres Françaises* (p. 111) Jean-Aubry writes:

M. Joseph de Smet faisait paraître de 'Typhon' une traduction dans la revue 'Progrès', et il s'apprêtait à traduire 'Nostromo', ce qu'il fit au cours des années précédentes: la guerre isolant M. de Smet en Belgique laissa dans l'ignorance de ce fait ceux qui assumèrent définitivement la charge de la traduction française des Œuvres Complètes de Joseph Conrad: ce qui explique pourquoi *Typhon* fut ultérieurement traduit par M. André Gide. . . .

11. *Conrad to Dawson*

Capel House,/Orlestone,/Nᴿ Ashford.

1 Augt 1911.

My dear Dawson.

We shall be delighted. Why not take your ticket from Paris only to Dover or Folkestone. A train which stops in *Ashford* leaves half an hour or so after the Continental mail train. If you let me know I shall meet you in Ashford. You could sleep here and continue to London say after lunch next day—by the fast afternoon train.

Wife sends kind regards.

Yours cordially

J. Conrad.

Marwood just been and sends you greetings.

Drop us a line in time. For wire: *Conrad Hamstreet* is sufficient address. *Change in Ashford.*

12. *Conrad to Dawson*

Capel House. Orlestone/Nʳ Ashford.

17 Aug. 1911.

My dear Dawson.

I am no end sorry to have acted tactlessly. I had not read the whole book. I knew that G. was no negrophile in the common meaning of the word.[1] Neither is he a man *"out after dollars."* I quite understand all you say and so will he when I show him your letter (he's in Paris just now)—and pray believe in my most genuine regard for your opinions, for your feelings for your judgement and your sincerity.

In fact my dear fellow neither he nor I would have had anything to say had you printed your letter to me as an article, or made a most condemnatory analysis of the book in your paper. Your hands are free now.

I would have written at once but there is a most tragic affair going on in our house. A friend arrived last *Sat* for a week end—and now is

---

1. Apparently Dawson had accused "G" of being a "negrophile." Evidence on the matter is sparse, but I conjecture that "G" was Perceval Gibbon, and the book *Margaret Harding*. See pp. 47–48.

lying dangerously ill in our house.[2] The worry and strain drives me almost crazy. There are also other circumstances which make this affair particularly poignant. I can say no more just now. Pray pardon the delay in answering your letter, and believe always in my inalterable feelings of friendship and regard.

Yours in haste

J. Conrad.

Wife sends kindly greetings.

2. Conrad wrote Galsworthy that on 12 August,
Last Saturday, Norman Douglas (who had returned to London from Italy 5 days before) came for a week-end. But he arrived in a state of high fever and hardly able to stand. . . . On Monday we sent for a nurse (after Jessie and I had been up with him for two nights and a day). To-day he does not recognize anybody, his temperature after most appalling ups and downs has reached 105°, —and here we are.
(Jean-Aubry, LL, II, 133–134; the letter should be dated 18 August). In his letters to both Galsworthy and Dawson, Conrad implies—contrary to Douglas's recollection—that originally a weekend visit from Douglas was planned. Cf. p. 57.

13. *Conrad to Dawson*

24–8–'11
Friday.

My dear Warrington Dawson

Just a word to say that the negotiation with Progrès "a abouti"— thanks to your friendly office, tact, wisdom and diplomacy. What could be more admirable than your speeches to Mme D[emachy]![1]

Yours is a jolly letter. What activity, what go there is in you. What mental alertness. You are a wonderful fellow. Yes. You can do anything you like I believe. And why I should be supposed to be in the way I want to know. *Your* individuality will make your work. When you touch Africa you shall make it yours—and yours will be better no doubt than mine—and at any rate very different—not so much in the shadows as the *H[eart] of D[arkness]* is.[2]

Marwood sends his regards.

Au revoir—a bientôt[.]

Yours

J Conrad.

1. See letter No. 8
2. While in Africa in 1909 Dawson had planned an African novel. He began writing it at Gill Farm, Ruckinge, Kent, in the spring of 1914, and called it, at various times, "The Rock," "The Shrouded Height," and "Border-lines."

138

14. *Conrad to Dawson*

Capel House,/Orlestone,/Nᴿ Ashford.
30 Sept '11

My dear Warrington Dawson

Just a line on this scrap of paper to thank you for your letter which gave me immense pleasure and to thank you still more for your friendliness to my boy. He joined the school-ship just a week ago and you shall hear from him before long.[1]

I am no end flattered by the Princesse's appreciation of the Duel and much honoured by the gracious invitation.[2] Please say so at a fitting opportunity. It looks to me as tho' you were determined to make me a success in the *grand monde* in which you move. I am instructing Methuen's to send you a copy of Western Eyes due to appear on the 5th Oct. You shall also have a little later on a small vol of Reminiscences[3] which will be published by Nash in 3 weeks or so.

I am only so so. Can't work. Wife sends her friendly regards.

Tout à vous

J. Conrad.

1. On 22 September Conrad left Borys on board the *Worcester*, a nautical school-ship at Greenhithe. Subsequently Borys did write to Dawson a few times. His letters of 1 and 8 November 1912 (Nos. 29 and 32) give a glimpse of the relationship between the two.
2. The lady who liked this story from *A Set of Six* (London, 1908) was Princesse Marie, daughter of the Duc and Duchesse de Rohan.
3. *Some Reminiscences* (London, 1912).

15. *Jessie Conrad to Dawson*

Capel House,/Orlestone,/Nᴿ Ashford.
October 11ᵗʰ 1911

Dear Mʳ Dawson.

Conrad, who has been in bed for several days, nursing a bad cold, asks me to write to you. He would very much liked to have accepted your kind invitation but it is quite impossible for him to travel just now. His cold is getting better now and he hopes soon to start work again. It is awfully kind of you to write to Borys, he values your friendship most highly. We have such good news of him and he seems perfectly happy. The snap shots of Jackolo[1] I wanted you to have[,] also the one of the house. We often talk of you and shall look forward to seeing you when next you are in England. With very kind regards. Believe me dear Mr. Dawson,

Very sincerely yours.
Jessie Conrad

1. The Conrads' younger son, John, who was five at the time.

16. Dawson to Conrad[1]

1 bis rue Hardy, Versailles,
17th Oct, 1911.

Conrad—my peerless Conrad—I am stunned by your audacity![2] Audacity of conception, daring to je [sic] just and pondered in dealing with a question about [which] the world insists upon being hysterical; audacity of essential detail in reaching a conclusion so unexpected and yet so bewilderingly real, so convincingly moral.

Two days ago, before finishing, I wrote to Mrs Conrad that I was so held by the sheer power of the story that I couldn't yet express a critical opinion. But that domination of the power was framing the opinion which came of itself, all carved out by the incidents and reflections on the way, when I reached the end. It must have been the end in perspective which puzzled me. I talked to myself somewhat in this wise: "A tragedy, of course; but what?— How?— Suicide? No; my Conrad is perfectly aware that suicide is no solution, that apart from its immoral evading of responsibilities it is in itself futile, cowardly, contemptible; such a character as Razumow is not chiselled out by a great artist to be despatched in any tawdry way such as that. Murder, then? That is possible; but that would be the matter-of-course thing, above which my Conrad always rises even in a short etching, so how much heavier are his exigencies in a granite block such as this! Besides, death would put him face to face with the spirit of Haldin; Razumow has dwelt so much on that spirit presence, that the thought would inevitably occur to the reader and would make Razumow's death seem a species of beginning rather than an end. Most writers of the day would not stop to consider this;

1. From Dawson's carbon copy. Hence the letter is unsigned.
2. Dawson had just read *Under Western Eyes* (London, 1911).

but Conrad would. So, I fancy it will not be death. Then—what? Not mere remorse, for that has already worn him down almost past suffering further subjectively; if he lives, there must be some other form of expiation."

Then I was caught in the whirl of Miss Haldin's search for him, of his talk at the house—I had no more time for speculation. I did not understand more than he did, when Nikita attacked him; I was shocked, stunned; I followed his mad wanderings through the streets —his *silent* wanderings, I followed him breathlessly, in a bewilderment akin to his; I wondered if there were blood marking his tracks —Conrad, *he too* must have looked down for blood, must have feared to slip in it, must have failed to understand when he saw none! The blows had deafened him where they had been meant to take his life. Then, suddenly, Nikita's announcement in the room— "I have burst the drums of his ears for him!"

Man—I sprang from my chair! Then I sat down again, and re-read every word of the scene before I could go on—re-read, fascinated, hypnotised as completely by the beauty of the art this second time as I had been by the vivid reality the first time.

Then, his end—the deaf, crippled philosopher—half-respected and well-cared for—death in life—and the stil[l]ness of eternity in which to meditate!

For the scheme as a whole, there is not a point neglected, not a thread which fails in its perfect working-out; so much, I expected from you because it was you. What arrests my attention and commands my admiration most, is your fairness of balance. "The Secret Agent" was a foundation on which I based hopes that you would remain fair, but after all, that was a story, and this was to be an exposition. You had reasons to abhor Russian oppression, you had opportunities to know grim facts about it; but you had had the advantage of many years of detachment from it all, and of seeing something of the inside life of professional wreckers. I expected you to keep the *mental* balance of it all perfectly; but feared for the human possibilities of the working-out. But you triumphed over every obstacle, remaining true, fair, and moral throughout. The abuses of autocracy and democracy, of tyranny and of anarchy, get each their due in measured terms which stamp the dominating thought upon the reader's mind—that there is wrong in right and right in wrong and all depends upon the use which is made of either.

I must stop here; I am amazed by *my* audacity in rattling off to you my impressions; I shall try to do some pondering too, try to raise myself to your plane, my Conrad, before I write seriously of "Under Western Eyes".

I was talking of it to-day to James W. Riddle, who was for several years U.S. Ambassador to Petersburg; I lunched with him, and you were the subject of a long talk between us. I did not give away the plot of the book, because I want him to buy it; but I discussed with him your conception of Russia. He was deeply impressed by your idea of *cynicism* when I explained it fully to him. Did you know that I spent several months in Petersburg during the Russo-Jap War? That enabled me to talk more intelligently than I could otherwise have done.

I have noticed in the course of my walks that Brentano, Galignani, and Smith's Libraries all have "Western Eyes" prominently displayed in their window-fronts. May the shekels rain upon you as your just reward!

Thy friend,

17. *Conrad to Dawson*[1]

CAPEL HOUSE,/ORLESTONE,/Nᴿ ASHFORD.
21 Oct. 1911.

My dear fellow

You have warmed me through and through with your wonderfully appreciative letter.[2] I just drop you these few lines to thank you without delay for a great and rare pleasure. I have been beastly seedy for days. Wife has told you—didn't she. I am most grateful for your invitation so truly brotherly but I can't jump at it (as I would like to do) just now.[3]

Mille amities. The house sends its love.

Yours always
J. Conrad

1. Original in Ralph Foster Museum, School of the Ozarks.
2. I.e., No. 16.
3. Jessie had declined for Conrad in her letter of 11 October (No. 15).

18. Conrad to Dawson

Saturday[1]

My dear fellow.

You will pardon the delay. I am pushing on desperately with my novel now six weeks overdue.[2] I am not going to write you exhaustively for the same reason—and I know you will not take it amiss.

I have read the MS. I have read it twice. And I can safely say that I have appreciated it without missing any material point. The question before us is however the question of expediency.

On meditating it over carefully I discover, stated shortly, that what stands in the way of that work is this: that the treatement [sic] is not light enough. It is witty and in places there is even profundity (in the comments)—but no lightness. There is I must say a sort of discord between the subject and the style which is the style of the man who wrote the Scar & the Scourge. And this is which [sic] puts off publishers and editors. They don't see its high qualities. They only feel that it does not fit in with their idea of what the treatment of such a subject should be.

I don't agree with them "au fond." My conclusion however is that the MS should be kept back as material for future use in a mood of the frankest fun.[3] You, mon cher, in my view, are not only a serious artist but an artist dans le genre sérieux. At any rate at present. And I think that a man who has written such two books as those you have published may well forego the immediate publication of this MS. Later on when the things near your heart, and therefore in accord with your temperamental manner of expression, have been uttered, then you may take up a lighter vein and no doubt you will find in yourself a more light-hearted mood. Voilà. This briefly is le vrai fond de ma pensée. I think that abstention just now is the more dignified policy. You ought to try to faire grand. It is in you. Keep

1. I am unable to date this letter. A note by Dawson says it concerns The True Dimension, which he finished on 10 May 1914, but Victory, the novel Conrad was working on in May, 1914, was not then "six weeks overdue." Conceivably Victory may have been "overdue" during the preceding autumn, when Conrad took nearly a ten-week pause in his work. With misgivings, therefore, one might suggest that Conrad read Dawson's unfinished MS then. It is much more tempting to place the letter before that of 25 November 1911 if one suspects, as I do, that despite Dawson's note it refers either to his much-travelled, often-rejected "Exiles of Elysium" or, still more probably, to an early form of The True Dimension called "The Purser's Shilling," which Dawson was writing in 1911. See Conrad's comments in No. 84.
2. Chance or Victory, depending on date of letter.
3. Conrad underlined the word twice.

to that gift. There will be always time enough to discover yourself as an excellent jester. Think of the public which you have yet to conquer. It mustn't be put in doubt of what you are really. A matter of policy. I tell you all this in the fulness of the sincerity which is due to you as écrivain and of my affection for the man[.]

Yours ever
J. Conrad.

19. *Conrad to Dawson*

Capel House,/Orlestone,/Nʀ Ashford.

25 Nov '11.

My dear Warrington Dawson.

I am distressed by your letter; but I don't think I am guilty as much as you seem to think. If there is any man I would wish to help it is you. But my dear fellow you are mistaken if you think I have the slightest influence. I don't know really who are the men of whom you speak. I did certainly get some reviewing to do for my friend [Norman] Douglas some time ago. But that was purely be [*sic*] the accident of meeting once or twice the editor of a newspaper whom I have not seen since. My dear fellow I am profoundly unknown here—or at any rate completely uninfluential. My own stories get refused. I have a little vol now which I have been unable to place for months.[1]

Reading your letter (the one which came with the MS)[2] I saw that the MS had been already offered to to [*sic*] several publishers; and amongst them those of whom I had been thinking. I don't know many of them. To go to them again would have been to go to meet a rebuff both for you and me. And having lately got some few knocks on my own account I knew I would do no good. I am now having a row with Methuen about certain matters connected with the publication of that miserable novel of mine.[3] I have been so outspoken with that beastly firm that any interference of mine in favour of your work would be simply fatal to its chances.

1. Perhaps *'Twixt Land and Sea*. Though it appeared the next year, this "little vol" did not take the form that Conrad planned.
2. "Exiles of Elysium" or "The Purser's Shilling"? Cf. No. 18, n. 1.
3. *Under Western Eyes*.

I am very sorry for having offered my opinion on the MS. I can see its quality. I can also see why these men have declined it. But indeed my dear fellow I had no idea you attached so much importance to the immediate placing of that MS. From our conversation I imagined you had other works ready or at any rate not far from being finished. I don't know how I got that impression. I can only repeat that I am sorry. I wrote to you in all sincerity if under a complete misapprehension of the real state of affairs. And now I can only express my profound contrition at having disappointed your expectations. Whether you will forgive me my clumsiness I don't know. But whether or no I can assure you of my unalterable regard and sympathy[.]

Yours always
J Conrad.

20. *Conrad to Dawson*

CAPEL HOUSE,/ORLESTONE,/Nʀ ASHFORD.
29 Dec '11

Dear Warrington Dawson.

Our best wishes of health and prosperity for the coming year. Thanks for your card. I am immensely flattered by your choice for the "conference" but I feel profoundly how unworthy I am of the distinction.[1] But still I would come over for the pleasure of hearing you speak (if at the cost of enormous blushes) if I could possibly manage it. But it is not possible. On ne peut pas lutter contre la force des choses. Everybody (including the two boys) sends most affectionate greetings.

A vous de coeur
J. Conrad.

1. On 3 March 1912 Dawson delivered a lecture on Joseph Conrad to the St. Geneviève Club, Paris.

21. *Jessie Conrad to Dawson*

CAPEL HOUSE,/ORLESTONE,/Nᴿ ASHFORD.

March 11ᵗʰ 1912

Dear Mʳ Dawson.

Conrad who is very busy finishing his novel,[1] asks me to thank you very much indeed for your letter and for your kindness in the matter of your lecture.[2] He sends his love to you and will write to you himself in a very short time. We have been a houseful of influenza even Borys, on board the Worcester, did not escape. I saw him a week ago and he sent messages to you for Conrad to forward. He seems to be working very hard. Conrad wished me to tell you that no American editor has been here. With kindest regards and warm remembrances.

Sincerely yours,

Jessie Conrad

1. *Chance*, finished 25 March.
2. Dawson's Conrad lecture, delivered eights days earlier. See preceding letter.

22. *Conrad to Dawson*

CAPEL HOUSE,/ORLESTONE,/Nᴿ ASHFORD.

9 Ap. '12

My dear Warrington Dawson.

I was touched by the friendliness almost more than by the generous appreciation of the lecture.[1] Forgive me for not writing sooner to thank you. But all these[2] words of thanks do seem cold when set down black on white. However you know me well enough to believe that I am neither insensible nor ungrateful.

And now more thanks for the book.[3] You have a most attractive French style—and very French it is too and yet with something individual—and even racial—glowing through it and adding to the fascination of the perfectly simple diction. Of course one is aware of the deep feeling under the quiet, correct I may say, poise of the phrase. And one can not help feeling with you, all the way with you—even apart (in my case) from the complete accord of thought

1. See the two preceding letters.
2. Perhaps "mere."
3. Dawson's *Le Nègre aux États-Unis* (Paris, 1912).

146

—from the conviction your perfectly unrethorical [*sic*] prose carries to my mind. I can indeed congratulate you with all my heart on that work so seriously emotional[,] so fairly stated as to its main (human) points and so discreetly eloquent. Marwood (who is a great reader) when bringing the book back said to me that this was the first work of real value he had read on the subject. This was his first remark. He said also other intelligent things in praise of the book which I won't repeat, since they are only the amplification of his first statement. He asks to be remembered to you kindly.

The Editor of the English Review (Austin Harrison—the son of the positivist philosopher,[4] you know) got your address from me. He means to ask you for an article. If I were you I would write it for him[.] It wouldn't be bad if you had an organ in England where you could now and then express the *Southern* point of view on various American questions. The circulation of the E. R[.] is running up fast. However you will see what he says and what you think of him. I have just finished my long novel.[5] No more this time.

Yours as ever

J. Conrad.

My wife's cordial regards. When are you coming over?

4. Frederic Harrison, long president of the English Positivist Committee and one of the founders of the *Positivist Review*.
5. *Chance*.

23. *Conrad to Dawson*

CAPEL HOUSE,/ORLESTONE,/NR ASHFORD.

6 May 12

Trés cher.

Thanks for your good letter. It is a funny story that of G. Richards.[1] That man's infernal cheek knocks me over. You have said the right things in this matter. I have not been feeling very well lately. It's very good and dear of you to ask me over and I would love it; but

1. Probably Grant Richards, i.e., Franklin Thomas Grant Richards, a devil-may-care publisher and author. Though no further allusions are made to him in the correspondence, Conrad's phrase "infernal cheek" fits well with the judgment passed by the London *Times* in Richards's obituary of 25 February 1948 (p. 7): "his wild methods in finance . . . scandalized even the Carey Street officials."

147

just at present it is impossible. I must at once start a series of short stories. It's convict labour! No more this time. Affectionate remembrances from us all.

Yours always
J. Conrad.

24. Conrad to Dawson

Capel House,/Orlestone,/Nʀ Ashford.
10 July '12

Mon trés cher.

This is good news. We are all looking forward to your visit here. I shall let Borys know to-night.

Certainement—if health and other things permit. I'll be delighted to be made known to Lord Plymouth.[1]

But as you know I am a man peculiarly liable to be af[f]licted by a "nigger in the fence" whatever my purpose may be.

Au revoir then. We expect to hear from you very soon with a firm date. Au revoir à bientôt[.]

Yours ever
J. C.

Wife's kind regards.

1. Robert George Windsor-Clive, Earl of Plymouth, to whom Dawson introduced Conrad.

25. Conrad to Dawson

Capel House,/Orlestone,/Nʀ Ashford.
2 Aug '12

Dear Warrington Dawson

I was glad to get your letter. You must now let us know at what date your engagements will permit you to come and see us.

You are very kind. Borys is now away fishing at Marwoods and then he has an invitation to the seaside. The two days between these two absences we would like to keep him with us. I have started a long short story[1] and am tied down to that task after months of loafing. Couldn't you come here directly you return from St Fagan Castle?[2] Anyway we leave the dates to you but please let us know soon.

Au revoir— A bientot we hope[.]

Yours always
J. C.

PS Jessie's kind regards. I want to hear all the news of your work —of things done and things planned.

1. Probably the short story which developed into the novel *Victory*.
2. One of Lord Plymouth's homes, near Cardiff, Wales.

26. *Conrad to Dawson*

CAPEL HOUSE,/ORLESTONE,/N^R ASHFORD.
12 Augst '12

Mon cher

Il nous tarde de vous voir! Would you mind the heroic enterprise of taking the 10.15 am train from Char[ing] + on Sunday next (arrives *Ashford* 11.40) and stay with us till after lunch on Monday, if you can.

I or Borys will meet you in *Ashford*.

We shall talk de omnibus rebus and mostly of our work—or yours rather for mine is done such as it is.

Tout à vous
J. Conrad.

27. *Conrad to Dawson*

23 Aug. '12

My dear W. Dawson.

Pinker[1] will expect us on Monday about noon[.] I shall arrive Char[ing] + at about 11.45.

I have this moment heard from Mavrocordato (sub-Editor of the

1. James Brand Pinker, Conrad's agent and friend.

E.R[.]) that Harrison is away in Scotland.[2] This is a bad time of
the year to catch people in London. However we shall call at the
E.R[.] so that you may make the acquaintance of Mavrocordato[,]
a very nice fellow and worth twenty Harrisons anyhow. Au revoir.

Yours always

J. C.

2. Conrad's letter of 9 April (No. 22) had mentioned Austin Harrison's interest
in seeing an article from Dawson for the *English Review*. The current sub-editor was
John Mavrogordato.

28. *Conrad to Dawson*

CAPEL HOUSE,/ORLESTONE,/N^R ASHFORD.

Thursday.

My dear Warrington

I am no end sorry; but it is no use pretending, this blamed fit of
gout has got me fast and cant be shaken off in two or three days.
It is with the greatest reluctance that I had to send the wire; and
that I must give up all hope of hearing Mr Powell play on the 19th.[1]

I am bitterly disappointed. Please tell him.

Glad you are at work. Don't forget I'll have to hear these new
Chaps too, when you come down. A bientôt[.]

Yours always

J. Conrad.

1. Tracing John Powell's public concerts given on a nineteenth has not yielded
a date for this letter. Though Conrad says here that he will not attend, a plausible
guess may still be November, 1912. On 23 November 1912 Mary Withey reported to
Dawson that she had seen Conrad at Powell's stunningly successful concert in
Æolian Hall on the nineteenth of that month. The "Chap[ter]s" mentioned here
would refer, then, to Dawson's "The Sin." Conjectured date: 31 October 1912 (see
No. 30, n. 1).

29. *Borys Conrad to Dawson*

H.M.S. Worsester,/Off Greenhithe,/Kent.

Nov. 1st. 1912.

Dear Mr Dawson.

Thank you very much for the knife, it is the very thing I wanted.
Now that you have sent your address in America I shall of course

write to wish you a Merry Xmas, and also I will write before that if I may. There is not much news now, so soon after you have been down; but I will drop you a line again before you go. Mr. Pinker has just sent me a fine book entitled, "The British Battle Fleet" by a man named Jane.[1] It is quite a new book I think, but it interests me very much indeed; and it has some very fine coloured plates and photographs. The chaplain is fairly calm now but the other day some mischevious spark put some peper in the duster which he cleans the blackboard with. Of course the result was a violent fit of sneezing which did not improve his temper, although he did not suspect anybody. I have no more news just now but will write again soon[.]

Always your sincere friend,
Borys Conrad.

1. Frederick Thomas Jane, *The British Battle Fleet* (London, 1912).

30. *Conrad to Dawson*

Capel House,/Orlestone,/N^r Ashford.
Friday.[1]

My dear Dawson

You are very good to us & to our boy. Believe in our heartfelt appreciation of all you do and say. We are inexpressibly touched by your sympathy and by that friendship you extend to our child. I don't wonder at his being at ease with you; you have the gift of putting people at ease. Even a boy of his age could not fail to respond to the warmth of your heart and the absolute sincerity of your whole personality. It is irresistible.

What do you say to running down here by the usual train (10.5 am) on Sunday? I—we—want to hear the story (if you can finish it by that time) from beginning to end. Can you do it? Will you?

1. Though I cannot date this letter, the Dawson story that Conrad expected to "hear . . . from beginning to end" was probably "The Sin," which Dawson assuredly did read aloud to Conrad. Dawson was working on it in late October and early November, 1912, the last page being dated Saturday, 2 November. Before another week elapsed, Dawson sailed for the States on the *Philadelphia*. Perhaps, then, the "Friday" when Conrad wrote this letter was 1 November. The possibility is enhanced by Borys's reference on that date to Dawson's recent kindness to him; this is the subject with which Conrad begins.

Miss Capes will be here; an old girl but as intelligent as they make them.² How do you feel about it? But don't let this suggestion stand in the way of your finishing the work. That goes before everything.

If we don't hear from you *by wire* on Saturday (say till 4 o'clock) we'll take it you can't come. But perhaps then you could run down for a night during the week—with the MS if possible. *Any* day.

Our affectionate regards[.]

Yours ever
J. Conrad.

Thanks for cutting.³ Very fine.

2. Miss M. Harriet M. Capes, dedicatee of *A Set of Six* (London, 1908) and editor of *Wisdom and Beauty from Conrad* (London, 1915).
3. Probably one of Dawson's newspaper articles.

31. *Conrad to Dawson*¹

Bon voyage and good luck. Many thanks for your letter & enclosures. Am glad MS shorter than we expected.² Jessie's best wishes. Jack's love.³ Let us know of your movements.

Affectionately yours
J. C.

Friday⁴

1. A picture postcard note.
2. "The Sin."
3. John Conrad.
4. I.e., Friday, 8 November, the date of the postmark.

32. *Borys Conrad to Dawson*

H.M.S. Worcester,/Off Greenhithe,/Kent,
Nov. 8.th. 1912.

Dear Mr Dawson,

Thank you very much indeed for your letter. I could read it without the slightest difficulty, and I hope to write you your Xmas letter in French. This is just a line to wish you 'bon voyage,' and no sea-sickness. I shall write to you again very soon, and I hope you will answer in French when you can. I was very glad to hear that Father was better, and I hope you slept well in my room. I have no time for more now; but shall always think of you on your journey.

Yours very affectionately,

Borys Conrad

33. *Conrad to Norman Douglas*[1]

CAPEL HOUSE,/ORLESTONE,/N^R ASHFORD.

Sunday.

My dear Douglas.

Glad you have got into some diggings. You ought to come down to see us now this worry is off your mind.

I am sending you Dawson's MS of The Sin. It's now not 19000 but 18000 [?] words. The shortened parts have been retyped except in parts where you'll see the blue pencil. As a matter of fact that thing doesn't stand shortening much. But some time when you are not printing a Masefield Poem you may manage to put it into small print. It's quite good enough. Or has Masefield leased the ER for 7–14–21 years?[2]

Assure your sick Chief[3] of my sympathy in his corporeal trials.

My work drags. Borys has been in the sanatorium with "flu" a fortnight. John has a horrible cough and is very much out of sorts. Jess too is not herself and makes me a bit anxious.

---

1. Original MS in the University of Texas Library. Written some time between November, 1912 (when Dawson turned "The Sin" over to Conrad), and mid-March, 1913 (when Conrad informed Dawson that he had sent it off to the *Review*). My guess is that it was a March letter because, (1) having waited until mid-March to shorten "The Sin," Conrad probably would have informed Dawson as soon as possible that the job was done; and, (2) in the letter of 16 March, as in this one, Borys is at school and both boys are sick.

2. Conrad had no taste for John Masefield, though "Possibly Masefield's closhy puts and bloody liars put *The English Review* on its feet at last . . .." (Richard Aldington, *Pinorman: Personal Recollections of Norman Douglas, Pino Orioli and Charles Prentice* [London, 1954], p. 69).

3. Austin Harrison.

Yes. We ought to talk plans over if the thing is to come off at all. Sketch something (a scene or two) no matter how roughly, elementarily[,] cursorily—if you feel at all like it.[4]

Pardon this scrawl[.] Love.

Yours ever
J Conrad.

4. Apparently a reference to one of Conrad's several plans to collaborate with a friend on a play.

34. Conrad to Dawson

16 Mch '13

My dear Dawson.

Just a few words to meet you.[1]

My dear fellow I have done what I could to shorten The Sin. It is gone to ER with the strongest possible letter I could write.

I had quite a circus with those people; I will tell you all about it when we meet. Pray my dear friend forgive my interference with the MS, and believe it hurt me more than if it had been my own.

The novel—Good! Yes! Trés fort!![2] As Pinker could not have done much with it before Easter I held it up here for a second reading.

I know you have pardoned me my brutal silence. I had a fiendish time of it ever since you left. We are both profoundly touched by the unwearied evidences of your friendship and active good will towards me.[3]

Both boys are ill. B at school. John here. B is better but poor John has a rough time of it with bronchitis. Shall write soon[.]

Yours ever
J Conrad.

1. Dawson had just visited the States and was on his way back to France.
2. "The Novel of George," published as The Pyramid (London, 1922).
3. Dawson had written an article full of praise for Conrad in the New York Times of 2 February 1913 (p. 51).

35. *Jessie Conrad to Dawson*

CAPEL HOUSE,/ORLESTONE,/NR ASHFORD.
April 3rd 1913.

Dear Mr Dawson

You are now probably at home again. I do hope your sister has quite recovered and that you are no longer anxious about her. Your novel arrived, but seems to me to be incomplete.[1] The last page is numbered 241 and ends with the paragraph: "If I'm not careful tonight, there may be trouble" Arthur said to himself. But an instant later, his thoughts held no place for such as the Marquis d'Azincourt.

———————

I seem to remember that in your letter you said you had finished the novel and it occur[r]ed to me that perhaps the remainder has been mislaid.

Conrad is not very well and very depressed[.] I will keep the MS. carefully till I hear from you. We are looking forward with great pleasure to seeing you and Mr Powell here. We have all had very bad colds, indeed the winter though very mild has been very trying. John is making huge strides in the path of knowledge and feels rather important. Conrad is going to write to you but I thought in a matter of this kind delay might cause you some trouble.

With kindest regards and rememberances from us all.

Your very sincere friend
Jessie Conrad.

P. S. The "Sin" Conrad has shortened and it is now in Mr Pinker's hands. The MS of your novel is quite complete up to the number I have mentioned. Page, 241.

1. "The Novel of George." Cf. preceding letter.

36. *Conrad to Dawson*

CAPEL HOUSE,/ORLESTONE,/NR ASHFORD.
3 Ap. '13

Trés cher ami.

Jessie made a mistake. The last chapter in our possession is XXV *Lord St May asks some questions*.[1]

1. "The Novel of George."

The last lines are: *"Can you give me the promise now dear?"* To *which Evelyn made answer "I promise."*

I decided to hold the MS till it is complete because in my opinion the showing around of an unfinished MS does no good. I know it is done sometimes and has been done once in my own case, years ago. But not by an agent. It was a friendly move. I did think [?] rather anxiously over your copy and decided to hold it till I hear from you. Naturaly I had a conversation with P[inker]—more than one. However I did not tell him the MS was not complete. I simply told him it was in my hands till after the holidays.

The Sin after cutting down was sent direct from here to the E. R[.] with the strongest possible letter making its acceptance a personal matter. Those fools (confidal) got hold of A. Bennett now and are giving him space for a series.[2] We are awaiting news of your arrival in France.

Yours always
J. Conrad.

2. Four Arnold Bennett essays preceded "The Sin": "The Story Teller's Craft: I. Seeing Life," XIV (April–July, 1913), 17–29; "II. Writing Novels," 349–360; "III. Writing Plays," 556–568; and in XV (August–November, 1913), "IV. The Artist and the Public," 331–342.

37. Conrad to Dawson

12 Ap. '13

Cher ami.

You will find 2 letters of mine and one of Jessie's.[1]

You are very good to me. I don't know how I deserve of such a staunch friendship from a man like you.

We will talk at large when we meet. This is only a word of affectionate welcome on our side. Our love.

Yours ever
J. Conrad.

1. Nos. 34–36.

38. *Conrad to Dawson*

CAPEL HOUSE,/ORLESTONE,/N^R ASHFORD.
1 June '13

My dear Dawson.

I had to prepare for the press my novel—the work of a week or a little more.[1] It was absolutely necessary to let a couple of days pass before taking up your work[2] in order to clear my ear and my mind of all the stale echoes of my own writing. N'est ce pas?

Hence the delay. Also I had to read the copy twice at least—don't forget. Because the first reading is never sufficient for a complete understanding of a work of art. Neither truly are two readings sufficient—but as a matter of fact ¾ of the work had *four* readings —two of the copy from the US and two now.

Well, I am confirmed in my impressions. Allure trés-belle and well sustained. Subject admirably in hand and the work as a whole (from the point of view of an "intelligent reader") extremely interesting. I am not going to talk of character painting and of the descriptive passages. Avec un homme de votre talent cela va sans dire.

Remains the method—the sheer method (as distinct from subject and style)—the only part of our art in which advance or at any rate novelty (of effects) is possible.

But my thoughts on that matter can have no practical bearing on the novel as you have written it. Mind I don't condemn the method—as the novel stands. Indeed from a certain point of view it is impeccable. No. I am thinking of the general question of which I can't write but which we must have a little talk about in view of future work. That is if you care for it—I mean the talk. Well cher ami my sincere congratulations. It's a distinctive piece of work, full of thought and movement, expressing an artists vision[.]

Tout a vous

J. Conrad.

---

1. *Chance.*
2. "The Novel of George."

39. *Dawson to Walter Hines Page*[1]

8 Duchess St./W.
20th June 1913.

Dear Mr. Ambassador,

If you have not forgotten meeting me on your visit to Charleston last January, & your talks with Col. Roosevelt about me, I hope you will honour with your presence the first public meeting of a Society[2] founded, as a plea for healthy art, by the American pianist & composer John Powell, pupil of Leschetizki,[3] & myself, with the collaboration of other well-known musicians, Benno Moiseiwitch [*sic*], Vernon Warner, Zimbalist, etc. You will see by our programme that the Earl of Plymouth is introducing me; & we have some of the best-known musicians in London, all members of our Society, to contribute their talent.

It would mean a great deal to us to know that you, who have done so much in America for one branch of art—and my branch!— are willing to encourage our effort which, beginning with music, is intended to include all the arts.

Yours very respectfully,
Warrington Dawson

1. U.S. Ambassador to Great Britain. Original letter in Houghton Library; printed by permission of Harvard College Library.
2. The Fresh Air Art Society. See pp. 66–76.
3. Theodor Leschetizky was an important Polish pianist and teacher. His pupils included Paderewski, Gabrilowitsch, and Schnabel, as well as Powell, Moiseiwitsch, and Warner.

40. *Conrad to Dawson*[1]

CAPEL HOUSE,/ORLESTONE,/NR ASHFORD.
20 June 1913.

My dear Dawson.

If your manifesto related to music only I would sign it out of hand from sympathy and confidence I have in your (and Powell's) feeling for rightness in expression.[2] But the creed of 14 articles aims

1. This letter is given particular attention in Part One, pp. 71–74.
2. Conrad alludes to the fourteen-point Declaration of Principles which had been printed as a flyer to advertise the Fresh Air Art Society.

at all art, at art representative as well as interpretative (music) as it appears plainly from Art VII. And there as an artist I would be involved not in a declaration of my confidence in men who say those things, but in a positive confession of faith. A serious matter if there ever was one.

And the fact is my dear Dawson (when I say Dawson I mean Powell too) that I don't believe in the oneness of life. I believe in its infinite variety. And if you tell me that I am a shallow person thinking of forms and not of essence, I will tell you that this is all we have got to hold on to—that form is the artist's (and the scientist's) province[,] that it is all we can understand (and interpret or represent) and that we can't tell what is behind. As to the Eternity of Art—I don't suppose it is more or less eternal than the earth itself. I can't believe in the eternity of art any more than in the eternity of pain or eternity of love (subjects of art, those) whose emotions art (and of all arts music) brings home to our breasts. Art for me *is* an end in itself. Conclusions are not for it. And it is superior to science, in so far that it calls on us with authority to behold! to feel! whereas science at best can only tell us—it seems so! And thats all it can do. It talks to us of the Laws of Nature. But thats only one of its little jokes. It has never discovered anything of the sort. It has made out with much worry and blundering certain sequences of facts beginning in the dark and leading God only knows where. And it has built various theories to fit the form of activity it has perceived. But even the theory of evolution has got a great big hole in it, right at the very root. And it is amusing to see the scientists walk round it with circumspection for the last sixty years, while pretending all the time that it isn't there.

You don't suppose that I am fool enough to deny the *fact* of evolution. All I say is that the "truth of life" is not in it wherever else it might lay; and that "truth to life" (Art V.VI.VII) is too vague an expression to link art's achievement to. For me the artists salvation is in fidelity, in remorseless fidelity to the *truth of his own sensations*. Hors de là, point de salut.

All these things I have said in the plainest words in print and they are also implied in every line of my writings. For what I believe in most is responsibilities of *conduct*. *My* responsibility, not Life's, is what I acknowledge—or else my dearest boy I would sign your credo with both hands without more ado. And indeed all these things of opinion and belief I've tried to put before you shortly do not prevent me from feeling the warmest sympathy for what you and Powell would be at. I know that both you and I aim at sincerity—in the last instance. The difference is not great. But a Credo is a Credo and (unless nothing matters that one sets one's hand to) must be treated seriously, as an act where our conscience takes all the responsibility.

Apart from fundamentals as declared in the first seven articles, to which I have formulated my attitude[,] I think that Art VIII is as it were detracting from the generally lofty moral attitude you take. Unless esoteric one must take it medically. Why insist upon if I may [say] so the obvious unless for the sake of the street? Sound body (which includes nerves, heart, liver and mind) is just as necessary for the pursuit of burglary or for digging ditches as for the pursuit of art. And let me remind you that almost every new effort of art has had morbidity, unhealthiness thrown at it like a brickbat. It is the moral attitude of the Philistines. There are millions of perfectly healthy people who are stupid, for whom all art other than oleograph reproduction is morbid. There are sound minds of quite unspeakable meanness of view in matters of art. Creative minds too—or at any rate critical. I am thinking now of a Buchanan barking at certain painters[3]—of an atrocious life of E. A[.] Poe written by a man professing himself to be his friend.[4] A perfectly sound man in the average cant of the day. *Truth* you say[.] Well, Truth it is! The soundness of art is not the soundness of a game. Suffering is an attribute[,] almost a condition of greatness, of devotion, of an altogether self-forgetful sacrifice to that remorseless fidelity to the truth of his own

3. Conrad is thinking here of Robert Buchanan's famous attacks on the pre-Raphaelites, the most notable of which appeared in *The Contemporary Review* ("The Fleshly School of Poetry: Mr. D. G. Rossetti," XVIII [1871], 334–350). This mainly concerned writing but dealt also with painting. Using the pseudonym "Thomas Maitland," Buchanan said that Rossetti

> belongs, or is said to belong, to the so-called Pre-Raphaelite school, a school which is generally considered to exhibit much genius for colour, and great indifference to perspective. It would be unfair to judge the painter by the glimpses we have had of his works, or by the photographs which are sold of the principal paintings. Judged by the photographs, he is an artist who conceives unpleasantly, and draws ill.

4. Conrad refers to the memoir by Poe's literary executor, Rufus Wilmot Griswold. The death of Poe on 7 October 1849 was followed first by Griswold's commentary in the New York *Tribune* (9 October) and later by his "Memoir" in Vol. III of Poe's *Works* (New York, 1850). The whole affair is recorded by Joy Bayless, *Rufus Wilmot Griswold* (Nashville, Tenn., 1943).

sensations at whetever [*sic*] cost of pain or contumely which for me is the whole Credo of the artist.

I suppose you may be saying to each other: this man has disappointed us. All I can do is to beg you to consider that I meet your sincerity with mine and that by saying what I say I am only faithful to truth which is your ideal as well as mine. Pray believe, both of you, in my great regard and unalterable affection.

Yours as ever

J. Conrad.

PS. B[orys] writes he had a good time—a great time! with you. Our tenderest thanks to you for your goodness to him.

41. *Conrad to Dawson*

CAPEL HOUSE,/ORLESTONE,/Nᴿ ASHFORD.

Saturday.[1]

My dear Dawson.

Writing yesterday in the midst of various interruptions I am afraid I forgot to answer your letter. You must forgive me. I was frightfully worried with one thing and another—nothing of importance, but distracting.

Frankly I don't know whether you (both of you) would want to see me at the meeting now.[2] Still I'll be in London on Monday and will be at Pinkers at about noon. If you think I had rather not then drop me a wire there or a telephone message for me—any time in the morning—in non committal words as *Mr Dawson thinks not* or something equally cryptic to Pinker's office people.

I shall be busy with Pink: for some little time. A newspaper cutting from US reached me qui me donne furieusement a penser. I will tell you all about it when you come here. Indeed I will be glad to hear what you think of it. Jessie thanks you ever so much for your invitation but as a matter of fact, strangely enough she who has no engagements as a rule, has one for next monday which she can't break. As to me I would break bread with you (after dissent-

1. I.e., 21 June 1913.
2. Dawson, on behalf of Powell and himself, had invited both Conrad and Jessie to attend the Fresh Air Art Society meeting of 23 June. He also invited, among others, Conrad's friends Sir Sidney and Lady Colvin; Colvin sent regrets but invited Dawson for lunch two days later (letter of 21 June 1913).

ing from your principles) with the greatest pleasure but I must take Pink to lunch in order to have him all to myself. But unless I hear to the contrary I will turn up at the Hall in good time[.] I may not agree with your metaphysics but, whatever happens, I have the greatest sympathy for your action. You will tell me then on what day we may expect you here.

Yours affec^{ly}

J Conrad

42. *Conrad to Dawson*

CAPEL HOUSE,/ORLESTONE,/N^R ASHFORD.

Tuesday[1]

Trés cher.

I am positively grieved but the thing is impossible. My oldest friend is coming tomorrow to stay till Friday night.[2] A friend of over thirty years' standing through good and evil fortune. We don't see each other oftener than once or twice a year. I can't get away from home.

On Saturday we have arranged to give Mrs Retinger an outing on the river before she goes back to Poland. They sleep here and are going to town on Sunday morning by the 10.20. Then at 11.30 a young man called Richard Curle (he writes—a queer creature) comes down for the day. He will go away at 8 o'clock.

So do you, dear Dawson, come on Sunday by the 10 am train from Char[ing] +. I shall meet you in Ashford 11.30 same train with Curle. That can not be helped. But after he's gone we shall have a good long evening together. See? And then on Monday we shall speed you on your way since go you must.

Jessie sends an affectionate message to you and Powell.

Ever yours

J. Conrad.

1. Despite its hints I have been unable to date this letter. Because it comes after Curle's first visit (December, 1912) and before the Conrads' trip to Poland *with* Mrs. Retinger (July, 1914), the year 1913 seems probable. Since the river "outing" for Mrs. Retinger would seem more appropriate in mild weather, perhaps the general period was the close of Dawson's visit to England in May and June, not that of the visit he made in November and December.
2. Conrad regarded G. F. W. Hope—at one time a weekly sailing companion—as his oldest friend.

43. *Conrad to Dawson*

Friday.[1]

Dear Dawson.

Do come on Sunday as arranged[.] *You* never tire me. And if you give up the idea of the Southampton route you will call again on your way to Folkestone.

Yours

J. C.

1. This undated note may have followed the preceding letter. Relevant evidence would be, (1) the arrangements for a Sunday visit, (2) Dawson's reluctance to crowd Conrad's schedule, and (3) Dawson's imminent departure.

44. *Conrad to Norman Douglas*[1]

CAPEL HOUSE,/ORLESTONE,/NR ASHFORD.

Friday, 4 July '13

My dear Douglas.

What about Dawson's story?[2] I have given him to understand that it was going in this year, since that was the impression I received—or else I am damned if I would have taken the odious trouble of cutting it down, on myself.

It can be set up in small type anyhow.

The fact is that for want of a definite pronouncement I find myself so com[m]itted with Dawson that I don't want this play of mine[3] to appear in the *ER* unless you can tell me positively that *the Sin* will be published too—say in October.[4] I simply can't let you have it, not from ill will, but because that young man will think that I have shouldered out his stuff—after promising him to do my best for him with Harrison.

Will you please explain this matter to your chief. Meantime I am sending you the play to look at but with the distinct understanding that I can't let it go in except as above.

1. Original in University of Texas Library.
2. "The Sin." Cf. letters No. 30–31, 33–36.
3. "One Day More," printed in August number of *English Review*, XV (1913), 16–35. The play was based on the story "Tomorrow," which had appeared first in the *Pall Mall Magazine*, XXVII (1902), 533–547.
4. "The Sin" *was* printed by the *Review* in October (pp. 384–411).

Please preserve this letter and the envelope too. I don't keep copies of my correspondence, and I want to be able to produce this if necessary.

Yours ever in haste
J. Conrad.

45. *Conrad to Dawson*

CAPEL HOUSE,/ORLESTONE,/N^R ASHFORD.
Wednesday.¹

My dear Dawson

Just a word to tell you that I have finished your Mother's book. Admirable. Whether the public will have the sense to appreciate it I don't know (and in the public I include the common rewiever [*sic*]) but it is a wonderful disclosure of personality and a poignant record of the time. Once one had read oneself into it with the first score of pages one is carried away by the narrative with ever-increasing interest to the very last immensely effective pages of this war drama seen from the non-combattant side through a young girl's eyes.

Very fine! Very feminine[.] Perfectly touching in the charm of its naïveté and the complexity of the sentiments of that inexperienced soul suddenly initiated and yet preserving its freshness its elasticity and its courage. And how fascinating that invincible belle humeur which nothing but the terrible gloom of the last hours can overcome.

In the light of these brave and tragic pages of the past, nothing seems more trivial than the Gettysburg celebrations of to day.

Yours affectionately
J. Conrad.

PS. Send us your instructions for return of proofs—and a word as to your movements.

---

1. This was one of four Wednesdays between 23 June (when Conrad met Dawson in London) and 23 July (when Conrad forwarded the proofs he had just read at the time of the present letter; the proofs were of Sarah Morgan Dawson's *Confederate Girl's Diary*, ed. Warrington Dawson [Boston and London, 1913]). Because the first three days of July, 1913, marked the fiftieth anniversary of the Battle of Gettysburg, Conrad's allusion to "Gettysburg celebrations of to day" might refer specifically to Wednesday, 2 July.

46. Conrad to Grace King[1]

CAPEL HOUSE,/ORLESTONE,/Nᴿ ASHFORD.
23 July 1913.

Dear Miss King.

The proofs of Mrs Dawson's war-diary are going off by the same post with this letter.

A very interesting document. Whether it will take with the public I dont know. I mean in this country. But the public is rather capricious even in the U.S[.] I believe. One can never tell.

It is *very* good and dear of you to say these kind things about my work. A word of commendation goes a long way towards comforting one who is getting a little tired of the unending task.

Believe me, dear Miss King, your very obedient servant and well-wisher.

J. Conrad

1. Grace King, a friend of Mrs. Dawson and Warrington, was a New Orleans writer whose fiction was a late contribution to the local color movement. In 1913 she was travelling in Great Britain. In 1946 her papers were loaned for microfilming to the Southern Historical Collection of the University of North Carolina Library (Chapel Hill) by Miss King's nephew, Mr. Carleton King of New Orleans. The present letter is reproduced from the UNC film.

47. Jessie Conrad to Dawson

CAPEL HOUSE,/ORLESTONE,/Nᴿ ASHFORD.
July 25ᵗʰ 1913.

Dear Mr Dawson.

Miss King's letter arrived on Wednesday saying she had a few quiet day's in which to read and enjoy your Mother's journal. She said also several very kind and friendly things of Conrad's work. The M.S. was dispatched to her by registered post yesterday. *To night Borys returns for his holiday*—a truly great moment for me—Conrad has gone part of the way to meet him and I am awfully glad for he has been working so hard correcting the proofs of Chance. The house presented a curious aspect the other night: Conrad his hands dug deep in his hair—cursing I'm afraid—printers—proof readers etc, casting collar and tie into the waste paper basket, and slowing [i.e., slowly] relaxing into utter despair. It was a task but with my help he finished it in a fortnight. He sends you his love and is of course very much depressed now that it is over and very worried as to his work in hand. It is awfully difficult to cheer him up but I am trying very hard. It seems to me some time I will need a space of utter quiet and calm to understand truly what has gone before.

We want badly to hear of you and to know you are feeling less tired than when we saw you.

Both boys send their love—also Conrad—who last is not least.— I, my warm regards and sincere friendship[.]

Yours sincerely
Jessie Conrad

48. *Jessie Conrad to Dawson*

CAPEL HOUSE,/ORLESTONE,/N^R ASHFORD.
July 28th 1913.

Dear Mr. Dawson

Your letter has just arrived. Conrad wishes me to write to you at once and to beg you not to let his promised visit alter any arrangements you may wish to make. Last Saturday he returned from an appointment in town with the most severe attack of gout he has had for the last two years. This makes any fixed plan impossible for some weeks and both he and Borys are desperately disappointed. I will write again to you in the course of the next week and let you know how my invalid progresses.

Meanwhile our affectionate remembrances to you.

Believe me, very sincerely yours
Jessie Conrad.

49. *Conrad to Dawson*[1]

Dear D.

I suggested, if I remember rightly *Sidor* but there is also *Ossip* both sufficiently characteristic[.][2]

Am getting bet[t]er.

Love from us all[.]

Yours
J. C.

1. This is a card, undated but postmarked 2 August 1913.
2. Conrad had suggested a number of names which Dawson might use in his "Grand Elixir" (published as *The Green Moustache* [Chicago, 1925]).

166

50. *Conrad to Dawson*

CAPEL HOUSE,/ORLESTONE,/N^R ASHFORD.[1]

Trés cher.

Many thanks for your letter and enclosure. Pray don't be discouraged by the peregrinations of your work.[2] It has been the fate of much fine imaginative work—as you know. But remember that in the end value will tell—and you *are* giving value.

I have had a fiendish time. It may be put shortly as: Six weeks, going for the seventh, with *not a line* written. You understand that with this enormous hole in my work to fill up every idea of a 'spell off' must be given up. It must be—and there is no more to be said. Bodily suffering is nothing but it is the "worry that killed the cat" —as sailors say. I haven't moved an inch from here. Too seedy to go about. I haven't even seen Pinker—so I don't know for certain what he is doing either with your work or mine. The beggar does not write. However I know that he isn't idle. Patienza!

A great (and dreary) peace broods over the silly landscape. I am to-day downstairs at my desk, oppressed by the sense that all this is of no use. Pen, ink, paper—unnutterable [*sic*] futilities; and I gaze at the sunshine itself with a jaundiced eye. I feel as if I wanted to get drunk and break windows or go out and burgle a house—do something to assert myself and prove that I am not a mere tame writing-rabbit (lapin savant). I have just finished looking over revise proofs of my book. Comme c'est bête—Mon Dieu!

I imagine that by this time you've had enough of this kind of letter. So I won't take up another piece of paper. Borys & Jack send their love. Jessie as you know is always your very particular friend—

---

1. Until more evidence is brought to bear on this letter it may be dated tentatively between 28 July and about 15 August 1913. The "spell off" which Conrad cannot have is probably the one which Jessie provisionally refused for him in her letter of 28 July (No. 48). In her letter of 25 July (No. 47) she earlier informed Dawson that she and Conrad had finished work on the proofs for *Chance*, and in the present letter Conrad tells Dawson that he has "just finished" with the "revise proofs"; probably these two letters were not written very far apart. On the other hand, Conrad tells Dawson that he is in his sixth week without writing; on 2 August (Jean-Aubry, *LL*, II, 149) he told Arthur Symons that he had been in bed a week (which corroborates Jessie's news to Dawson of Conrad's falling ill on 26 July [reported in letter No. 48]) and that he had not written anything for a month (since *ca.* 2 July). Since Conrad now tells Dawson that he has written nothing for "Six weeks, going for the seventh" (which sounds as if he is calculating fairly accurately), he would seem to be writing *ca.* 15 August.

2. A Dawson note identifies this as "The Novel of George."

but she isn't at hand to send messages. It's extraordinary how that woman understands you. We often talk of you and *always* keep you in the 'friends' room' of our minds.

Ever yours
J. Conrad.

51. *Conrad to Dawson*

Saturday[1]

My dear Warrington

They have sent me the proof of the Sin with notification that they are cutting down to 28 pp of text. I have tacitly assented to it without referring to you. However beastly the mutilated work may appear to you you must remember that no such effect can be produced on the readers who don't know what they are deprived of. And then my dear how could I have argued? The whole last nº consisted of 152 pp[.] You get a sixth of the space as it is—and this has been given to no one within my recollection of the Harrison administration. They have cut down statesmen and philosophers and novelists. You are not alone in this experience. I hope you will forgive me for not making a better fight of it.

Yours ever
J Conrad
Delighted to hear of your Mother's diary in Heinemann's hands. *PS* as to your novel[2] mon cher je n'ai rien a dire que patience et courage.

1. August, 1913? Conrad's comment that the last *English Review* contained 152 pp. refers to the issue of either July (pp. 507–658) or August (pp. 1–152).
2. "The Novel of George."

52. *Jessie Conrad to Dawson*

CAPEL HOUSE,/ORLESTONE,/NR ASHFORD.
September 23rd 1913.

Dear Mr Dawson.

Conrad asks me to tell you that he has got the M.S. and will read it in a few days and will write to you.[1]

1. "The Grand Elixir," which Dawson finished in August.

Borys has gone back again and has just written to say that he is a Petty Officer.[2] I know it is a position he was most anxious to fill and his letter is full of satisfaction. I suppose you will soon be coming to England again and when you do, I hope you will come to see us. If you see Mr Powell, do please remember us to him very kindly and saw [i.e., say] how pleased we should be to see him any time.

With very kind regards, believe me dear Mr Dawson.

Yours very sincerely

Jessie Conrad

2. I.e., on board the *Worcester*.

53. *Conrad to Dawson*

CAPEL HOUSE,/ORLESTONE,/N^R ASHFORD.

24 Oct 1913

Cher ami.

I am sending to day the *Grand Elixir*[1] to London.

Pardon the delay. I was so seedy mentally this last month or more than [i.e., that] I was not fit to tackle *any* reading.

I don't know that I am much better. However I felt I could not delay any longer. That the story is clever, that the writing is in many respects admirable there can be no doubt. The only question in my mind is the question of *direction*. Are you using your undeniable and maturing talent to the best advantage—I mean practically, pour vous faire une place digne de vous—and that by the speediest methods?

Thinking over all these matters it came into my mind whether it would not be rather good for you to throw your next fiction into the autobiographical form, which gives certain facilities and also imposes certain restraints. Your gift as a raconteur will get full play while the necessity to keep your man *credibly convincing* will impose on you certain limitations from which your imagination will not suffer in the end. And then look at the advantage of *direct* expression for your thoughts and feelings. Pensez-y mon cher. You want something to steady you artistically. But all this is matter for talk more than for correspondence.

1. I.e., *The Green Moustache*. This is the letter Jessie promised in her note of 23 September (No. 52).

Keep us in mind as we keep you. Let us know what is happening to you. I see the *Diary*[2] advertised to-day in the D. Teleg: as published.

Yours affectionately
J. Conrad.

2. Sarah Morgan Dawson's *A Confederate Girl's Diary*.

54. *Jessie Conrad to Dawson*

CAPEL HOUSE,/ORLESTONE,/Nᴿ ASHFORD.
October 28th 1913.

My dear Mʳ Dawson

I write to you for Conrad who is busy, and rather overwhelmed with business letters which I cannot answer for him this time. We are awfully pleased that you are coming over and shall certainly look forward to seeing you here. Will you try to persuade Mʳ Powell to come with you when you come if he can spare us a few hours. Please give him our love when you see him.

You will perhaps say what day would suit you, I think we have no pressing engagements and we are nearly sure to be at home till after the 21st Nov.

With our warm greetings to you[.]

Always sincerely yours.
Jessie Conrad.

55. *Dawson to James Brand Pinker*[1]

France.
6th Nov, 1913.

Dear Pinker:-

I am coming to England at the end of next week to deliver an address at Wolverhampton, where a friend of mine is standing for Parliament,[2] and I had intended to wait until then to talk with you of several collaborations I have undertaken and which, I think, promise well financially. But a note in print about one of these collaborations, which appeared, it seems, in the Morning News and Leader

1. From Dawson's carbon typescript, presented to Duke by Dr. Herbert Barry. I have corrected typing errors.
2. Ivor Windsor-Clive, son of the Earl of Plymouth. Dawson's "address" was on "Joseph Conrad: A Great Contemporary."

of the 4th inst, has attracted enough attention for the Cazenove Literary Agency to write appreciatively of the importance of the book and ask to handle it. I am, of course, writing to Mr. Cazenove—with whom, by the way, I have never had dealings—telling him I am not free to accept his offer. But it occurs to me that, with the help of the paragraph in question and of information I can give you, you might be able to do something immediately in this particular affair.

You will probably be able to get a copy of the paper in question. I have not seen it, but from Cazenove's letter I judge that the matter was rightly presented. It concerns a collaboration with Auguste Rodin for collecting in book form his genuine notes, untouched, but only coordinated, about art, life, nature, etc, such as he has made them throughout much of his life. I enclose copies of my correspondence with M. Rodin on the subject.

The important consideration will be to draw the attention of publishers to the fact that this will be the first and only book by M. Rodin himself. Recent volumes, biographies, studies such as "The Real Rodin", etc, and Paul Gsell's "Art", show him as seen and interpreted by other people;[3] there will appear shortly in French, and, I suppose, in an English translation, a work attributed to him, on Architecture, in which as usual a collaborator has rewritten and generally "interpreted" everything the Master had to say.[4] Concerning this last work, M. Rodin said to me a few days ago, "I would not make a public statement which would injure the interests of the friend whom I have authorised to make use of some of my ideas, but I tell you that my supposed "ideas" are being so re-written as to represent very little of what I said or believe. My real book will be what you are to do with me, because I know from long experience that you respect not only my ideas but also my form."

I think some words as to my relations with M. Rodin would help to make publishers understand.

I first met him in 1899, when he was preparing for the 1900 exhibition an exhibit of his own, outside of the grounds, because, after the sensation of the Balzac statue, he had been refused any official orders or privileges. I called as a newspaper correspondent to write an article about his work, but he was struck by my comments and invited me out to his house at Meudon. He told me that I had the knack of expressing in words just what he had expressed in stone or

3. Gustave Coquiot, *Le Vrai Rodin* (Paris, 1913), and Gsell, *L'Art* (Paris, 1912).
4. *Les Cathédrales de France, avec Cent Planches Inédites hors Texte*, introd. Charles Morice (Paris, 1914).

bronze, and he soon took to discussing with me the works on which ... [part of line missing] if he had truly expressed what he wished. When, after the 1900 exhibition, he sold a number of his statues and small groups to foreign museums, he made the condition that my descriptions of them should be inserted in the catalogues so that they should be understood.

From that time on I was frequently with him while he was working; I used to go out sometimes as often as two or three times a week to breakfast with him at Meudon at 8 A.M., then spend an hour or so with him in his studio or discussing art and nature before the panorama of the Seine valley which his villa commands, and then we would go in to Paris together, he to his studio there, I to my newspaper office. On account of my artistic grasp, he offered to take me as pupil. I had, however, decided at the age of four that my career was to be literary, I had been seriously working for it, acquiring technique and taking every step with a view to that alone, since I was ten years old, I had commenced to find myself at the age of twenty-two, and I did not feel justified in taking the risks either artistic or financial of changing my mode of expression. I therefore did not accept his offer, but our close friendship has continued through the years.

Some ten or eleven years ago I was first privileged to see his notes, and I recognized their great value; I proposed to him then that he should allow me to prepare them for publication. He promised me that I alone should do this work when he was ready for it, but did not feel that the time had yet come when the public was prepared. Recently, he proposed that I spend January and part of February with him either in the south of France or in Italy doing this work. I promptly accepted, and exchanged with him the letters of which I append copies.

It is difficult to say, just yet, what the length of the book will be. I shall, of course, draw it up in French first, and then translate it myself. My task will be to coordinate and unite in chapters the various subjects he has treated. I know already that there will be one on "Impressions of antiques in the Louvre"; another on Nature; another on Feminine Beauty; another on Ideas of Art; etc. His wording is wonderfully picturesque and its value has heretofore been destroyed by "improvements"; I shall not only respect it in the French, but use to the uttermost my knowledge of both the French and English languages to render in English all its colour and beauty.

172

I am hoping that on the strength of this book you may be able to force an opening for either "George" or "The Grand Elixir", telling the publisher that I don't want to give the Rodin book unless one of my own novels goes with it.

Of the other matters alluded to at the beginning of this letter, I shall speak when I see you. I shall cross via Havre-Southampton on the night of the 13th, arriving on the morning of the 14th and going to 8 Duchess St, Portland Place. I should be glad if you could make an appointment with me for Friday, since I believe you are not in town Saturday, and I expect to leave Monday for Worcestershire.

Yours sincerely,

56. Conrad to Dawson

10 Nov. 13

Mon cher.

Lady Phyllis received your MS all right en foi de quoi I send you the note she was good enough to write to me.[1]

Fate willed it that only yesterday I destroyed the proofsheets of Chance which have been lying about for weeks now. As I hate paperasses of all kinds I flung them into the waste paper basket and they are gone beyond recall. Am awfully sorry. Chance as you know has not appeared yet—or else you would have had a copy. This being so perhaps it would be better not to speak of an unpublished book. Qu'en pensez-vous?

I have read your letter with mixed feelings. Sorry that you should take the view you take and glad to see the serenity of your mind contemplating the worst.[2] Without controverting your statement of facts one is reluctant to accept the tone or under-tone of renunciation sounded in the letter. However it isn't discouragement—which is wise since no one can see into the future.

We must have a talk. Will you my dear fellow come here on the day of your arrival, for the night. Take the train (either in Dov: or

1. After reading "The Grand Elixir" Conrad had forwarded it to Lady Phyllis Windsor-Clive, to whom the book was later dedicated.
2. The failure to get "The Novel of George" into print?

173

Folk:)[3] *next after* the boat train and the puffer[4] will meet you in *Ashford*.

Our affectionate regards.

Always yours
J. Conrad.

PS We expect you to leave Paris Thursday morning and sleep here Thursday night. Please write or wire which route you take *Dov:* or *Folk*.

3. Dover or Folkestone.
4. Conrad's car.

57. *Dawson to Walter Hines Page*[1]

HEWELL GRANGE,/REDDITCH.
19th Nov.

My dear Mr. Ambassador,

I am coming to London on the 21st, to be at 8 Duchess St, Portland Place; I shall be there for ten days, & I should be grateful if you would ask your secretary to drop me a line & tell me what would be an appropriate time for me to call on you, for I know how busy you must be. I not only want to see you for the pleasure of continuing our conversations of Charleston last January & London last June, but I want to give you a copy of my mother's Civil War Diary which Houghton, Mifflin have just published, & also to ask you if you could honour with your presence the meeting of the Fresh Air Art Society on the 28th. Lord Plymouth, whom I am now visiting, is coming up to London expressly for it, although still only convalescent from his recent serious operation.

Yours very respectfully,
Warrington Dawson

1. Written on Lord Plymouth's stationery from his home in Worcestershire. Original in Houghton Library; printed by permission of Harvard College Library.

58. *Lord Plymouth to Dawson*

HEWELL GRANGE,/REDDITCH.
Jan. 1, 1914.

My dear Dawson.

Many thanks for your letter. I am not sorry to start a new year &

174

to see the back of the old one. My own affairs were particularly difficult to manage & I don't feel as if I had come out of 1913 unscathed. Now I send you all good wishes for a most successful year to come. I am much interested to hear of your talk with Conrad. I think the writers of fiction are apt to become idealists & to float in the air of an attractive socialism far above the stoney path that practical people are treading; and then we become rather impatient with one another. Don't you think so? I am glad to think that you and Conrad are exceptions and look at things as they are.

I wonder if you would kindly drop into an envelope Rodin's address & send it to me. I cannot remember it.

Yours vy sincerely
Plymouth.

59. *Jessie Conrad to Dawson*

Capel House/Orlestone/Nr Ashford/Kent.
January 19th 1914

Dear Mr Dawson.

You must be thinking very badly of us for not having written before, but we have had a sick house generally for over six weeks. Even now Conrad is in bed in one room with a sharp attack of gout and Borys in another with a bad feverish cold. I wander from one to the other doing what I can to ease them both. I am glad to say both seem to have improved slightly to-night and I hope Borys will soon be able to rejoin his ship for his last term on board. John sends his love to you and very many thanks for your kind thought of him at Christmas. I posted you a copy of "Chance" on Saturday which I hope will have reached you by this time. There were ever so many reviews of it on the day of publication more than we have ever had before. Conrad sends his love to you and as soon as he can hold his pen without pain he is going to write to you himself. Meanwhile I send you our very warmest New Year wishes.

Believe me always

Your sincere friend
Jessie Conrad.

60. Conrad to Dawson

17 Febr. '14.

Mon trés cher.

We have been rather anxious but the good report on your convalescence has done away with that.

I hope Jessie explained how damnably busy I've been. Since you were here with Powell I have done a big lot of the novel[1] and finished two short stories both presenting some difficulties which you as homme du métier will detect at once when you see them. I've just heard that the Metropolitan has taken one of them for pub[on] in June-July Nos. The other the Pall Mall Mag is nibbling at on this side.[2]

Meantime *The Island Story* the novel now in hand has got itself sold on the strength of the 75000 w already written, to Munsey's Mag.[3] So now I have to buckle-to and drag without intermission till I have dragged the 30-40 thou: words out of myself with groans and imprecations.

Seven editions of Chance = 12000 copies (to date)—which for England is very good and for me something absolutely fabulous.

You are very dear in your comments on Almayer's Folly—and I am even more touched by your feeling about my poor Nigger who never got his own in either country.[4] Yet who knows if the hour of justice is not about to strike! I have just heard that Doubl: Page have bought the book from Dodd Mead and are going to publish it uniform with *Chance* this very year! Whether simultaneously I don't know. The pub: of *Chance* in US is fixed for the 26 Mch. What will happen there? The peace of my future years, the fate of the children hangs in the balance—for I can't write forever and there is not much time left to pursue fortune to follow up a first success!

All our loves to you. It's late and I've been writing all day.

Yours ever
J. Conrad.

1. *Victory.*
2. "The Planter of Malata," *Metropolitan* (June–July, 1914); and probably "Laughing Anne" (i.e., "Because of the Dollars"), also published in the *Metropolitan* (September, 1914).
3. *Victory* (subtitled *An Island Story*) appeared in *Munsey's Magazine*, LIV (1915), 112–240.
4. *The Nigger of the "Narcissus"* (New York, 1897 [pub. as *The Children of the Sea*] and 1899; and London, 1897 [seven copies to secure copyright] and 1898).

61. *Conrad to Dawson*

CAPEL HOUSE,/ORLESTONE,/Nᴿ ASHFORD.
25. Ap. '14

Trés cher.

Delighted to hear you are coming. Do call on the way for a quiet evening and night before plunging into the whirlpool of London.

Jessie has already in view a place which may do for you for a quiet stay in the country[.] A mile from here. She hasn't actually seen it; but it is a farmhouse where a clergyman we know stays every summer for a month. So it must be at least possible. There are no children.

It would be jolly to have you dropping in of an evening. Another place, a house in the woods may be worth looking at.

I say nothing more reserving everything for viva voce. Borys and John send their love in which the Old Folks join[.]

Yours ever
J. Conrad.

We shall meet your train at Ashford when you give us a definitely firm date.

62. *Jessie Conrad to Dawson*

CAPEL HOUSE,/ORLESTONE,/Nᴿ ASHFORD.
May 14ᵗʰ 1914

Dear Mʳ Dawson.

It would be awfully nice if you and Borys journeyed down together on Saturday. I am not quite sure what time he can leave but I am writing to him by this post to wire you directly he knows.

His address is should you wish to let him know of any alterations in your possible plans. "Quernmore" Victoria Road[,] *Norwood S.E.* Conrad says he will be very pleased indeed to see you and have a long talk. Forgive haste, and believe me dear Mʳ Dawson.

Your sincere friend
Jessie Conrad.

63. Conrad to Walter Hines Page[1]

CAPEL HOUSE,/ORLESTONE,/N^R ASHFORD.

15 May 1914

M^r & Mrs Joseph Conrad regret infinitely their inability to accept H.E. the U.S. Ambassador's and Mrs Page's invitation to dinner on the 2^d of June.

1. Original in Houghton Library; printed by permission of Harvard College Library.

64. Jessie Conrad to Dawson

CAPEL HOUSE,/ORLESTONE,/N^R ASHFORD.

May 18th 1914

Dear Mr Dawson.

I have this morning seen Mrs Seely and finally inspected your possible rooms, and have induced her to make some few small alterations, which I believe would add not a little to your comfort. Mrs Seely is prepared to let you have the bedroom, the small room for writing and the use of a room downstairs for meals (unless you prefere them upstairs) for 30/- per week. This seems to include attendance breakfast, lunch and afternoon tea. We will send over for you a bath, bathsheet and a reading lamp, and of course any other little thing you may need if you let me know. I have told her that you would not require the rooms before next Friday week and that I would let her know your date of coming for certain if you decide to take the rooms. I believe you could be very comfortable[.] You would certainly be quiet and we should enjoy having you near us. If there is anything further I can do for you in this matter you know I am always ready to do it.

Please remember me very kindly to Mr Powell and give him our love. He knows we shall be very pleased to see him if he has the time to spare. Conrad sends his love to you.

Forgive haste as I want to catch our evening post and the time is short[.]

I remain

Always your sincere friend
Jessie Konrad Korzeniowska[1]

1. For the first time to Dawson, Jessie uses here her Polish name (Conrad's original name was Józef Teodor Konrad Korzeniowski, coat of arms Nałęcz). Probably her increased awareness of her Polish connections resulted from the Conrads' plans to go to Poland later in the year.

65. *Walter Hines Page to Dawson*

EMBASSY OF THE UNITED STATES OF AMERICA
London, 16 May '14

Dear Mr. Dawson:

Mr. Conrad has, most courteously, declined our invitation to dinner. No doubt it causes him much trouble to come in at night—etc.
etc. etc— I am most anxious to meet him & he ought to see Mr.
Doubleday[1] while he is here.— I wonder if I am acting within the
bounds of propriety (I'm sure I am) if I commission you to induce
him to come to luncheon with us—preferably with Mrs. Conrad, but
with or without her—on Thursday May 28, at 1:30? I am just arranging a very small luncheon on that day—you, the Conrads, Mrs.
Humphry Ward & one or two more to meet the Doubledays.[2]— Isn't
this a proper commission to give you, my friend?

Sincerely yours
Walter H. Page

1. F. N. Doubleday of Doubleday, Page & Company.
2. The guest list at one point included the Kiplings, who apparently did not come.

66. *Jessie Conrad to Dawson*

CAPEL HOUSE,/ORLESTONE,/NR ASHFORD.
May 25th 1914

Dear Mr Dawson

I made the inquiries of Mrs Seelly you asked me to. Your postal
address will be Gill Farm Ruckinge Nr Ashford Kent. There are two
deliveries daily 8.45 am. 2.15. pm. Postman will also take letters and
telegrams when he calls and you can buy stamps from him. Your
telegraph office is the same as ours Hamstreet. Mrs Seelly says your
rooms will be quite ready for you on the 29th. If you let me know
your train in Hamstreet the car shall meet you and I will arrange with
the carrier to take your box to the farm.

Conrad is working and so far is well so that I hope nothing will
interfere with our coming up on Wednesday afternoon.[1]

Our warm remembrances to you and Mr Powell whom we shall
love to see after the 5th.

Yours always sincerely
Jessie Conrad

1. I.e., 27 May, the day before the Doubleday-Page luncheon.

67. *Conrad to Dawson*[1]

Jessie went out this morning and not back yet to dress Afraid impossible arrive in time Reply Conrad Norfolk Hotel Surrey St Strand

1. A telegram sent on 28 May from the East Strand Office, received at the Western District Office, and presumably delivered to Dawson at his boardinghouse, 8 Duchess Street.

68. *Ellen Glasgow to Dawson*[1]

HOTEL CURZON,/CURZON STREET,
MAYFAIR,/LONDON. W.
May 30th 1914

Dear Mr Dawson,

Thank you so much for your notes, and for your efforts. We should be deeply disappointed to return to America without meeting Mr Conrad, and I hope we may arrange to call on him at Capel House. But, if he dislikes an intrusion upon his quiet, I trust you will tell us so very frankly.

When you come back to town won't you come to tea with us some afternoon.

Very sincerely yours,
Ellen Glasgow

1. Printed by permission of First & Merchants National Bank, Richmond, Virginia, executor of the estate of Ellen Glasgow.

69. *Dawson to Walter Hines Page*[1]

Gill Farm,/Ruckinge,/Near Ashford./Kent.
11th June, 1914.

Dear Mr. Ambassador,

I hear that my dear friend Col. Roosevelt is coming to England. I am here in the wilds of Kent, seeing no newspapers & consequently cut off from events; but I presume that he will be visiting you in London, & will arrive a day or two before his lecture on the 16th.[2] I have

1. From the original in Houghton Library; printed by permission of Harvard College Library.
2. Roosevelt lectured to the Royal Geographical Society at Burlington Gardens on his expedition to Brazil. Page secured the promise of a ticket for Dawson from the president of the Society.

written to him in Madrid[3] to let him know that I am in England, & to ask him to arrange if possible for me to hear his lecture. I know this is difficult, but in Paris for the Sorbonne, after we came back from Africa, he got me in either with the family or with the Embassy —he told me it would be with one or the other, & I only know that it succeeded, for I received an invitation. It occurs to me that I ought to let you know of my letter to him, in case such arrangements are in your hands, but I don't want to worry you unduly.

On Monday the 15th I return to town, to

8 Duchess St, W.

Telephone Mayfair 4861.

Since the day after I had the pleasure of lunching with you, I have been down here, in the farmhouse next to Conrad's[,] he working on the novel he is finishing, & I on the one I am beginning,[4] each day, & in the evening I go over to dine with him. It has been a very wonderful experience.

Looking forward to seeing you when I return to town next week, & with best regards to Mrs. Page, I am, dear Mr. Ambassador,

Yours most respectfully,
Warrington Dawson.

3. Kermit Roosevelt was married in Madrid on 10 June.
4. Conrad's *Victory* and Dawson's "The Rock."

70. *Jessie Conrad to Dawson*

CAPEL HOUSE,/ORLESTONE,/N^R ASHFORD.

June 22nd 1914

Dear Warrington

We are both so very busy or I should have sent you a line before. We still miss you very much, we got so to look for you in the evening. Borys seems to begin to feel the strain although fairly confident of success.[1] Where do you want me to send your M.S. when I have finished reading it?[2] I shall tell you how much I have enjoyed

1. Borys had left the *Worcester* with a first-class certificate "both in school and seamanship" (Conrad to Galsworthy, 5 May 1914, in Jean-Aubry, *LL*, II, 154), and he was now being tutored for an entrance examination to the Faculty of Applied Science at Sheffield.
2. Perhaps *The True Dimension* (1916), which Dawson completed at Duchess Street on 10 May; but see letter No. 18 and its first note.

reading it when I send it back. I hope also to have the photographs of "Ivy Walls" and the "Someries" to send you[.] With our warm remembrances to you and Mr Powell. I am always

Your sincere friend
Jessie K. Korzeniowska

71. *Jessie Conrad to Dawson*

CAPEL HOUSE,/ORLESTONE,/N^R ASHFORD.
July 3rd 1914

Dear Warrington

So very many thanks for the jolly photographs, and for the offer of more. I would love to have them. I never saw a better picture of the house and the ones of Conrad and the boys.[1] So far the news from Sheffield is very good. Conrad seems to be keeping well and Borys seems very confident of success, or at any rate most hopeful. I am horribly lonely, and greatly disgusted, for the Saturday before they left, they lost a tap (an oil tap) and the engine got hot and melted the bearings, so the car has been laid up all the time they have been away. John sends his love to you. I will send you our address in Poland if we really go. With warm greetings[.]

Sincerely your friend
Jessie Conrad

1. These pictures are reproduced in the present volume.

72. *Conrad to Dawson*[1]

My dear Warrington

Jessie is extremely busy in getting things ready for the journey—and I also am busy in my own ineffectual manner attempting to ar-

1. This postcard (sent in an envelope and therefore not postmarked) was written in July, 1914, some time between the third (when Jessie last wrote) and the twenty-fifth (when the Conrads left for Poland). I conjecture a time near the latter of these two dates. On 22 July Conrad wrote to Mrs. (later Lady) Iris Wedgwood mentioning Borys in terms very similar to those in this letter: "Under various pretences he gets into the car at daybreak and goes off somewhere, only getting out of it for meals and to go to bed about midnight" (Jean-Aubry, *LL*, II, 156).

range various affairs. Let then this short word suffice to assure you of our affection and convey our thanks for the outward proofs of your friendship. Keep us in mind as we always keep you in mind[.] The boys send their love. They are both much excited. John yells from morning till night; B rushes about in the car on errands of his own contriving mostly. I am recovering from the heavy strain of finishing the novel.[2] Can't say I feel very cheerful but I am quiet. Just quiet.

With love too from the 'Old Folks[.]'

Yours ever
J. Conrad.

2. *Victory.*

73. *Conrad to Walter Hines Page*[1]

CAPEL HOUSE,/ORLESTONE,/NR ASHFORD.

15 Nov '14

Dear Mr Page

Illness, which seized upon me directly I put foot on English ground, prevented me from calling to thank you for your efforts on my behalf and apologise for the trouble I have given.[2] Since our return home some ten days ago I have been in bed; and this is the first day I can sit at a desk and handle the pen.

With the assistance of your Colleague in Vienna we started on our way out of Austria on the 7th October.[3] I had a very anxious

1. Original in Houghton Library; printed by permission of Harvard College Library.
2. Since Austria was at war with Great Britain, the Conrads had used the American embassies in Vienna and London to keep in touch with home and to expedite their departure from the Continent.
3. Conrad refers to Frederic C. Penfield, to whom he later dedicated *The Rescue* (1920). "It so happens that Mr. Penfield had been for many years one of the legion of Conrad's admirers, and therefore his interest in being of service to the novelist was just that much greater, and a warm friendship sprang up between the two immediately" ("Conrad in Poland," *Bookman* [New York], XLVI [September, 1917–February, 1918], 659).
On the same day that Conrad wrote this letter to Page, he wrote also to Galsworthy (Jean-Aubry, *LL,* II, 163):

> we started suddenly, at one in the morning, on the 7th Oct. in a snowstorm in an open conveyance of sorts to drive 30 miles to a small railway station where there was a chance of finding something better than a horse-truck to travel in with *ma petite famille.* From there to Cracow, some fifty miles, we sat 18 hours in a train smelling of disinfectants and resounding with groans. In Cracow we spent untold hours sitting in the restaurant by the railway station, waiting for room in some train bound to Vienna. All the time I suffered exquisite tortures. . . .

time till we got into Italy, but our way has been made as easy as possible by Mr Penfield who has been kindness personified in our time of need.

Our detention would have been very disagreeable but for the fact that we were in a Polish province and therefore amongst friends. My wife stood the stress and strain extremely well. She joins me in warmest regards to Mrs & Miss Page and yourself. Believe me, dear Mr Page,

Very gratefully yours
Joseph Conrad.

74. Jessie Conrad to Dawson

CAPEL HOUSE,/ORLESTONE,/N^R ASHFORD.
December 14th 1914

My dear Warrington.

We are so anxious for news of you, and to know where you are. All our wierd experiences we must tell you when we see you. I am so thankful to be here and to have all my boys safely in England. We have been home just over a month, were a month on the road and things don't seem to have improved much. I am awfully anxious about Borys who is determined to do something useful for his country and as you know he is under age to serve. Who could have foreseen such a terrible thing as this war[1]—and where is the end?

I am sending this to Duchess Street begging that it may be forwarded to you if possible.

Our affectionate greetings and remembrances my dear Warrington.

Always your friend
Jessie Conrad

P.S. Can you also give us news of Mr Powell?

---

1. Dawson, for one. He had predicted it in a public talk given in Boston in March, 1913.

75. *Jessie Conrad to Dawson*

CAPEL HOUSE,/ORLESTONE,/N^R ASHFORD.
December 28th 1914

My dear Warrington

It was a great relief to have your letter this morning and to know that one more valued friend was safe at the moment. Here it is awful one dare not write to ask for news for fear of pulling open a fresh sorrow. Conrad sends his love he was not well all the journey and has been very bad since we really got home. He has bad gout in his right hand and is quite helpless. He will be very pleased to see you when you come over and to have a long talk with you. Forgive this short note I am hardly able to get a moment to write letters. The boys are well and send their loves with me to you. May the New Year bring us all some promise of peace.

Always your friend
Jessie Conrad

P.S. Joseph Retinger[1] expects to be in Paris on Friday or Saturday he said he would write asking you to see him somewhere and give you all the latest news.

1. Retinger was a politically minded, highly educated young Polish friend of the Conrads. He had earned two doctorates—one in law in Cracow and one in the humanities at the Sorbonne. In later years he wrote *Conrad and His Contemporaries* (New York, 1943).

76. *Conrad to Dawson*

Capel. 11 Aug '15

Mon trés cher.

Infinite thanks for your good letter and for the book which has given me the greatest pleasure.[1]— My mental state has been deplorable I may safely say, though as a matter of fact it is improving. One gets used to things intellectually deadly as Mithridates got used to poison. Enfin! . . I am able to work now; very slow of course. Jessie and the children send you their love. The Borys child being now fixed for Sheff^d University is awaiting the decision of the war office. His eyesight is the only point of anxiety in his plans. Should he fail

1. Probably not one of Dawson's.

in that he will enter at once the workshops of the Sheff^d Engineering Faculty which are turning out war material now. I am driven nearly distracted by my uselessness. Believe in my firm affection.

Always yours

J. Conrad.

77. *Jessie Conrad to Dawson*

Dec. 31st 1915

My dear Warrington

We are so sorry to hear of your long spell of ill health. We are often talking of you and wondering how it is with you. I wish you were coming to England in time to see Borys before he leaves. He is perfectly happy and all his heart in his work. I shall send you his photogra[ph] as soon as I get one and will write you a long letter from where we are going to see him next week. No time for more now. Take care of yourself and come over soon to see us.

Yours affec.

Jessie

This was taken early in the year[.]¹

1. Jessie's note is written on a picture postcard depicting Conrad, John, and herself in the study at Capel House. The picture was taken by the Cadbys, whom Conrad had spoken of earlier as "a couple in great repute as photographers. Very artistic" (to Alfred A. Knopf, 20 July 1913, in Jean-Aubry, *LL*, II, 148). The photographing episode was recorded verbally by Carine Cadby in "Conrad's Dislike of the Camera and How It Was Conquered by Will Cadby," *Graphic*, CX (1924), 728. See illustration No. 15.

78. *Jessie Conrad to Dawson*

CAPEL HOUSE,/ORLESTONE,/N^R ASHFORD.

January 26th 1916

Poor dear Warrington

We are all of us so very distressed to hear such bad news of your health, but I hope you can send us a more cheerful account of yourself, dear boy, before very long. Conrad sends his love and is going to write to you[.] He has a little gout again in his right hand and is not anxious to hold a pen.

186

I shall also send you some special photographs of Conrad and the boys, early next week but without a letter. Borys is very happy and doing his work whole heartedly. He looks much older and is taller than his father—his mother of course is quite out of the running. Even John is level with my nose. One thing my hair is rapidly going grey so I shall soon have a little dignity by virtue of my grey hairs. If only this awful war were over. I am sure your dear Conrad would come to France to see you.

Here we have had rather a sick household since last August. Conrad has been gouty and I have been troubled with my heart, which I am glad to say is stronger now and except for a little rheumatism I am as usual. Do you remember you promised to send me your Mother's book? I mention it only for fear it may have been lost as it has not arrived.

How much one misses one's friends, the real friends whose presence one enjoyed so much. It seems everywhere so sad, you daren't write to people for fear of opening wounds healed only so recently. Borys expects to leave any day, they are only waiting, for their guns. Now dear Warrington, do take the greatest care and send us news please.

Always affectionately your friend
Jessie Conrad Korzeniowska

79. Conrad to Dawson

Capel House,/Orlestone,/Nʀ Ashford.
12 Feb 16

My dear Dawson.

Your news adds a darker shade to the gloom and oppression of the bitter hours through which we are living.[1] To tell you the truth

---

1. After 1915 Dawson's physical condition was never good, and sometimes it was very bad. Analyses varied, but on 12 February 1916 Dawson reported to Bernard Bernard:

> It has been discovered that the mass of muscles in the sacro-lumbar region, on the left side, against my spine, is hardened & choked, [as a] result of that old injury; the treatment consists in breaking up the resistance twice a week, & you can imagine how little is left of me afterwards. It would appear that this should relieve the condition of my left leg (now twisted under me & much weakened so that it's practically useless) but there may be further trouble lying deeper.

I was quite stunned by what you had to tell us about yourself. I am trying now to react in the direction of optimism, but my anxiety remains and I do truly wish I were near enough to see you, grasp your hand and hear your voice. But I am a strangely useless personality.

I am glad to hear that you can work—if only a little. But you are a man of firm character. As to me, apart from my health which has been bad (in the usual way) my mentality seems to have gone to pieces. I can do nothing—which of course is not a matter of importance except for myself. We had a letter from Borys the other day—in great distress about you, and asking us to send you his love. He expects orders to proceed "overseas" any day now. For some time past I have been rather anxious about Jessie, but still she keeps her end up in a wonderful way. Pardon this scrappy and disconnected scrawl. I am ashamed but I can do no better. Pray give us soon if only a line of news about yourself.

Yours ever affectionately

Joseph Conrad.

PS Jessie will send you (in a day or two) your copy of *Victory* which has been laid by for you ever since the day of publication.

80. *Jessie Conrad to Dawson*

CAPEL HOUSE,/ORLESTONE,/Nᴿ ASHFORD.

Kent

March 3ʳᵈ 1916

Dear Warrington

Your present of your Mother's Diary arrived on my birthday[1] and is a greatly prized book. I have read and have been very touched by your preface, and now I am reading the book with the deepest interest.

We were very glad to get your slightly better news of yourself although I fear you have some time yet of pain and weariness before you. Still if you are able to work, and work to to [*sic*] your own satisfaction it will help you very much I know. You will be interested to hear that Borys is now "somewhere in France[.]" I have just sent him your address and I hope you will hear from him in a few days. Joseph Retinger is ill in Paris, but as soon as he is will

---

1. I.e., 22 February.

[*sic*] enough I have asked him to call on you for me. We miss you so very much and it seems very lonely as most of our intimate friends are away somewhere.

John sends his love to you. You would not know him he is so long[,] nearly up to my nose. When you write to John Powell please remember me very kindly to him.

Now my dear Warrington take every care of yourself and we hope to see you soon.

Your affectionate friend
Jessie Conrad

81. *Jessie Conrad to Dawson*

Capel House
April 4th 1916

So many thanks for the book.[1] C. is writing to you in a day or so[;] he is not very well. Have you heard yet from Borys? He said he was going to write to you the last time we heard. I do hope you are better and I wish there was some prospect of seeing you over here soon. What is your news of Mr Powell? The time drags wearily on and I want to see my boy so much it seems so long since he left. Do write when you can.

Your aff. friend
J.C.

1. Probably Dawson's *True Dimension*, which had come out earlier that year. Though Jessie goes on to say that Conrad will write soon (presumably commenting on the book), Conrad apparently did not mention the novel for over a year. See No. 84.

82. *Jessie Conrad to Dawson*

CAPEL HOUSE,/ORLESTONE,/NR ASHFORD.
Kent
April 20th 1916.

Dear Warrington

Conrad asks me to send you his love and to explain why he has not yet written to you. He has gout again in his hands, due I believe to the excitement of last week. I wonder do you know Mr Jo Davidson? His bust of Conrad was a great event last week.[1] I went up to see it and I was glad the dear man didn't come for it *was* a day. I came in for all sorts of compliments that rightly belonged to him. I wish you had been in England.

We saw a very good review of your book in the "New Statesman.'[']² Conrad will have much to say to you when he can write. By the way I sent you soon after Christmas Borys' photograph in uniform and a p[ost]. c[ard]. of a rather good group of the rest of the Clan Conrad. Did it ever reach you? I ask because I sent them also to friends in Switzerland and they were stopped by Censor. Why? Borys address is—

> 2d Lt. A. B. Conrad 594 Coy M. T. A. S. C.
> attached 34th Siege Brigade. R. G. A.
> France B. E. F.

He writes us this week that there are changes impending mostly to his advantage but this address should find him and he will give you the fresh one if necessary. It is such a relief that he is well and so cheerful and happy. It would be too awful if he were miserable.

I do hope you are really getting better and that one day soon you will be again in England with us.

Your affectionate friend
Jessie Conrad

1. If Jessie's memory may be trusted, it was at this event that she met a charming American aviator who, the following Sunday, brought Jane Anderson down to Capel House for the first time (*Joseph Conrad and His Circle*, 2nd ed. [Port Washington, N.Y., 1964], p. 196).

2. Gerald Gould, *The New Statesman*, VII (1916), 42–43, spoke of *The True Dimension* as

> a remarkable performance. It contains no trace of the amateur or the beginner. The writing has force, breadth and distinction. But what is most remarkable of all is the novelty of the theme. . . . So skilfully indeed is the atmosphere realised, so persistently is the suspense maintained, that right up to the end, and after it, one remains doubtful whether the theme is a thrill or a joke. . . . The analysis of . . . Morton's character is really brilliant. . . .

83. Jessie Conrad to Dawson

CAPEL HOUSE,/ORLESTONE,/Nʀ ASHFORD.
Kent
December 27th 1916

Dear Warrington

Your letter has followed me from place to place and that is the reason I haven't written to you before. We are greatly distressed that your health is still so unsatisfactory, I had hoped by this time to hear that you were quite recovered. It is difficult to tell you much in a letter. A country woman of yours who is a great friend of ours is now in Paris.[1] I have asked her to call on you and tell you all there is to tell and to bring us news of you.

With our very best and affectionate good wishes for 1917.

Affectionately
Jessie Conrad

1. Probably the beautiful Jane Anderson. Jane was American, she recently had become a "great friend" of the Conrads, she often flew over to Paris, and Dawson did meet her.

84. Conrad to Dawson

Sunday.[1]

Cher ami.

"Mortonism" est une belle idée, as you make use of it;[2] but the fact is (I mean a *fact* not a criticism) that your metaphysical connections with the subject-matter of the F[ourth]. D[imension]. are not graspable to *my* mind. If you remember, some years ago, when I read the work in type-script, I tried to convey this to you.[3] Vous n'êtes pas un homme ordinaire—moi je le suis (with a certain quality of tension, of vision, which make me what I am). Therefore almost at every turn I run up against my limitations. What saves me is that I am aware of them. At the present time more than ever. That is why I have consistently refused for the last 2 years to write anything for the newspapers. In fact I can't do it. Even on matters not literary. Of the three papers I undertook for the Admiralty I wrote one.[4] For the rest I am afraid I'll have to break my word. A l'impossible nul n'est tenu. I can't come to terms with any sort of writing. The short book I've sent you was finished in 1914.[5] I have

1. I.e., Sunday, 22 April 1917. The envelope of the letter is postmarked Monday, 23 April.
2. The word "Mortonism" is derived from Dawson's character named Morton in *The True Dimension*.
3. Cf. Conrad to Dawson, No. 18.
4. Jean-Aubry explains that Conrad "accepted the Admiralty's invitation to visit several naval stations in the United Kingdom and to put on record some account of the war-work of the R.N.V.R." (*LL*, II, 165).
5. *Within the Tides* (London, 1915).

done nothing since practically. 2 short stories—about 18000 [words] in all in two years.[6] Voilà la verité.

I can assure you that in my shrinking there is no timidity as to saying what I think. And least of all any fear of compromising myself—against which your letter seems to be arguing. I should have thought you knew me well enough not to suspect me of *that* kind of wor[l]dliness.

I suffer from it so little that if you ever cared to write yourself a critical exposé of your philosophy (as contained in your art) and send it to me I would be stimulated (peut être) to add thereto some par[agraph]s: de ma façon and sign it and would see it published in every newspaper in the world not only without tremors but with sincere pleasure. This is not a cynical joke. It would be curious. Years ago I thought I would like to do it for myself if the thing had been practicable. Explain my own work in all its "nuances" which no critic however able and sympathetic could be expected to detect. I mean Explain it—not puff it. But you wouldn't suspect me of that sort of thing.

My dear I never doubted of your recognition. It's coming—if it has not come yet quite. The story you sent me (I am glad to have it) I remembered of course very well. It isn't the sort of thing that is ever forgotten.[7]

Nous voilà donc Alliés! It is a great piece of luck for England and France.[8] That's the sort of feeling one has: a piece of luck. And perhaps it isn't right to feel like that; but the way the thing came about, the contradictions of expressions, the mist of words[,] the years of reserve so impartial (officially) as to be almost dreadful do leave that impression on one's heart if not on one's mind. En fin! Le sort en est jété—and old Europe will have to reckon with a quickened Americanism; that is if Americanism cares to assert itself continuously in the future. But in any case it is a tremendous event.

Yesterday (Sat) at 12.15 AM Jessie and I sitting up late listened to the gunfire from Dover—a great burst of it which was over in 20 minutes; but we only heard to-day the news of two German destroyers sunk. Poor Jessie is not very well. The strain is telling on her. Last January she snatched the fearful joy of having the boy here

6. "The Warrior's Soul" and "The Tale."
7. In *The Crimson Pall* (Chicago, 1927), p. 9, Dawson identified this "story" as *The True Dimension*.
8. The United States declared war on Germany on 6 April 1917.

for 8 days. He was impatient to get back to his guns and his men. Ever since he went to France in Jan 1916 he has been in command of the MT section of a 6 in howitzer battery. He celebrated his 19th birthday here. He said to me "I am a veteran". And its true in a way. He was in the very first batch of the youngsters appointed to be MT officers with heavy guns. It was quite a new thing then—so new that in his own words they: "had to learn their work under fire".

I don't know how you will receive this letter. With anger may-be. But perhaps it will not last and so pray remember that in this house there is warm affection and eager welcome for you, always.

There are periods in one's life—public and private—that don't stand being set down on paper even for a friend. I can't talk to you about myself just now; and when better days come then one will want to talk of other things. Still, some day—peut être—— Meantime I am yours as always

Joseph Conrad.

85. *Jessie Conrad to Dawson*

CAPEL HOUSE,/ORLESTONE,/NR ASHFORD.
July 26th 1917

My dear Warrington

You have been much in our minds and thoughts even if we haven't written for some time. There is very little news, this horrible time of stress and worry drags on. Borys was hoping to get a short leave and go to Paris he is only two hour's journey from there and he intended coming to see you. His last letter was written in a great hurry and he said all leave impossible at present. I am sending you his latest photograph, you will hardly know him. Conrad and your friend John are both well. Conrad is going to write to you very soon. Meanwhile this brings our affectionate good wishes to you dear friend.

Always your friend
Jessie Conrad

86. *Jessie Conrad to Dawson*

4 C. Hyde Park Mansions[1]/Marylebone Road/N.W. 1
December 30th 1917.

My dear Warrington

I was greatly relieved to have your letter. I was feeling very anxious about you and almost feared to write. It is indeed good news that you are able to do something. I know so well how awful it is to be compelled to keep still when one's every instinct is movement. Do be careful, dear boy, not to do too much because if you throw yourself back again you will find it doubly hard to bear.

You must forgive Conrad for not having written and take my letter as an expression of our affection for you always. Since the war poor Conrad has seemed quite unable to write letters and now I'm afraid I have completely spoiled him in that respect. He is very pleased you are going to do those articles in the 'Bookman' for America.[2] He knows that you th[o]roughly understand him. Here we are anxiously waiting for some good thing to happen to cheer us and give us courage to face the New Year. Borys expects to get leave early next month. Your little friend John is as tall as I am and is now a school boy. We shall be here till the end of Febuary so as to enable the surgeons to try to repair me. It is a long and tiring business and the prospect is not very rosy. Anyhow they are going to give me a good stiff joint and they hope a painless one. I am longing for the time to come when I can with all due respect put my crutches aside.

Now my dear Warrington I send you our warm and affectionate greetings and good wishes for 1918. Believe me with love

Always as ever.

Jessie Conrad.

P.S. Lady Millais and Sir John send you good wishes and re-membrances.[3]

---

1. On 2 December 1917 Conrad informed Richard Curle: "We are at this address for 3 months so that Jessie should be treated for her unlucky knee joint. Of late she was fairly in the way of becoming a cripple for the rest of her days" (*Conrad to a Friend* [London, 1928], p. 58).

2. The articles never appeared.

3. Lady Mary and Sir John Everett Millais were good friends who lived at nearby Leacon Hall in Warehorne. They were the daughter-in-law and grandson of the famous painter.

87. Jessie Conrad to Dawson

3 Devonshire Terrace/Marylebone W. 1

July 14th 1918.

My dear Warrington

It is such a long time since I have seen your handwriting, I wonder, did you have my last two letters?

I shall try to give you all our news in order. First of all your dear Conrad has finished another long book called "An Arrow of Gold," and is fairly well considering all his anxiety about me.

I came into this Nursing Home three weeks ago for a serious operation on my knee. The wretched limb has been steadily getting worse for over a year and a month ago it was decided that they must operate at once. Sir Robert Jones performed the operation and removed the knee cup [sic] and some other septic parts of the bones, then dove tailed them to make a stiff joint.[1] He used a complete set of carpenter's tools—and truly the pain was and still is awful. I am getting on slowly, the wound will not discharge as it should and it is to be opened for the second time this evening. Since Friday they have been putting terrific pressure on it but unfortunately to no purpose. *When* it is better I shall be able to walk without any pain, which seems to me to be an impossible state of things after all these years.

Our dear Borys came home on special leave for the time to be with Conrad and John was here from school. Borys was due to return a week ago but a sharp attack of influenza has kept him here still. I wish you could see your two boy friends. I think you would be pleased with them.

I wonder will the war one day be over and will you then come to us as you used to do—ever so long ago.

If you ever hear of John Powell please remember me very kindly to him and say how much we hope to see him again, at Capel House after the war.

We all send you our love and every good wish. Always affectionately

Your friend

Jessie Conrad

---

1. Sir Robert Jones, a well-known orthopedic surgeon from Liverpool, became a friend of both Conrad and Jessie. Conrad, by the way, gave a somewhat different account of the operation to Sir Sidney Colvin; he said Sir Robert "excised all the cartilages, but without touching the bones, and made a new socket" (27 June 1918, original in Perkins Library, Duke).

88. *Jessie Conrad to Dawson*

Spring Grove/Wye/Nr Ashford/Kent
March 31st 1919.

My dear Warrington

Your welcome letter makes us very sad. I am so sorry your health is still so bad. It would indeed be good to see you and have a nice long talk over old times. Here we have just moved into this house but in six months we go to our real home where we hope to stay a long time. You would enjoy the new house if you could only get over. There we shall have central heat and electric light and be really comfortable.

It was a bit of a wrench to leave poor old Capel but the last year there holds so much pain and anxiety that I really was glad to leave it. The terrible months of the war and our great anxiety about dear Borys seem to belong somehow to the house. Then nine months ago I had a very serious and painful operation on my knee and again, the house seems to have had some share in the nightmare. I can move a little now with crutches an[d] an iron splint which adds just 7 lbs to the limb. I feel very wretched sometimes and one needs a great deal of faith to believe in a final cure. Still Sir Robert Jones says I shall walk so I must hope a little longer.

Your Conrad and the boys are well. Borys gets his discharge this week. He would have a message to you if he were here. I think you would be pleased with them both. John comes home on his holiday on the 9th. He is nearly as tall as Borys, and a great dear. Conrad sends his love and would so much like to see you. I'm afraid there can be no chance of his coming to France just yet. But one day Borys is going to take us all over the various fronts when he can, and it is possible for us to travel.[1] Do, my dear, Warrington write again soon and believe you have some really affectionate friends over here. With love.

Yours affectionately
Jessie Conrad

P.S.   I had a card at Christmas from John Powell. Is he likely to come over?

1. In 1921 Borys accompanied his parents as far as Rouen (they were going to Corsica) and showed them "a part of the battle area, the part on which nearly all his Service had been passed" (*Joseph Conrad and His Circle*, p. 222).

89. *Jessie Conrad to Dawson*

Spring Grove/Wye/Kent
September 15th 1919.

My dear Warrington

First of all please forgive me for not having written before. Conrad as you know is a terrible person to write letters and I generally manage to keep them well in hand. We were very relieved to know you were at least a little better, and next year I hope you will be well enough to come over once again to England. Both your boy friends Borys and John are well. Borys is discharged from the Army, but I am glad to say, that with the exception of a little fever, now and then, is well. John has grown very much and I think you would like him even at this age when boys, like colts are all arms and legs. Conrad has been certainly much better in health since Major Campbell R.A.M.C. an old friend took him in hand.[1] It is largely a faith cure between ourselves but none the less complete and comforting. We are leaving here for the address enclosed on the 2nd of October.[2] I will send you some photographs of it when we are settled. There is a nice room ready for you and the gardens are very charming.

Your ears must burn very often for many people ask after our friend Warrington Dawson. Lady Millais and Sir John wished me to remember them very kindly to you.

I wonder what news of John Powell you may have. I have not heard from him since Christmas[.] Will you give him my love if you write to him. Do write soon and give us news of yourself and let it be good please. My prospects are rather disturbing. I think you know that Sir Robert Jones performed a serious operation on my knee fifteen months ago. The bones refuse to knitt [*sic*] and he is to operate again in November in Liverpool. It's a long weary wait. I know I have your sympathy dear friend. We all send our love to you.

Affectionately
Jessie Conrad

1. Major Kenneth Campbell, Royal Army Medical Corps, an ophthalmic specialist. Campbell had a residence at nearby Wittersham, Isle of Oxney, Kent, as well as a London address. Borys Conrad, however (in a letter to Randall, 26 August 1966), emphasizes that Campbell

> was *not* my father's physician. He was a friend, but, being a doctor, it is not surprising that my father should have discussed his health with him. Any professional advice which he may have given would have been in consultation with Dr. Fox, who was the family doctor at that time. My father would have been most punctilious on this point.

2. Oswalds, Bishopsbourne, Kent.

90. *Conrad to Dawson*

SPRING GROVE,/WYE.
22-9-19

Dearest Dawson.

I asked Jessie to write you at once. As to myself—well! But what is one to say? I am not either very well or very happy—I don't mean in my "domesticity." That is secure for all time. But I have la sensation du vide. Not perhaps le Vide Eternel, though after sixty one may well begin to grow aware of it a little, but of a certain inward emptiness. For 25 years I've been giving out all that was in me. But apart from that I have the feeling of approaching isolation. I don't say loneliness; I shall, I imagine be always looked at now—but from a distance, as if set apart by my predestined temperament like some strange animal confined within a fence for public view. Through my fault—or is it simply Fate?—I have missed all along the chances of closer contacts. But why continue—except only just to say that I have been and am now missing you very much. I trust you won't think I am complaining of things or people. That *would* be outrageous on *my* part! But man, I suppose, is the only animal that is *never* satisfied, perhaps because he's the only one that does not live on bread alone.

Nothing has given me greater satisfaction than your good words about the Arrow.[1] You were often in my thoughts while I wrote. It was unavoidable.

I need not protest to you that I tried to be scrupulously fair in my treatment of the Blunts.[2] The antagonism of feeling had of course to come out since it is the very foundation of the story's psychology.

Borys sends you his warm greetings. John can hardly remember you. He is now a tall schoolboy. Jessie's love.

Always with affection

Yours
J. Conrad.

1. *The Arrow of Gold* (1919).
2. John Mason Key Blunt and his mother. See p. 101.

91. *Dawson to John Powell*[1]

EMBASSY OF THE UNITED STATES OF AMERICA
Paris,
23rd Sept, 1919.

Dear John,

For various reasons, it has been difficult for me to write, in all these years; one was that I knew I was getting slowly but steadily worse, in spite of seeming improvements at various times, & I did not want to tell you, & did not want to deceive you. So I let others do the talking. But now, I believe I am saved, thanks to the brains & the initiative of quite a young doctor who had the opportunity to observe me for a long while, & who has succeeded in relieving much that eminent celebrities never could affect, & in really bringing back a little of my strength. Even among those who saw me propped up in a chair or hobbling on two sticks, few could suspect how weak & infirm I was. I don't think I can ever be really active again; the spine has weakened too much for that—not the bone, the ligaments; but I am sure I can, with time & care, regain a certain amount of activity, instead of looking back each half-year & remembering what I had been able to do the half-year before & could no longer do!

The State Department has just given me important promotion as "Special Assistant," I am the only one of that rank at this Embassy. So I am continuing my official work here; I like it, & just at present am fitted for nothing but a sedentary life.

Jessie Conrad has several times sent her love to you, when writing to me. Borys came unscathed through the war.[2] Conrad's health is improved. But oh, my dear, have you seen "An Arrow of Gold"? If not—don't! He did not send it to me. When I first bought it & opened it & saw the dedication to Richard Curle, I thought my beloved Conrad had been ashamed to send it to me on that account.[3] But as I read—I said to myself—that the dedication was all right & there was another reason for not sending it to me! And yet, "The Shadow Line" was truly worthy of him. I hear, by the way, that the English reviews of the "Arrow of Gold" have been lengthy & effusive. Popularity . . . .[4]

1. Original in Alderman Library, University of Virginia.
2. Cf. p. 96.
3. See pp. 86–87.
4. Dawson was not alone among Conrad's friends in holding this view. Gals-

199

At times, I have heard echoes of your success. Some have told me that you have "come into your own." May it be true, my dear—if not already, then very soon. I have spent some wonderful hours with you, which were not forgotten in my years of deepest darkness. But it was only a physical darkness, for I always saw beyond: not on other planes alone, but on this one too, where so much exists which I love & admire & reverence, & in which it has been my privilege to share while striving not only with my mind & spirit, but with my bruised & wasted flesh.

I say with Mother—"God Bless you, John!"

Your Frank.[5]

---

worthy, e.g., confided to Garnett that the *Arrow* had "No guts"; "I can't put up, like the younger generation, with these later books" (*Letters from John Galsworthy 1900–1932*, ed. Edward Garnett [London, 1934], p. 236).

5. Powell's nickname for Dawson.

92. *Jessie Conrad to Dawson*

The Sefton Nursing Home[1]
70 Huskisson Street/Liverpool
16.12.19.

My dear Warrington

We are both terribly distressed to hear of your continued ill-health. I do wish you would come over and see this wonderful surgeon Sir Robert Jones. He operated on my wretched knee last Tuesday week, and found an abcess on the bone which had been causing endless pain and trouble. It is simply wonderful to be free from pain and to know I shall soon be able to really walk. I think when one has found such unexpected relief from a clever man's treatment, one is desperately anxious for one's friends to be cured too.

Be sure, my dear friend, we often speak and think of you and long to see you again. We all send you our love and greetings[.]

Always affectionately
Jessie Conrad.

1. The entire Conrad family had gone up to Liverpool, home of Jessie's surgeon, for the third operation on her knee. Despite her optimism in this letter, it was only a "little more than three months after my Liverpool adventure" that she "once again prepared for the ordeal of meeting the surgeon's knife" (*Joseph Conrad and His Circle*, p. 218).

93. *Conrad to Dawson*

OSWALDS,/BISHOPSBOURNE,/KENT.

5.4.20

My dear Dawson.

I was very touched by your letter to B[orys]. Very remorseful too at my apparent neglect. But both Jessie and I ought to be excused. I have been more or less laid up since my last. As to Jessie after the bright prospects following the operation in Dec^{er} last she needed all her fortitude to face the development of a new complication which crippled her completely again; in fact laid her up with horrible pain for some three weeks.

She was operated again on the 31 Mch, Sir Robert Jones coming down from Scotland on purpose, here. The relief was immediate— whether it is the last of her troubles we don't know. But the prospects are good and she is making a good recovery so far.

I won't say much more now. I am far from being well myself and we all had a horrid time of it for a month past looking at her sufferings. I am just beginning to recover my tone somewhat. 1919 was a bad year and 1920 looked as if it was going to be worse. But perhaps we have at last turned the corner.

Love from us all[.]

Yours always
J. Conrad.

94. *Conrad to Dawson*

OSWALDS,/BISHOPSBOURNE,/KENT.

July 9th. 1920.

My dear Warrington

Only the other day I dispatched to you a copy of my latest book.[1] Powell spent the night here, was perfectly delightful as usual; and, we thought, very little changed as far as appearance goes.[2] As to the rest he is the dear fellow he always was. He carried off a copy of the American edition of The Rescue, but the one I sent you is the first Eng.

1. *The Rescue* (1920), inscribed "With love from Joseph Conrad."
2. Borys met Powell in Canterbury, and Curle arrived that evening. Details of the visit were recorded in the Richmond *Sunday Journal* of 25 July 1920, p. 20.

I shall this evening begin reading the typescript Powell left with me.[3] I assure you, my dear fellow, that I have grown so slow in everything I do that I have the greatest difficulty to find time, real free time, for anything beyond the daily task. But I have now found time for you and shall drop you a line when I have finished. At a cursory glance the beginning pages seem certainly arresting.

I will say no more because I hate dictating a letter to you and my wrist won't allow me to write more than a few lines at a time.[4]

Jessie who's improving slowly (but still laid up) sends her love in which I join[.]

Ever yours,
J Conrad

3. On 12 July Dawson wrote to Powell: "I heard from Conrad to-day, in date of July 9th, saying that he was to begin reading 'The Manor' that same night, & would write to me shortly" (original in Alderman Library, University of Virginia). Probably this is the story published as *Adventure in the Night* (1924).
4. This is the earliest dictated Conrad letter in the Dawson Collection. Conrad's hand-scrawled additions (salutation, final sentence, complimentary close, and signature) corroborate his reference to gout.

95. *Conrad to Dawson*

OSWALDS,/BISHOPSBOURNE,/KENT.
30.12.20

Dearest Warrington

Infinite t[h]anks for sending me the text of the Interal Commission's findin[g]s in the famous North Sea Inquiry. It is marvellous you should have remembered a wish uttered so many years ago. May you find your life easier your hopes brighter your courage and endurance better rewarded this year. All here send you their best and most sympathetic wishes.

We will be leaving on the 23 Jan for Corsica where we, that is Jessie and I, propose to stay for a month or so. John goes to Tonbridge School this term, and B[orys] will take up his work in London; so we will have no one with us but a nurse-compon for Jessie.

Perhaps on our return journey we will be able to look you up. But our outward route must be (for various reasons) through Rouen Orleans and so on.

Just before your letter arrived Everitt (of D. P. & Co) was here and we conversed in a most appreciative and hopeful spirit your novel they are going to publish shortly.[1] I hope my dear fellow its merit will be recognized not only by fellow-spirits but by ordinary minds of the general public.

Ever affectionately yours

J. Conrad.

1. S. A. Everitt of Doubleday, Page & Co. spoke with Conrad about Dawson's war novel, *The Gift of Paul Clermont* (1921).

96. *Dawson to Sir Sidney Colvin*[1]

October 25th. 1921.

Sir Sidney *Colvin*,
   35, Palace Gardens Terrace,
   Kensington,
      London, W.

My dear Sir Sidney,

Your pleasant note in acknowledgement of Ambassador Wallace's book[2] gave me great pleasure, showing as it does that you have not forgotten me.

One of my greatest regrets in the state of my health to which I fell victim in the course of the war, is that my physical activity having totally disappeared, I am no longer able to go to England and so have not been able to continue my acquaintance with you, commenced so auspiciously at Joseph Conrad's, and continued so pleasantly in your own house.

I have read with deep interest your magazine articles, notably the Stevenson series.[3] What you say of Stevenson and his modelling has been of use to me. I had never tried modelling but took it up on your suggestion and have found it a great resource in my state of helplessness. But I find that I run only to faces, faces—of various types and periods. I don't know how I do them, yet they have character. I play

1. From Dawson's carbon typescript.
2. *The Speeches of the Hon. Hugh C. Wallace, American Ambassador to France, 1919–1921, Collected with a Foreword by Warrington Dawson* (Paris, 1921).
3. Colvin wrote "Some Personal Recollections" for *Scribner's Magazine*, LXVII (1920). In the third section (pp. 338–354), devoted to Robert Louis Stevenson, "my closest friend of all" (p. 69), he recorded that when Stevenson "could not talk, read, or write, he amused himself moulding little scenes with figures and landscapes in relief" (p. 353).

with a small lump of clay and presently it seems to me that a type of face is looking out from the lump. I work to make it appear as if I were freeing a prisoner from a cell.

Heinemann is going to publish early in November my novel of France before and during the war, THE GIFT OF PAUL CLERMONT, in which Rudyard Kipling has taken so much interest. Indeed, just for your own information, it is entirely due to him that this book, which he read in manuscript, is being published by Doubleday in America and by Heinemann in London. He was very anxious to see it appear because of the picture it gives of France at a time when we all feel that too much cannot be revealed about the real heart of France to the English-speaking world, British as well as American. I have asked Mr. Pawling[4] to send a copy to you and I should be deeply grateful not only for my own sake, but for the sake of the cause, if you could do anything to help it on its way. Not that it is a theme novel—perish the thought! But it is a novel which poured itself out of me because all that I had seen and felt had to find expression and its natural form was the form on which I have specialised.

Yours ever sincerely,
(signed): Warrington Dawson

WD/MC[5]

4. Sidney Pawling, a partner of the publisher William Heinemann.
5. "MC" was Marguerite Castéra, one of the numerous ladies who served for a while as secretary to Dawson.

97. *Conrad to Dawson*

OSWALDS,/BISHOPSBOURNE,/KENT.
30 Nov. 21

Mon trés cher.

Now I have absorbed it I send you my thanks for the gift of Paul Clermont.[1] It is a very charming and touching performance which one likes more the deeper one gets into it. The development of the boy is done with masterly simplicity as to means. The war part is certainly very fine and deeply moving in its economy of sentiment

1. It should be noted that Conrad's remarks here are less strained than they often were when he had to comment on Dawson's work. This book was simply better.

and charm of expression. Indeed the whole my dearest Dawson is beautifully written. The descriptions of the country are bien senties. And what is wonderful in a book with so many people in it, every single character comes off as a creation. They live.

My congratulations. I won't go into details now; but France has in you a wonderful friend—that is one strong general impression amongst others. The fact of the dedication to Joffre pleased me very much.[2]

I exist wearily, work with difficulty and am not having a good time—so to speak. The bright spot is Jessie's recovery after years of trouble. We talk of you often and think of you always with affection and sympathy. Believe my dear friend ever yours,

Joseph Conrad.

PS Jessie's dear love.

2. See pp. 96 and 107.

98. *Conrad to Dawson*

OSWALDS,/BISHOPSBOURNE,/KENT.

29.3.22

My dear Warrington

I write a few words at once to thank you for your dedication which touches me by its generous expressions.[1] But it would have been a more intimate and a closer Communion if you had merely written "To my friend" above my name as only from one craftsman to another can be done.

My dear, I am sorry at what you say of the late Pinker.[2] That he should have in any way damaged your prospects is deplorable. But I do not feel remorse in the matter; for if you remember the only time we talked on the subject (outside the road gate of Capel) my advice to you was *not* to go to him. A year or more later I heard from him that he was acting for you.

1. Conrad refers to Dawson's dedication of *The Pyramid*. See p. 108n.
2. Pinker had died in New York on 8 February 1922, and Conrad was very much touched. Not only had the two men closed their old rift, but in recent years they had grown quite close. Dawson, however, blamed Pinker, at least in part, for his own lack of success. Pinker had had a chance to peddle *The Pyramid* as early as 1913.

I do not believe that any publisher would have a particular confidence in my judgment. What exactly would you like me to do.

Jessies love.

Affecly yours

J. Conrad

99. *Conrad to Dawson*

Oswalds,/Bishopsbourne,/Kent.

June 2nd. 1922.

My dear Dawson.

I dictate this letter because I really don't know when I will be able to write in pen and ink, my right wrist having been bad for a long time now and showing no signs of serious improvement.

Neither will I be very long in what I have got to say now. I find it very difficult to express myself to the typewriter. Shortly then, my dear Dawson, I have given the fullest and most friendly consideration to the letter you have written me. Facts as the proverb says are stubborn things. I now find from repeated attempts that the form of writing consisting in literary appreciation of other men's work, implying analysis and an exposition of ethical and aesthetic values on which all criticism and even a mere panegyric must be based, is not in my way. And the deeper my untutored feelings are affected the less I am able to put them in a form that would influence peoples minds. If you have looked at my volume of collected papers, on the side of 'Letters', you will see how few they are and how utterly useless anything I could write would be to give a start to a literary reputation.[1] Whatever I say I can only talk about myself; not because I am a megolamaniac but because I am not sufficiently cultured to talk with authority to the public about other men. Whenever I have attempted it the effort has been out of all proportion to this miserable result. I won't enlarge further on the state of affairs which is generally known. I dislike writing, I don't believe in my own wisdom, and I shrink from putting forth my opinions to the general public. I am like that. I cannot help it. It is temperamental; and it is closely associated with the unliterary complexion of my mind. The only

1. In the preceding December Conrad had sent Dawson a copy of his *Notes on Life & Letters* (London, 1921).

thing that ever qualified me to take a pen in hand is the possession of a certain creative gift. And even in that I am not secure. It has never been a source of gratification to me; on the contrary, it has brought me many hours of unhappiness in the doubts and heart searchings it has forced me into at every step.

The above confession is strictly entre nous. To be conscious of one's own deficiencies is not a crime, though I admit it is a great hindrance to the carrying out of many good intentions. In that sense it may be called a weakness—but enough of this.

On the other hand, my dear Dawson, whenever it has happened to me to address my friends intimately and personally on the subject of their work I have always written with perfect sincerity of feeling, however inadequately expressed; and to what I have written in private I will of course stand to in public. Therefore my dearest fellow if you think that the publication (whole or in extracts) of what I have said to you in the open intimacy of our friendship may be of any use I would be glad if you would deal with it to the best advantage.

Now specifically as to "The Rock".[2] I have read about half of the MS and I can say here at once that it has from the first engaged my interest, both by treatment and expression. The descriptive parts are first-rate. The two scenes between Vera and Errington on board and during the shooting trip are very good. As to the book's chance of success it is impossible for me to say anything; the more so that I have not finished it yet; but it is all very characteristic, very 'Dawsonian', and is penetrated through and through by your characteristic earnestness of emotion. As to criticism of details my dear Dawson, I don't suppose you want it; and in any case I would offer it with great diffidence if I were to offer it at all. For in those matters I am not, by any means, sure myself. This mainly for the reason that having a pronounced temperament and a sort of personality in my writing which has not been acquired but was inborn (and therefore is very masterful) I know that I would be prejudiced in many ways by the mere fact of being what I am.

Pardon all the delays in my correspondence, my dear friend. I have been laid up four times since New Year's Day. I have been unable to

2. The novel Dawson planned in 1909. He began to write it in May, 1914, was interrupted by the war, resumed work in August, 1920, and finished in January, 1922. On 18 May 1926, a long while after Conrad's death, Jessie reported to Dawson that she had just come across two typed copies of it.

finish anything for the last two years; which is for me a cause of serious worry. When I have a chance of a few days' work I absorb myself in it in a sort of desperation, and then feel too tired to put two consecutive thoughts together.

Jessie (who is still very crippled) sends her love[.]

Every affectly yours
J Conrad.

100. *Jessie Conrad to Dawson*

OSWALDS,/BISHOPSBOURNE,/KENT.
June 27th 1922.

My dear Warrington

You are so often in my thoughts and we so often speak of you that it seems you must know it quite well. It was such a great disappointment to miss you when we came from Corsica. I should certainly have managed to find you out but I was so very much a cripple. This November we mean to try to get to the South of France and, who knows, we may come through Versailles as we shall go by car. The few snap shots I am sending you John took last holidays. It is his first attempt at photographs. You would be very much interested in both boys. Borys who is nearly 25 and John just 16 in August. Of course they make me feel rather old and sometimes I find it hard to believe I am really their mother. Even John now can drive a car. He is taller than his father or brother[.] This last four or five years have been very full of pain and now that I begin again to move with a little ease I wonder how I managed to exist.

I wish so much that we could have some better news of you. Only the other day dear Lady Millais was asking after you and sends you her very warm remembrances and sympathy. I expect you know that her only son died over two years ago.[1] She has been very wonderful about it but he was everything to her.

Do write me a nice long letter and if you have a photograph of yourself send me one.

---

1. Sir John died on 30 September 1920 at the age of thirty-two. Despite bad health he had rejoined the navy (from which he had retired in 1911) and served on the H.M.S. *Amethyst*. In 1917 he retired again, this time with the rank of Lieutenant Commander (London *Times*, 1 October 1920, p. 10).

My cookery book comes out next January.[2] Do you remember the little farmhouse where you stayed that summer before the war? I don't think the world will be ever the same again do you?

Much love from all[.]

Affectionately
Jessie Conrad

2. A *Handbook of Cookery for a Small House* (London, 1923). "The recipes in this book are calculated for a household of four persons" (p. 3).

101. *Jessie Conrad to Dawson*

OSWALDS,/BISHOPSBOURNE,/KENT.
August 9th 1922.

My dear Warrington

Conrad is in town and asked me to tell you that there is nothing he wishes altered in his letter before you publish it.[1]

We are so grieved to know you are not getting better. I wish so much there was some prospect of our coming to see you this winter. Should some wonderful chance give us the means of spending the winter in the South be sure we would look you up on our way. Trains are rather an impossibility for me now. I am still tormented by this horrid periostitis and have been having very painful injections now ever since Febuary. The poor old knee is simply a pincushion.

J. C. (as we call Conrad) is not at the moment very well and needs a real rest.

I wish you could see this garden it is lovely in spite of the bad weather. Haven't you some snap shots of your home to send me so that I can picture you in it.

Both boys are well. John whom you knew as a kiddie is now 5 ft 9 ½. When you write do give me your latest new[s] of John Powell it is so long since I have heard from him.

I must close now as we have to send to Bridge to post on Wednesdays our post office being closed.

With love from us all and every good wish.

Yours very affectionately
Jessie Conrad.

1. Evidently the document which served as Conrad's foreword to Dawson's *Adventure in the Night* (1924).

102. *Jessie Conrad to John Powell*[1]

OSWALDS,/BISHOPSBOURNE,/KENT.

January 14th 1923.

My dear Mr Powell.

We were more than pleased to hear from you and I am very proud to have a copy of 'my piece,' as you used to call it.[2] How I wish I could ever play it. I have a wonderful memory and I can recall whole parts of it to my mind and see you vividly as you played it at Capel House. Is there any chance of your coming again to England? Please do not fail to let us know. You may have heard that Conrad is considering the prospect of going to America in April. I have very mixed feelings about it. I like to know that he feels the energy to go but I rather distrust his ability. Frankly I shall be very anxious while he is away. If his health stands the strain (and as we all know a change is often a great tonic) I shall feel happy that I have put nothing such as an objection in his way.

I am much better and if I am extremely careful to be moderate in my efforts I get along quite well. But of course it is only after all a mended limb and the strain is easily felt and resented. Your young friend John (your namesake by accident) is returning to school on Friday. Borys is in Manchester, tomorrow he is 25.

I am very distressed to think of Warrington and I wish I could go to see him. It was always a pleasure to be with him. Somehow one has a feeling that you might be brothers.

You will be tired by such a long yarn. I send you my love and New Year Greeting.

Always affectionately
Jessie Conrad.

1. Original in Alderman Library, University of Virginia.
2. I have found no Powell composition dedicated to Jessie. Probably "my piece" refers merely to one that she especially liked.

103. *Conrad to Ellen Glasgow*[1]

OSWALDS,/BISHOPSBOURNE,/KENT.

4. Ap. '23

My dear Ellen Glasgow
Let me address you like this in affectionate remembrance of our

1. From the original in the Alderman Library, University of Virginia. Conrad sailed for the United States later this same month.

meeting at Capel House, and because of our fellowship in the Craft. Thank you for your charming letter which has touched us both deeply. Poor Mrs C (as we all call her) is in no state to travel. She was much better last year but now there came a sort of relapse— renewed inflamation of the deeper tissues in the limb which has been operated upon so many times. She just can move about the house—and no more. I am most reluctant to leave her; but I have accepted Mr & Mrs Doubleday's invitation to spend 3 weeks with them at Oyster Bay and I could not think of drawing back now.

I fear my dear and unforgettable friend that it will be impossible for me to come as far as Richmond—this time. I have had two very bad years and now feel as tho' I were made of brown paper. It is not the sort of thing that gives one much confidence for travelling. No doubt Mr D. has made a few engagements for me; but I will have to keep very quiet for the most part. I wish I could borrow for a month one hundre[d]th part of our Hugh's spirits and vitality.[2] But such a transaction is impossible in this imperfect world. Pray pardon me and believe me always your faithful and affectionate[3] friend admirer and servant

Joseph Conrad.

PS Jessie will be writing and sending you a few photographs of us all in a day or two.

2. Hugh Seymour Walpole, novelist and man of letters, was a friend of both Conrad and Ellen Glasgow. Not only was he prolific, but in 1919 he had made the first of a series of lecture tours in the United States, boosting the sales of his books and generally making himself popular. Unlike Conrad he had the "spirits and vitality" to visit Miss Glasgow.

3. Some of the letters in Conrad's abbreviation are illegible, but "affectionate" is clearly the word he intends.

104. Conrad to John Powell[1]

EFFENDI HILL/OYSTER BAY, LONG ISLAND
NEW YORK

My dear Powell

I take the first quiet moment since our return from the New England tour to drop you a line.[2] I found here a letter from my

1. Original in Alderman Library, University of Virginia, postmarked 28 May 1923.

2. Conrad travelled through New England during the last half of his stay in America.

wife who asks me to give you her "very special love", and hopes that she will see you next year in England.

I join in that message and in that hope with all my heart. You are one of our "precious friendships" and you know that they are not many. I was made happy by seeing and hearing you this time[3]— and I am grateful to you for giving me the opportunity.

And now, my dear fellow—Goodbye! May success attend all your activities and give you the happiness your great gift and your warm heart deserve.

Always your old friend
Joseph Conrad.

3. Powell played at the Doubledays' home while Conrad was a guest there.

105. Dawson to Conrad[1]

19 rue du Maréchal Joffre,/Versailles.
Seine et Oise.
July, 20, 1923.

I had not the heart to write to you during all your American adventure. When we talked of it in the years gone by, you and I were to have gone together! And I am here on my back, more helpless than ever, told the miracle may yet happen—while I measure out the years and tell myself I must keep busy as long as I remain here!

The Chicago publisher[2] who has been bringing out "THE PYRAMID" serially will bring out the book in volume form, as well as my book for children, and "THE SIN"—(you remember our fun with the ENGLISH REVIEW?)—and he is talking of reprinting "THE SCAR" and "THE SCOURGE."

In connection with "THE PYRAMID", I shall publish our correspondence.[3] But there is so much of my own expression of opinion in it that I am wondering if you would let me add to your reply to my letter these lines of what you told me after reading "THE PYRAMID" (under another name, I've made the change).[4]

1. From Dawson's carbon typescript. Salutation and complimentary close were probably written in by hand.
2. Dawson's friend Bernard Bernard.
3. When Dawson became involved with Kipling regarding this book, he apparently decided it would be impolitic to publish in it the Conrad-Dawson "correspondence." He withheld the latter until his *Crimson Pall* (1927).
4. See pp. 63–64 and 77.

They would make a real and even thundering reply to my letter, and they mention the three books in which this particular publisher is interested. They also interest me particularly because the novel I am just finishing, whose scene is France and which is called "The Virgin of Ivory" comes nearer to being a critical novel than anything I have done.

And I must go on writing, or I'll just die stupidly like anybody else, and I don't want to do that!

May I use this text? Please say yes—after you have taken out anything you may not want to stand for now.

106. *Conrad to Dawson*

OSWALDS,/BISHOPSBOURNE,/KENT.

July 29th. 1923.

My dear Warrington.

I met John Powell in New York and we talked of old times, mostly in affectionate reference to yourself, and with genuine sorrow at the heavy trial that fell to your lot. You were very much in my thoughts over there. From that land of novel experience and generous kindness I turned my eyes more than once towards Versailles where my second American friend (Crane was the first, in time)[1] gave us all—as I told J. P.—a great object lesson in serenity, courage, and undaunted fortitude.

My greatest regret was not to be able to visit the South. The time was short and the health too uncertain for that. So at least it seemed to me. Perhaps if you had been by my side—who knows! But this doesn't bear thinking about.

Certainly, my dear Warrington! You may do exactly what you like, and what you think best, for the object in view.[2] Though, of course, I can not remember what I may have said in our many and intimate conversations, I can raise no objections to the text of the type-written pages you have sent me, and I sincerely rejoice that there is a publisher who seems to be taking the matter up properly. It appears, then, that good things can come even out of Chicago!

1. Conrad had met Stephen Crane in 1897.
2. Conrad refers to Dawson's requests in the preceding letter.

Does the "Virgin of Ivory" (trés bien, ce titre) enter into the scheme of the contemplated publication?

You are mistaken in thinking that you are no longer a memory for the boys.[3] Even to John who was a very small boy when he saw you, you are a very living personality, as is evident from his talk. They both inquire after you constantly. I am living in hopes of coming over to France, (I mean Paris) in a not distant future; but there are many things in the way. You will be, of course, the first to hear of it directly the way is clear.

Jessie joins me in the expression of warm sympathy and love. She will be writing to you herself before long. She is still very crippled and often in pain—but there is some improvement.

Ever yours

J. Conrad.

3. Cf. No. 90.

107. *Lillian M. Hallowes to Dawson*[1]

OSWALDS,/BISHOPSBOURNE,/KENT.

Dec. 10th. 1923.

Dear Mr Dawson,

Mr Conrad is laid up just now and is unable to write any letters by hand, so he has asked me to write to you without delay in answer to your letter to him. He sends you his love, in which Mrs Conrad joins, and asks me to say that of course he will be glad to accept the dedication of the book you propose.[2] He will write to you himself as soon as he is able, but he has had rather a bad attack of his old enemy, gout, which seems loth to leave him.

Yours faithfully,

L. M. Hallowes.

1. Miss Hallowes was Conrad's secretary from 1908 to 1924. "She used to declare that proofs would be found imprinted on her heart when she died" (Jessie Conrad, *Joseph Conrad and His Circle*, p. 228).
2. *Adventure in the Night* (1924).

108. *Jessie Conrad to Ellen Glasgow*[1]

OSWALDS,/BISHOPSBOURNE,/KENT.
Febuary 14th 1924

My dear "Ellen"

Forgive the liberty I have taken and if you will, use my name in a like manner. Please share this letter with our mutual friend John Powell, to whom I offer the same privilege.

So many thanks for your new book which I enjoyed so very much.[2] You have been my bed companion now for over a week. I first read the new book and then re-read all the rest with the greatest enjoyment.

I gave all your kind messages to J. C. as we all call him here and he sends you his love and his warm greetings. I am glad to say he is much better in health now than he has been for some time. This is a great relief to both the doctor, the boys and myself. There was a time when some very disquieting symptoms caused us all very grave anxiety. These have now happily disappeared and now apart from his love of gout, he is very well. The small boy you knew, John is now a young man standing 6 ft and is studying French in Havre, where he lives with a French pa[r]son's family of 10 children.[3] Who says the French birth rate is falling?

Borys the elder is now a married man with a son of his own.[4] This is perhaps the reason of my last twenty grey hairs. He is a fine baby and we are very pleased with him.

I am not unfortunately much improved in the matter of walking. And while my virtues are many and varied there still seems a difficulty in growing wings stout enough to enable me to flit gracefully instead of walking. The doctor's suggestion that I should walk on my hands I have dismissed as undignified.

With love to you and to "John".

Affectionately yours
Jessie Conrad Korzeniowska

1. Original in Alderman Library, University of Virginia.
2. *The Shadowy Third and Other Stories* (1923).
3. The Bosts, a "Serious, spartan French family," Conrad told Curle (20 September 1923, *Conrad to a Friend*, p. 207). Later Conrad wrote to Galsworthy that John "studies at the Berlitz Institute, draws at the École pratique des Beaux-Arts, and fences 3 times a week,—not to speak of driving the Br. Consul's car, having teas . . . with the British Chaplain and conversing with the Bost family (eleven of them)" (22 February 1924, Jean-Aubry, *LL*, II, 340).
4. The first Conrad grandchild, born in January, 1924, was named Philip James.

Borys had secretly married Miss Joan King in September, 1922, several months before Conrad's trip to America. Jessie, who learned the news just before he sailed, refrained from telling Conrad until his return.

109. *Jessie Conrad to Dawson*

OSWALDS,/BISHOPSBOURNE,/KENT.
February 23rd 1924

My dear Warrington

We were very pleased to have your letter and the photograph. You have not altered much since we last saw you in Capel House. I have been keeping this letter waiting hoping to have the photograph of Borys' little son to send you. But I'm afraid you would grow tired of waiting for news of your friends over here if I delay any longer. What do you think of John? The small boy you left [is] now six feet high. He is in Havre and I will put his address in this letter. Perhaps if you have time you would write him a few lines. He is living with a French family learning the language. Borys still feels the effect of his war service and worries us at times. J. C. is so much better now than he was a month ago. I am still in the hands of the surgeons. I am now having injections of cocaine three times a week and my limb resembles a cribbage-board more than anything else.

Did you know I had turned journalist? I have appeared now several times in the "Daily Mail" and had some very complimentary letters from the editor. Also I have been a regular contributor to a magazine of articles on cookery. I find a great relief in having some real work to do now that I am so tied to my chair.

I am moved to send you these two articles and as I have no other copies I would ask you to return them to me. Conrad had the surprise of his life one day when he opened his paper and saw my name there.

We had a hope of coming to France with the car and motoring South, but so far the surgeon will not give me permission to leave England until May. I hope this letter hasn't tired you out.

With love from us both. Always your friend

Affectionately
Jessie Conrad

P.S. Your new book has just arrived.[1] Thanks so much.

1. Probably *Opportunity and Theodore Roosevelt* (Chicago, 1924).

216

110. *Lillian M. Hallowes to Dawson*

OSWALDS,/BISHOPSBOURNE,/KENT.

June 23rd

Dear Mr Dawson.

Mr Conrad has been meaning to write to you for some time, but first of all Mrs Conrad's operation & now his own illness have prevented him from writing any letters.[1] He has been laid up for more than a week with a very bad attack of bronchitis, complicated with gout & is only just beginning to feel a little better. But he does not want to delay any longer in thanking you for the copy of "Adventure in the Night" which you have sent him, which unfortunately he has not been able to look at yet. Mrs Conrad's operation has been quite successful and the Surgeon hopes that it will effect a final cure on her knee. She is making excellent progress & hopes soon to be able to get about again.

Mr Conrad sends his most friendly greetings and is so glad to hear of the improvement in your health.

Yours sincerely
L. M. Hallowes.

1. On 2 June 1924 Conrad had told Doubleday that Sir Robert Jones was to come to Canterbury and operate again on Jessie's leg on 13 June (Jean-Aubry, *LL*, II, 344).

111. *Dawson to Jessie Conrad*[1]

February 20, 1929.

Mrs. Joseph Conrad,
   Torrens,
     Mill Lane,
       Marbledown[*sic*],
         Canterbury.

My dear Jessie,

It was a great relief for me to receive your letter of February 17th, even though the news is not very cheering. I have not only thought much of you but have been growing concerned for your sake, and I would have written again to enquire if I had not feared to worry you. Because I well know that there are distressing periods in life when

1. From Dawson's carbon typescript.

one would like to write news of oneself and really lacks the heart to do so, and the insistence of friends is then rather painful than helpful.

I am grateful that your twelfth operation has at least brought you some relief. What a long martyrdom you have had as a result of that unfortunate accident. But your fortitude, and the way you have continued throughout the years to play an important part in life, are truly inspiring to your friends.

I can well understand your feeling to see your two lads grown beyond the stage where they need your constant loving vigilance. You have far more to look back upon in life than most women could ever aspire to, but of course such an active mind and such an affectionate nature as yours need employment.

I wonder if some time you could find the leisure to write a short sketch of Conrad's friendship with me.[2] It is a field that remains practically unexploited even in the extensive Conrad literature which already exists. And yet you and I both know how much we meant to each other. It would be a help to me in getting before the public some day my own view of "my dear Conrad," a task rendered difficult by the very fact that so much has been written on what has now come to be conventional lines and I have things to say which are not generally said. But this consideration is not the main one I am holding in view. I am thinking that such a sketch by you would help now to get a new public in America for Conrad, if brought out in pamphlet form and widely circulated by my publisher, Bernard Bernard of Chicago.

Mr. Bernard is making a great effort with my works and notably is advertising them considerably in his magazine "Health and Happiness." It is his health and diet principles which I follow and which have enabled me to fight out with pretty fair success a battle for life against what among doctors is accepted as an incurable disease which ought to have put me in my grave many years ago—rhizomelic spondylosis of the spine. He is the publisher of his own health books as well as my novels, and undertakes little else, and he always runs in frequent mention of me or my works in the pages of his magazine. He has of late been advertising Theodore Roosevelt considerably because of my book "Opportunity and Theodore Roosevelt." He would

2. Jessie responded with "Friendship's Friend," included in the present volume, pp. 32–35.

certainly do as much and indeed more for Conrad if he had something from you about me which he could bring out as a booklet, and he reaches a public which ordinary publishers are unable to reach—thousands and thousands of people who buy his own books and read his magazine to guide them in their daily living and care for health.

I don't know just what you would care to say about me and my visits to you in the old days. "My dear Conrad" used to say to me in confidence: "it is surprising how well that little woman understands you!"[3] He never said more—but the expression recurred so often that it made a lasting impression upon me. It would certainly be interesting for me, after all these years, to know just what you saw in me for better or worse!

Luckily, I have not minded the cold. I am not dependent upon weather conditions except that I dislike heavy fogs which fortunately are scarce occurrences here.

It is a great disappointment to me to know that you cannot come to France just yet because I so much want to see you. We must hope for better luck very soon.

Ever with love to you, dear Jessie,

Most affectionately,

3. See No. 50.

112. *Jessie Conrad to Dawson*

TORRENS,/MILL LANE,/HARBLEDOWN,/CANTERBURY.
March 21st 1929

My dear Warrington

I am so pleased you liked what I wrote.[1] Of course make any use you like of it. I did not think of any payment from Mr Bernard for that. It was a real joy to do it for you and your generous thanks for it pleases me greatly. How I wish I could come over for a chat. I feel as if you would do me more moral good than anyone else. One is so apt to give things a wrong value when one is alone to brood over them. I will write in a day or so.

My love in haste[.]

Jessie Conrad.

Your very affectionate friend.

1. "Friendship's Friend."

113. *Jessie Conrad to Dawson*

TORRENS,/MILL LANE,/HARBLEDOWN,/CANTERBURY.
July 25th. 1929.

Dear Warrington

I was glad to have your letter of a few moments ago. You do not give me any news of yourself. I would like so much to know how you are. Do you know if John and Louise[1] are coming over in September as they intended? I have lost their address which I wish you would let them know when you are writing next.

We have been having such a dry hot summer everything absolutely dried up. It is getting really serious too.

I am very interested in the mistake as to my place of abode. Is it possible for you to set it right, as I am still so new to seeing myself in print that I would hate to miss even so small an article.[2] Shall I send you one I am doing for the 'Blue Peter'?[3] Perhaps they would take that for America if the American rights are free.

I am still hoping to come over some day and I shall certainly come to see you. I am not sure if I told you that John's wife is expecting a baby in October.[4] Never be surprised if you hear I have stolen a kiddie, the Mother hunger is very strong sometimes. I believe you miss having a human being dependent upon you, more than the person on whom you, yourself depend. Conrad was so very dependent upon me. I have had no news of Borys for nearly four months, but I'm trying to conclude that no news is good news.

My love to you[.]

Affectionately
Jessie Conrad

1. Powell had married Louise Burleigh on 25 April 1928. Miss Burleigh was a Richmond playwright and author, much interested in the little theater movement. She and Conrad had corresponded about producing "One Day More."
2. One of several bits of evidence that "Friendship's Friend" appeared in *Health and Life*, Bernard Bernard's physical culture magazine at the time.
3. Probably "Joseph Conrad's War Service," *Blue Peter*, XI (1931), 252–255.
4. This first child of John and Mary Conrad (the former Mary Grindrod) was named Richard.

114. *Jessie Conrad to Dawson*

TORRENS,/MILL LANE,/HARBLEDOWN,/CANTERBURY.
October 18th 1930

My dear Warrington

Nurse Budd sent me a cutting from the 'Daily Mirror' showing you receiving the Legion of Honour.[1] My love and congratulations. It is such a long time since I heard from you I begin to fear you have forgotten me. Do you remember suggesting that you and I should collaborate in a Life of Conrad. I have been steadily collecting facts and material. You suggested sending your secretary over to help. My dear friend I could not offer her hospitality other than as a paying guest but I believe we could make something quite fine between us. Also I could perhaps come over to see you, under her escort in my car which is the only way I can travel. I must still have a nurse always with me, and of course your stairs are truly formidable, but we might manage to get me [*sic*] to transport me up to see you again. If you thought seriously of this and that there would be sufficient remumeration [*sic*] for us both to justify the expense, it might be worth while for me to come over with your secretary. I have now an excellent chauffeur, who speaks French. People here are clamouring for a life and I have been asked by several people to collaborate. None of these people either knew or met Conrad so you see none could do the same justice as you yourself. I have lately met most of the Polish Embassy and a little while ago I met the great grandson of Prince Roman.[2]

Let me hear from you very soon please dear Warrington, say how your health is and if you have thought any more of the Life.

With my love to you.

Affectionately yours
Jessie Conrad.

P.S. I could send you some snaps of the new grandson[.][3]

---

1. On 15 October Dawson had been made a *Commandeur de la Légion d'Honneur* in recognition of his labors on behalf of Franco-American amity.
2. Prince Roman Sanguszko was the hero of Conrad's "Prince Roman," a story which appeared first in *The Oxford and Cambridge Review*, No. XVI (1911), 201–226.
3. John's son, Richard.

115. *Dawson to Jessie Conrad*[1]

19 rue du Maréchal Joffre
Versailles
Dec 17, 1930

Dearest Jessie,

Mrs. Hastings Jones[2] was here this afternoon, she is feeling better and says that since she plans to go to England next May she could arrange to be at your disposal daily for a month—she will be visiting near Canterbury and can motor to you daily—I of course paying her salary and X's[3] during that time, for the sake of our "collaboration[.]"

How would you like that? Do let me know.

With love, ever most affectionately

Warrington.

1. Original presented to Perkins Library, Duke, by Borys Conrad.
2. Frances Hastings Jones, Dawson's secretary and friend.
3. Crossings of the Channel.

116. *Jessie Conrad to Dawson*

Torrens,/Mill Lane,/Harbledown,/Canterbury.
August 1st 1932.

My dear Warrington

It is a long time since I have heard from you. Do send me a few lines to say how you are. It is eight years ago on Wednesday since I am all alone and perhaps this makes me more than usually wakeful. It is just 2. am, and I am desperately lonely and so I write to you. I want very much to come to see you once more. Fate is not very kind to us, I am getting less and less able to get about and I have no hope of any improvement. There is such a lot I would like to talk to you about if I could only get over again. I send you my love my dear Warrington.

Always affectionately,
Jessie Conrad.

117. *Dawson to Jessie Conrad*[1]

August 3, 1932.

Mrs. Joseph Conrad,
Torrens,
Mill Lane,
Hartledown[*sic*],
Canterbury.

Dearest Jessie,

I am too sorry to have seemed to neglect you. Constantly you are in my thoughts, and of course you are particularly so now, at this season which recalls my own intense grief at losing "my dear Conrad" who meant in my life what nobody else has ever meant or can mean.

For the past two or three years my researches for French 18th Century documents to help in Mr. Rockefeller's reconstruction of Williamsburg, colonial capital of Virginia, have been an exhausting task which not only demanded countless hours of extra work, but proved so taxing in many ways, particularly in demands for correspondence, that my relations with my friends suffered in the matter of letters. This work is now ended and I promise to write to you more frequently.

I often wonder how John is doing and if you are satisfied with the position he is making for himself in life. That observant and penetrating nature of his, combined with great sensitiveness and constant reactions to things on the surface, can scarcely go through life, I should imagine, without a certain number of jolts. But what a delightful character that boy has always had!

I scarcely dare speak of Borys when you do not mention him yourself.

I am engaged at present in very interesting literary tasks. My friend, Major [Georges] Ladoux, who was Chief of the French Intelligence Service during the War, has written his Memoirs, and I have just finished translating the first volume, which is to be published by Cassell in October. It will appear separately because it deals entirely with a remarkable French woman agent in Spain.[2]

---

1. From Dawson's carbon typescript.
2. *Marthe Richard the Skylark: The Foremost Woman Spy of France* (London, 1932).

This will be followed by a more serious book telling how the Secret Service was built up in France, and I am now engaged in translating that.[3]

I have also taken up singing once more and my voice is in particularly good trim. Beginning in October, I intend to reserve the second Sunday of each month for a musical afternoon where I shall sing and have other artists appear also for the entertainment of my friends.

I do wish that it were possible for you to come to see me. I feel convinced that if you lived on a diet like mine, you would find such an improvement in your general health that you would be able to do much that is now impossible for you, just as I have learned to do, even though the basic complication with me never changes any more than it could be expected to do in your case.

Ever, with deep love,
Most affectionately,
Warrington Dawson.

WD/LA[4]

3. Apparently *The Kaiser's Blonde Spy* (London, 1934).
4. L. d'Ambleon held a place for a while in Dawson's series of secretaries.

118. *Dawson to David McCord*[1]

January 30, 1933.

David McCord, Esq.,
52, Garden Street,
Cambridge,
Mass., U.S.A.

Dear David:

*   *   *

I wish that you would write something about me, some day. I am sending you a copy of replies I have just made to a questionnaire sent to me by the Editor of "Who's Who Among North American Authors," for a series of personal articles about living writers, which Miss Alberta Lawrence expects to serialize.[2] I do not know just how much interest should be attached to this project of hers, but it seemed a pity to neglect the opportunity.

1. From Dawson's carbon typescript. McCord was a cousin of Dawson.
2. Miss Lawrence was editor of the Golden Syndicate Publishing Co., New York.

On the other hand, I learn that Miss Grace King devoted several pages of her posthumous book of Memoirs[3] to comments on Mother and myself, and I am wondering if this, in conjunction with Miss Lawrence's proposed article, for which you might possibly look out, would give you an opportunity to take up with your publisher the question of my long-deferred African novel.[4] I am sending you the complete manuscript of the novel, and I would like you first to read it, so as to be able to form your own judgment about it. My own feeling concerning it is that this is by far the most important work of art which I have ever produced. Whether or not other people will be prepared to see it, I cannot say.

I mentioned it very briefly in my reply to the questionnaire, because although it has an interesting inside story, I thought it best to keep the material fresh for purposes of publicity when the book is published.

This book was the subject of long hours of conversation between Joseph Conrad and myself.[5] Although I was full of the idea at the time, I hesitated to write it, because I felt that his "Heart of Darkness" had said the supreme word about Africa and that it would be difficult to do anything else. He insisted, however, that I had ideas which must be expressed, and he kept repeating to me that when I came to write about them, I should make Africa "all my own."

He finally invited me to go down and make him, so to speak, a half visit, working on this book while he, on his side, was working on a book. The arrangement was that I should take rooms in a nearby farm-house, so that each of us should work independently throughout the day, but I should daily dine and spend the evening with him and that, furthermore, we should both drive out in his car in the afternoon when we happened to have finished our day's work by tea-time.

We made none of the conventional restrictions about "not talking of our work." Quite the contrary, we kept our liberty of thought to talk about everything which passed through our minds. I was one of the extremely few people to whom Conrad ever talked of his work while engaged on it, and he would even read to me passages from his unpublished manuscripts, a thing which he was resolutely opposed to doing in the latter part of his life. He thus became familiar with every turn and twist of the plot of "The Shrouded

3. *Memories of a Southern Woman of Letters* (New York, 1932).
4. "The Rock."
5. In the spring of 1914.

Height," and he knew in intimate detail all my ideas concerning the characters.

There was one character I had not foreseen when originally creating the plot, which had seemed to be complete as it stood. I vividly remember Conrad's shout of delight on the evening when I told him of my own surprise when Jack Errington went into his dining-room for breakfast at Lanoi and found Bob Ponsonby seated at a table tucking in a hearty meal. As a matter of fact, Conrad and I both immediately realized that this character had all along been essential to the plot and must have existed in the background of my mind before I had been fully conscious of it.

The question of form was one to which I gave particular attention for this novel. Conrad had always said to me that he considered me capable of creating a new novel form, which was necessary to renovate the English novel, and that it would probably come to me of itself. He thought that a new form was called for by my individual expression, which was not like that of other people. I told him that as far as this particular novel was concerned, no method was possible except the handling on two different planes. He and I agreed as to the dangers of the method, but we could not find any other possible solution.

I wish that he could have seen the finished novel, as I am sending it to you to-day. I am more fully aware than ever that the form is dangerous, because it is totally new. So many startling things have been done in the way of fiction during the twenty years which have passed since I discussed this point with Conrad that possibly the form of the book might not prove to be an unsurmountable obstacle to-day, as it would have been even a decad[e] ago.

I am enclosing for your mother a photograph I have just had taken of a family portrait which belongs to me, Frédéric Le Chevalier, who is a collateral of ours, having been killed in battle under the reign of Louis XIII, and never having been married. My picture is the original, which was recently much admired by experts I had in the house examining my entire collection. It has never been out of the family or of France, having been given to me some twenty-five or thirty years ago, along with other pictures, by a member of the family here.

Ever your very affectionate cousin,

WD:EB[6]

6. Ethel K. Bullard, one of Dawson's secretaries.

119. Jessie Conrad to Dawson

'Torrens'/Harbledown/Canterbury
2.1.36

My dear Warrington

This is to wish you everything of the best for 1936 and more than all that we may meet before the end of the year. It seems impossible in the face of our mutual disabilities, you held to your couch in France and I to mine in England. My powers of walking get less and less—but if only I can get the necessary funds together I have still the car and a keen spirit of adventure left. I should so much like to come over and to see you again. The world seems very much upside down and it does not look like righting itself in a hurry.

Both the boys and their families seem well. I hope to see Borys soon. His boy is doing well at school. John's two[1] are very intelligent and interesting.

Do write to me when you are able and remember me to your sister very kindly.

With my love to you my dear friend[.]

Affectionately yours,
Jessie Conrad.

1. John and Mary Conrad had had a second son, Peter.

1. Francis Warrington Dawson, Jr., *ca.* 1912.

2. Dawson and Theodore Roosevelt on safari
near Lake Naivasha, B.E.A.

3. Conrad relaxing on a Sunday at Capel House.

4. Capel House, the Conrad home from 1910 to 1919.

5. Conrad's study at Capel House, with his easy chair and writing table.

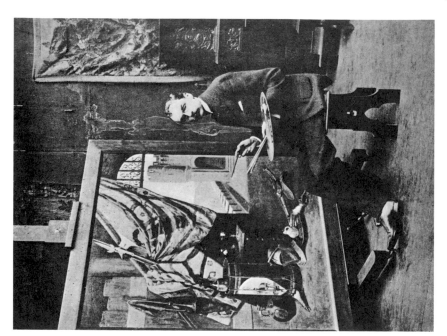

7. Frédéric Humbert, the aesthetically-inclined master swindler.

6. Thérèse Humbert, who with her husband created the swindling enterprise which Conrad used as background for *Chance*.

9. A friend of Dawson and Conrad: The Virginia pianist John Powell, *ca.* 1912.

8. Cadet Alfred Borys Conrad of H.M.S. *Worcester*, 1911.

10. Miss Ellen Glasgow's visit with Conrad in 1914,
photographed by Dawson.

11. Borys Conrad, photographed by Dawson
on the same occasion.

12. John Conrad (right) with his frequent playmate Robin Douglas, son of Norman Douglas.

13. In the garden at Capel House on the day of Miss Glasgow's visit.

14. A recent photograph of Gill Farm, Ruckinge, where Dawson went to be near Conrad.

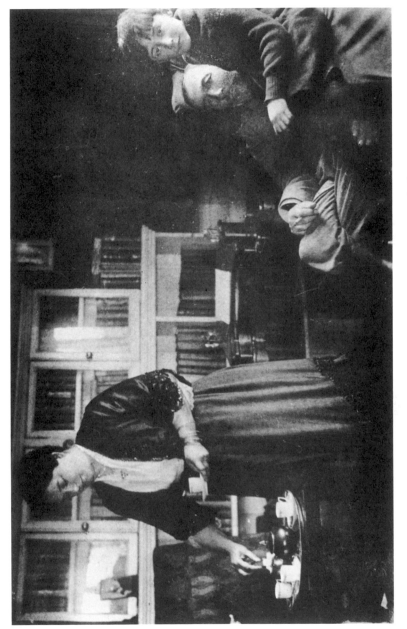

15. Joseph, Jessie, and John Conrad in the study at Capel House, 1915.

16. Dawson at fifty-one.

17. Jessie Conrad in her later years.

18. Dawson at eighty-one.

Bibliography

The first part of this bibliography is an abbreviated list of people who granted interviews or wrote letters which aided the author's research. It is the most gratifying part because it serves as a reminder of how many have been kind enough to lend time and thought to a project which, admittedly, will not startle that turtle on whose back the world rests.

The second section lists manuscript sources. Since three of the major collections involved were uncatalogued when the research was conducted, and since hundreds of documents have proved useful, it has seemed best simply to list collections here, and to cite particular manuscripts only at those points in the text where they are mentioned or quoted.

For both antipedantic and practical reasons the third part of the bibliography—printed sources—has been restricted to selected works by Conrad and Dawson. Conrad items are cited only if for some reason they have surfaced in the text. (To supplement these the reader may turn, for a good start, to Kenneth A. Lohf and Eugene P. Sheehy, *Joseph Conrad at Mid-century: Editions and Studies, 1895–1955* [Minneapolis, 1957].) Dawson's work is more thoroughly represented for the simple reason that a Dawson bibliography is available nowhere else. An exception is made, however, in the case of Dawson's voluminous journalistic work. Although Dawson generally did his best writing as a reporter, there has seemed to be little reason to list here more than a handful of his most relevant newspaper pieces.

One final point: If this third part of the bibliography looks suspiciously lean, or if, by its brevity, it seems to smack of scholarly ingratitude, the reader is invited to turn to the footnotes, where he will find a number of additional debts, large and small, catalogued according to subject matter.

1. *Interviews and Letters*

Dr. Herbert Barry, Jr. (nephew of Dawson)
Lucy B. Barry (grandniece of Dawson)
Joseph A. Bell (schoolmate of Dawson)
Lady Phyllis Benton (formerly Lady Phyllis Windsor-Clive, friend of Dawson and member of Fresh Air Art Society)
Burrows & Co., Ashford, Kent (suppliers of photograph of Gill Farm, Ruckinge)

Cyril Clemens (ed., *Mark Twain Journal*)
Borys Conrad (Conrad's older son, friend of Dawson)
Richard Curle (student and friend of Conrad)
R. M. Good (President Emeritus, The School of the Ozarks)
John D. Gordan (Conrad scholar and curator, Berg Collection, New York Public Library)
Edward Gough (son-in-law of Benno Moiseiwitsch)
Royal H. Jurgensen (curator, Ralph Foster Museum, The School of the Ozarks)
Dr. Bernard Lytton-Bernard (Dawson's friend and publisher)
Ernest C. Mead, Jr. (Professor of Music, University of Virginia; pupil of John Powell)
Sir Roland Oliver (friend of Conrad and son of Capel House landlord)
Earl Pruce (librarian, Baltimore *News-American*)
Dr. John M. Rhoads (Professor of Psychiatry, Duke University)
Archibald B. Roosevelt (son of Theodore Roosevelt and friend of Dawson)
Hilton Rufty (Professor of Music, University of Richmond; pupil of John Powell)
Helen Sanderson (friend of Conrad; wife of E. L. Sanderson)
Cmdr. I. C. M. Sanderson (son of E. L. and Helen Sanderson)
Marguerite Steedman (journalist who interviewed Dawson)
Alfred Vicher (Versailles friend of Dawson)
Thomas R. Waring (ed., Charleston *News and Courier*)
Vernon Warner (friend of Dawson and Powell, concert pianist, member of Fresh Air Art Society)

2. *Manuscript Sources*

Institutions

British Museum Library
Columbia University Library
Duke University, The William R. Perkins Library
Harvard University, The Houghton Library
New York Public Library, especially The Berg Collection
The Philip H. & A. S. W. Rosenbach Foundation.
St. Luke's Hospital (Morningside Heights, New York City)
The School of the Ozarks, Ralph Foster Museum
University of South Carolina Libraries, especially the South Caroliniana Library

University of Texas Library
University of Virginia, Alderman Library
Virginia Historical Society Library
Wellcome Historical Medical Library (London)
Yale University, Beinecke Rare Book & Manuscript Library

Individuals

Dr. Herbert Barry, Jr., and Miss Lucy B. Barry
Lady Phyllis (Windsor-Clive) Benton
Mr. Borys Conrad
Dr. Bernard Lytton-Bernard

3. *Relevant Works by Conrad and Dawson*

Joseph Conrad

L'Agent Secret, trans. Henry D. Davray, pub. in 13 installments in *Le Temps* (31 May—8 July 1910).
Almayer's Folly (London, 1895).
The Arrow of Gold (London, 1919).
Chance (London, 1914).
Conrad to a Friend, ed. Richard Curle (London, 1928).
Conrad's Polish Background: Letters to and from Polish Friends, ed. Zdzislaw Najder and trans. Halina Carroll (London, 1964).
Entre Terre et Mer, trans. G. Jean-Aubry (Paris, 1929).
"Freya of the Seven Isles," *Metropolitan Magazine*, XXXV (April, 1912), 20–28, 51–54.
"In My Library: The Life Beyond," rev. of *Existence after Death Implied by Science* by J. B. Hunt, London *Daily Mail*, 16 July 1910, p. 8. Cf. Dawson's views on psychism.
The Inheritors, written with Ford Madox Hueffer (New York, 1901).
"'The Inheritors.'—A Letter from Joseph Conrad," New York *Times*, 24 August 1901, p. 603.
"The Intimate Letters of Joseph Conrad . . . ," *World Today*, XLIX (1926–1927), 30–38, 134–143, 217–226, 319–328.
Joseph Conrad: Letters to William Blackwood and David S. Meldrum, ed. William Blackburn (Durham, N.C., 1958).
Joseph Conrad: Life and Letters, 2 vols., ed. G. Jean-Aubry (Garden City, N.Y., 1927).
Joseph Conrad on Fiction, ed. Walter F. Wright (Lincoln, Neb., 1964).
Joseph Conrad's Letters to His Wife (London, 1927).

Last Essays, introd. Richard Curle (Garden City, N.Y., 1926).

"Laughing Anne," *Metropolitan*, XL (September, 1914), 19–21, 57–61.

Letters from Joseph Conrad 1895–1924, ed. Edward Garnett (Indianapolis, 1928).

Letters of Joseph Conrad to Marguerite Poradowska, 1890–1920, trans. and ed. John A. Gee and Paul J. Sturm (New Haven, 1940).

Lettres Françaises, ed. G. Jean-Aubry (Paris, 1930).

The Mirror of the Sea: Memories and Impressions (London, 1906).

The Nigger of the "Narcissus" (London, 1898).

The Nigger of the "Narcissus" preface, privately printed (Hythe, Eng., 1902).

Nostromo (New York, 1904).

Notes by Joseph Conrad Written in a Set of His First Editions in the Possession of Richard Curle (London, 1925).

Notes on Life & Letters (London, 1921).

Notes on My Books (Garden City, N.Y., 1921).

"One Day More," *English Review*, XV (1913), 16–35.

"The Partner," *Harper's Monthly Magazine*, CXXIII (1911), 850–865.

A Personal Record (New York, 1912).

"The Planter of Malata," *Metropolitan*, XL (June–July, 1914).

"Poland Revisited," in *The Book of the Homeless*, ed. Edith Wharton (New York, 1916).

"Prince Roman," *The Oxford and Cambridge Review*, No. XVI (1911), pp. 201–226.

The Rescue (London, 1920).

A Set of Six (London, 1908).

The Shadow-Line: A Confession (London, 1917).

"A Smile of Fortune," *London Magazine*, XXV (1911), 801–836.

Some Reminiscences (London, 1912). Variant title of *A Personal Record*.

Suspense: A Napoleonic Novel (New York, 1925).

"The Tale," *Strand Magazine*, LIV (1917), 345–353.

"Tomorrow," *Pall Mall Magazine*, XXVII (1902), 533–547.

'Twixt Land and Sea (London, 1912).

Le Typhon, trans. Joseph de Smet, *Progrès* (May, 1911 . . .).

Under Western Eyes (London, 1911).

"Victory," *Munsey's Magazine*, LIV (1915), 112–240.

Victory: An Island Tale (London, 1915).

"The Warrior's Soul," *Land and Water* (29 March 1917), 29–39.

Wisdom and Beauty from Conrad, selected and arranged by M. Harriet M. Capes (London, 1915).

Within the Tides (London, 1915).

Bibliography

Youth: A Narrative and Two Other Stories ["Heart of Darkness" and "The End of the Tether"] (London, 1902).

Francis Warrington Dawson

Adventure in the Night (London, 1924).

Les Aventures de Buz et Fury (Paris, 1931).

Beaumains (Paris, 1936), b.w. *Éclaireurs de France, 1999: Pièce a Rythme Accéléré en Deux Actes* (Paris, 1936).

Buz and Fury (Chicago, 1923).

"Le Caractère Spécial de la Musique Nègre en Amérique," *Journal de la Société des Américanistes*, n.s. XXIV (1932), 273–286.

introd. and ed., *A Confederate Girl's Diary*, Sarah Morgan Dawson (London, 1913). Re-edited by James I. Robertson, Jr. (Bloomington, Ind., 1960).

Contes et Merveilles (Paris, 1962). On verso of title page: "Il a été tiré de cet ouvrage 20 exemplaires sur papier alfa, constituant l'édition originale et réservés a l'auteur."

The Crimson Pall (Chicago, 1927).

Les 2112 Français Morts aux États-Unis de 1777 à 1783, en Combattant pour l'Indépendance Américaine (Paris, 1936).

Et S'il Était Innocent? (L'Affaire Gaspard) Récit Romancé (Paris, 1960).

"Étude Psychologique sur les Races Noires de l'Afrique Orientale," *Progrès* (May, 1911), pp. 261–281.

Les Français Morts pour l'Indépendance Américaine de Septembre 1781 à Août 1782 & La Reconstruction Historique de Williamsburg (Paris, 1931).

"Francis Warrington Dawson [Sr.]," Charleston *News and Courier*, 7 December 1930, p. 6-C. A long biographical letter.

The Gift of Paul Clermont (London, 1921).

The Green Moustache: A Fantasy of Modernism (Chicago, 1925).

The Guardian Demons (London, 1928).

"A History of the Foundation of New Orleans (1717–1722)," trans. from the French of Baron Marc de Villiers, *Louisiana Historical Quarterly*, III (1920), 157–251.

"Joseph Conrad," New York *Times*, 2 February 1913, p. 51.

ed. and trans., *The Kaiser's Blonde Spy*, George Ladoux (London, 1934).

Le Linceul Rouge-sang (Paris, 1961).

"The Man," *Atlantic Monthly*, CXIX (1917), 333–337.

"The Man on the Altar: An Experience in Petrograd," *Atlantic Monthly*, CXVIII (1916), 777–786.

ed. and trans., *Marthe Richard the Skylark: The Foremost Woman Spy of France*, Georges Ladoux (London, 1932).

"Mr[.] Dawson Exposes Errors in New Book about Conrad," Charleston *Sunday News*, 5 July 1914, p. 23. Also in Boston *Evening Transcript*, 3 July, p. 12.

Le Nègre aux États-Unis, pref. Paul Adam (Paris, 1912).

Opportunity and Theodore Roosevelt (Chicago, 1924).

Paul Clermont's Story and My Own, Followed by The Gift of Paul Clermont (Chicago, 1928).

The Pyramid (London, 1922).

Le Rapt de la Vierge (Paris, 1960).

"Refugee: The Experience of a War Correspondent," *Atlantic Monthly*, CXVIII (1916), 131–137.

Le Sacrifice de Paul Clermont (Paris, 1925).

The Scar (London, 1906).

The Scourge (London, 1908).

Le Septième Crime (Paris, 1961).

"The Sin: An Allegory of Truth," *English Review*, XV (1913), 384–411.

The Sin: An Allegory of Truth (Chicago, 1923).

ed., *The Speeches of the Hon. Hugh C. Wallace, American Ambassador to France, 1919–1921* (Paris, 1921).

"The Spirit of Pershing's Army," *Outlook* (London), CXVII (1917), 372–374.

The True Dimension (London, 1916).

ed., *The War Memoirs of William Graves Sharp American Ambassador to France 1914–1919* (London, 1931).

Index

Index

Carlyle, Thomas, 127n
Carter, A. E., 69n
Carter, Josiah, 7n
Casement, Roger, 110n
Castéra, Marguerite, 204n
Cazenove Literary Agency, 171
Charleston, 62; Dawson's family in, 6–13 passim; Dawson's views on returning to, 29
Charleston, College of, 14
Charleston *Courier*, 9
Charleston *Daily News*, 9
Charleston *News and Courier*, 9, 11, 14, 15, 29, 94, 105, 117, 133
Charleston *Sunday News*, 37, 87
Cherville, G. de, 127n
Cholmondeley, Mary, 12n
Chopin, Frédéric, 59–60, 110
Civil War, 7–8, 10–11
Cladel, Judith, 79
Clark, Barrett H., 65
Clemenceau, Georges, 90
Clifford, Hugh, 130
Colvin, Lady Frances, 161n
Colvin, Sir Sidney, 161n, 195n. *See also* letter No. 96
Confederate Girl's Diary, A (S. M. Dawson), 11n, 12n, 78, 98, 164, 165, 168, 170, 174, 187, 188
Conrad, Borys, viii, 3, 4n, 33n, 39, 60n, 86, 107, 112, 146, 148, 153, 154, 165, 166, 169, 175, 177, 181, 182, 183, 187, 189, 202, 208, 210, 215, 216, 220, 223; friendship with Dawson, 50–51, 120–121, 139, 151, 161, 201; in World War I, 34, 95, 96, 102, 184, 185–186, 188, 190, 192–193, 194, 195, 196, 197, 199. *See also* illustrations No. 8, 11, 13, and letters No. 29, 32
Conrad, Mrs. Borys (Joan King), 216n

Conrad, Jessie, viii, 57, 79, 92, 95, 98, 100, 102, 107, 155, 161, 176, 179, 182, 199; aid to Conrad's friends, 57, 80, 81, 86, 138n, 177, 178, 179; collaboration with Dawson, 221, 222; after Conrad's death, 115–116; death of, 116; in Fresh Air Art Society, 75; friendship with Dawson, 32–35, 112–116, 122–123, 167–168, 219; health and operations, 102, 103–104, 111, 112, 113, 116, 136, 153, 188, 192, 194, 195, 196, 197, 200, 201, 202, 205, 207, 208, 209, 210, 211, 214, 215, 218, 227; as letter writer, 5; views on Dawson's friendship with Borys, 51,

121; views on Ford Madox Hueffer, 30; views on Perceval Gibbon, 47; visit to Dawson, 113–114; and World War I, 34, 96–97. *See also* illustrations No. 13, 15, 17
—, Writings:
articles, 47n, 96n, 216, 220
"Friendship's Friend," 32–35, 123n, 218n, 219, 220
Handbook of Cookery, A, 209
Joseph Conrad and His Circle, vii, 115
Joseph Conrad as I Knew Him, 96n

Conrad, John, 33, 39, 86, 112, 140, 153, 154, 155, 175, 183, 187, 189, 194, 195, 196, 197, 202, 208, 209, 210, 214, 215, 216, 220, 221n, 223, 227. *See also* illustrations No. 12, 15
Conrad, Mrs. John (Mary Grindrod), 220n, 227n

Conrad, Joseph: in Africa, 110n; aid in publishing Dawson, 56–57, 153, 154, 155, 156, 163, 168; bases of friendship with Dawson, 120–123; collaboration with Hueffer, 113, 114n; collected edition of, 82n–83n; comments on Dawson's writing, 63–65, 143–144, 169 (*see also* individual works under Dawson); "credo" letter, 71–74, 109, 158–161; Dawson lectures on, 51–53, 121, 145, 146, 170; death of, 111; dedication to, by Powell, 60, 61n; dedications to, by Dawson, 108, 111, 205, 214; discussions with Dawson, 42, 47–48, 50, 83–84; Ellen Glasgow's comments on, 85; Embassy luncheon for, 80–82, 179, 180; first meeting with Dawson, 29, 32–36 passim, 121–122; health and mental state, 29–31, 103, 104, 122, 129, 139, 147, 150, 166, 167, 169, 175, 183, 185, 186, 187, 188, 189, 197, 198, 201, 202, 206, 207, 209, 214, 215, 217; interest in teeth, 58; trip to America, 110–111, 210, 211, 212, 213; trip to Corsica, 104, 107, 196n, 202, 208; trip to Poland, 88, 178n, 182–184; and World War I, 95–98 passim; writing for *Progrès*, 135–136, 138. *See also* illustrations No. 3, 10, 13, 15
—, Views on: Americans, 3–4, 100–101, 121; autobiography in writing, 5; critical novel, 64, 65; Dawson-Borys friendship, 139, 151, 201; form in fiction, 63–65; music, 59–61, 110; own later

236

Index

Index

Howard, Leslie, 99n
Howells, William Dean, 69
Hubbell, Jay B., 20n
Huddleston, Sisley, 49n
Hueffer, Ford Madox (later Ford Madox Ford), 29–30, 35, 36n, 46n, 55, 58, 64–65, 95, 98–99, 113, 114n
Hueffer, Mrs. Ford Madox, 30n
Humbert, Eve, 44–46
Humbert, Frédéric, 40–46. See also illustration No. 7
Humbert, Gustave, 40–41, 44, 46
Humbert, Thérèse, 40–46. See also illustration No. 6
Humbert case: Conrad's use of, 40–46; Dawson's view of, 41–43, 45
Hunt, Violet, 30, 35
Huxley, Elspeth, 23n

Ibsen, Henrik, 68

James, Mrs. Arthur Curtiss, 110
James, Henry, 30n
Jean-Aubry, G. See Aubry, G. J.
Jervey, Theodore D., 79n
Joffre, J. J. C., 96, 106, 107, 205
Jones, Sir Robert, 195, 196, 197, 200, 201, 217n
Jusserand, J. J., 107

Karl, Frederick, 74
Keating, George T., 122n
Kennedy, Daisy, 67n
Kerry, Christl, 115n
King, Grace, 11, 75, 78, 225. See also letter No. 46
King, Joan. See Conrad, Mrs. Borys
Kipling, Rudyard, 37, 105, 106n, 108n, 112n, 179n, 204, 212n
Knight, Grant C., 69n
Knopf, Alfred A., 186n
Korzeniowski, Apollo. See title page

Ladoux, Georges, 89–90, 91n, 223
Laemmel, Rudolph, 90
La Nux, Paul V. de, 128
Lawrence, Alberta, 13n, 224, 225
Lawrence, D. H., 55n
Le Chevalier, Frédéric, 226
Lectures, Dawson's, 78–79, 184n; on Africa, 24n, 28, 52n, 62; on Conrad, 51–53, 121, 145, 146, 170; on Fresh Air Art Society, 52n, 67, 68, 70, 75, 76, 78; other subjects, 52n; style in, 52–53, 76; on Versailles, 52n, 104n
Leo XIII, Pope, 9
Leschetizky, Theodor, 59, 67, 158
Le Tellier, Maurice, 114n

Lightwood House, 6
Little Less Than Gods, A (F. M. Ford), 113
Lockwood, Frank C., 15n
Logan, S. Frank, 7n, 12n, 119n
Lohf, Kenneth A., vii, 131n
Lonn, Ella, 8n
Loubet, Émile, 16
Ludwig, Richard M., 114n
Lynch, Bishop Patrick, 10
Lytton-Bernard, Dr. Bernard. See Bernard, Bernard

McCabe, William G., 15n
McCabe's University School, 15
McCord, David, 83n. See also letter No. 118
McDow, Dr. Thomas B., 9, 12
McKenney's University School, 14
Mackenzie, Sir Compton, 55n
McKinley, Carlyle, 14, 14n–15n, 48
McMillan, William N., 27, 128, 129n
Macmillan Co., 82n, 84
MacShane, Frank, 55n
Malory, Sir Thomas, 13
Manly, Louise, 15n
Manoury, Adolphe, 17, 114
Margaret Harding (Gibbon), 47–48, 137n
Marshall, Archibald, 36
Marwood, Arthur P., 35–36, 95, 131–132, 133, 137, 138, 147, 148
Masefield, John, 153
Mathot, A. Z., 128
Mavrogordato, John, 55, 149–150
Mead, Ernest C., Jr., 61n
Meixner, John A., 99n
Memminger, Lucien, 92
Mercure de France, 38
Metcalf, John C., 82n
Methuen & Co., 139, 144
Metropolitan Magazine, 176
Meyer, Bernard C., 30n, 58
Millais, Lady Mary, 194, 197, 208
Millais, Sir John E., 194, 197, 208
Mitchell, Broadus, 9n
Mitchell, George S., 9n
Moiseiwitsch, Benno, 67, 158
Morf, Gustav: Polish Heritage of Joseph Conrad, source of verses quoted on title page
Morgan, James Morris, 10, 11, 51
Morgan, Sarah, 10
Morgan, Thomas Gibbes, 10
Morice, Charles, 171n
Morison, Elting E., 25n, 27n, 28n

Index

Index

Roosevelt, Theodore, Jr., 96
Rosenbloom, Sydney, 67, 70, 76
Rossetti, Dante Gabriel, 160n
Rostand, Edmond, 16
Rothenstein, Alice, 31
Rothenstein, William, 29n, 31, 86n, 103n, 121
Rouse, Blair, 112n
Russo-Japanese War, 17, 52n, 142
Rutherford, Mildred L., 15n
Ruyters, André, 103

Saint-Gaudens, Augustus, 16
St. Luke's Hospital (N.Y.), 15, 93–94
Sanderson, Capt. E. L. (Ted), 25–28, 29, 33n, 37, 130, 133
Sanderson, Mrs. E. L. (Helen), 26, 27–28, 29, 33n, 37, 75, 130–131
Sanderson, Cmdr. I. C. M., 26n
Sanderson, Katherine ("Mrs. Kitty"), 25
Sanguszko, Prince Roman, 221
Sass, Herbert R., 14n–15n
Schwab, Arnold T., 78n, 81n, 110n, 121n
Scribner's Magazine, 25, 27, 28, 131
Seelly, Mrs., 178, 179
Segonne, Lilian, 115n
Sharp, George Clough, 112, 120
Sharp, William Graves, 94, 96n, 97
Shaw, George Bernard, 69
Sheehy, Eugene P., vii, 131n
Simons, James, 7
Smet, Joseph de, 38, 136
Smith, Charles A., 82n
Smith, Frederick E. (Lord Birkenhead), 90
Smith's School, Mrs. Isabel, 14
Socialist strike riots (1901), 17
Soskice, David, 36n
Spring Grove, 102
Steedman, Marguerite, 90n, 117
Stevenson, Robert Louis, 26, 203
Straus, Jesse I., 98
Sutherland, J. G., 6n, 96n
Symons, Arthur, 69, 167n

Taylor, Jane Anderson, 95, 190n, 191n
Teeth, Conrad's interest in, 58
Tennyson, Alfred, 13
Thackara, Mrs. Alexander M., 92
Thackeray, William Makepeace, 24, 27
Torrens (ship), 26
Trappschuh, Bernhard. See Bernard, Bernard

United Press, 17, 24, 28, 88, 89
Urgent Fund for Serbian Wounded, 92

Vacaresco, Hélène, 53
Valentine, Edward A. U., 18–19, 121
Venn, J. A., 27n
Versailles: Dawson in, 4, 104–105, 114–115, 116, 118–119, 224; Dawson lecture on, 52n
Vicher, Alfred, 99n, 118
Vignier, Elizabeth, 12n
Visiak, Edward H., 58

Wallace, Hugh C., 97–98, 203
Walpole, Hugh, 3n, 103, 211
Ward, Mrs. Humphry, 179
Warner, Vernon, 67, 158
Washington, Booker T., 49n
Watson, E. L. Grant, 36n
Watterson, Henry, 9n
Wauchope, George A., 15n
Webb, Frank D., 19n
Wedgwood, Iris, 182n
Wharton, Edith, 39n
White, Ethelbert, 120
White, Henry, 24
Wilcox, Ella Wheeler, 85
Wilde, Oscar, 69
Wiley, Paul L., 99n, 114n
Wilhelmina, Queen, 17
Willcox, Louise Collier, 84, 85
Williamsburg, Va., Dawson's work in restoration of, 114, 223
Winawer, Bruno, 110
Winchester, Paul, 19n
Windsor-Clive, Alberta V. S. C. (Lady Plymouth), 53, 56n
Windsor-Clive, Ivor (Viscount Windsor), 52, 53, 54, 170
Windsor-Clive, Lady Phyllis (later Lady Phyllis Benton), vii, 52, 53n, 54, 75, 93n, 99n, 118, 122, 173
Windsor-Clive, R. G. (Earl of Plymouth), viii, 53–54, 56n, 67, 90, 148, 158. *See also* letter No. 58
Withey, Mary, 55, 150n
Wohlfarth, Paul, 31n
Woodward, C. Vann, 9n
Woolf, Cecil, 57n
World War I, 88; Conrad's activities during, 96; Dawson's activities during, 89–98 *passim*, 105; effect on Conrads, 192–194 *passim*; Jessie's comments on, 34
World War II, Dawson's life during, 116–117

Zimbalist, Efrem, 67, 158
Zola, Émile, 46n